HOW TO SURVIVE

THE MONEY PANIC

Martin D. Weiss

PROBUS PUBLISHING COMPANY
Chicago, Illinois

ISBN: 1-55738-087-2

Printed in the United States of America

1   2   3   4   5   6   7   8   9   0

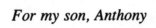
For my son, Anthony

Contents

Foreword

The world economy is living on borrowed time. After nearly half a century of persistent credit expansion, a major correction is long overdue. The trouble is, when it comes, most people won't know how to cope with it.

More than two generations have gone by since the Great Depression. As a result, there are very few people now living who experienced, firsthand, the financial chaos of the early 1930s, and actually profited from it. All of today's experts are the product of the postwar expansion.

Worse yet, the government's success in papering over one financial crisis after another in recent years has induced most Americans to ignore the ever-deepening problems of the nation's financial institutions. When the Money Panic finally comes, most people will be shockingly devastated.

For that reason, I believe this book is a Godsend to those who truly want to protect themselves against the inevitable collapse and to profit from it as well.

Why? Because behind this book is a father-and-son team—plus a powerful research think-tank—that will guide you step by step through the coming crisis:

Martin Weiss has correctly predicted every significant turn in interest rates over the last fifteen years. And, as you might expect, he successfully kept his clients out of the stocks well before the Crash of '87. The real "proof of the pudding," I believe, is the fact that he actually sold stocks short just four days before the 1987 Crash and then cashed in the huge profits the very morning after Black Monday, which turned out to be the bottom for 1987 and 1988.

His father, Irving Weiss, accomplished a similar feat 60 years ago. He is probably the only person active in the industry today who went short the market in 1929 and made substantial sums for his clients during the early 1930s.

In this book, you will find the information you *need* to survive and profit in the turbulent times ahead. It identifies for you, for example, the banks, insurance companies and brokerage firms with whom you can entrust your funds even in the worst of times. And it shows you what you can do right now to protect your savings, your investments and the value of your home.

One of the most valuable features of this book is the author's new, unique plan to help you earn up to 20% with no risk whatsoever. It's hard to believe, but it really guarantees full protection of capital, and is effective in both inflationary and deflationary times.

But that's just for starters. As I reviewed the manuscript, I couldn't help but notice that this book has accomplished several major goals:

First, Martin has ferreted out every possible danger and pitfall that could entrap you in the months and years ahead. This includes the hidden problems not only of the banks, the S&Ls, common stocks, bonds and real estate, but even the so-called "guaranteed investments" which have become so popular in recent years.

Second, the book has a practical and positive side. The author dedicates chapter after chapter to explicit instructions on where to find the very strongest banks in America, the safest money funds, the most liquid corporations, the best brokerage firms, insurance companies, utilities, etc. He gives all the specifics you need including names and toll-free phone numbers!

Third, this book provides you with a visionary—yet thoroughly rational—scenario of the future and how you can profitably anticipate critical turning points. Martin is willing to stake his reputation on the result of his years of research by dedicating one third of this book to describe in great detail what he professionally believes will happen in the different markets. Even if only a portion of his forecasts comes true, your comprehension of future events will be significantly enhanced.

Fourth, this book is completely up to date. It is based on brand new research with the latest data available now. It takes into account the results of the 1988 Presidential election. And it covers the latest episodes of the merger frenzy and the most recent S&L failures in Texas.

Fifth, this book is exciting to read. Like a thriller, it builds up to a climax. But unlike fiction, it's about things that will directly affect you and your future. So, it leaves no cliff-hangers.

Best of all, it is easy to understand. You don't need any previous knowledge of economics or investments to benefit from its advice.

I congratulate Martin for having written this book. It's a timely contribution to the investing public. And I congratulate you for having selected this book. Once you have read it, you will have discovered the road to financial prosperity.

T. J. Holt
January 2, 1989

Introduction

I have written this book to help you survive and prosper during the Money Panic.

The Money Panic is not the same recession repeating itself every few years until the far reaches of the next century. Nor is it the Great Depression returning to haunt us from the depths of the 1930s. The Money Panic is different from anything we have ever experienced: A boomerang reaction to decades of accelerated expansion; an outpouring of stockpiled goods; a sudden contraction in consumption, production and distribution; an historic shift in values and behavior patterns; and, most important, an explosive demand for cash.

Will our leaders have the will or the power to prevent it? Probably not. When they try to pump up the economy with more money, it brings back inflation and triggers a dollar collapse. When they try to cool off the economy, it chokes cash-starved corporations and creates an instant bankruptcy crisis. And when they do nothing, they forfeit the fate of the economy to the most powerful force of all—a gargantuan *three and one-half trillion dollars* in short-term debt coming due within the next twelve months.

In a letter to a U.S. Senator, one man has voiced growing concern that these huge debts may return to haunt us in the near future. In comments to reporters, another man has recently said that "there are more problems in our financial system than in any period since the Depression." Still another has spent much of his time telling Americans that "the entire structure of deposit insurance needs to be reassessed."

Who are these people and why are they saying these things? They are none other than the former Federal Reserve Chairman Paul Volcker, the former FDIC Chairman William Isaac, and the former Federal Home Loan Bank Chairman Richard Pratt—the men who, only several months earlier, were in charge of America's banks, S&Ls and the Federal Deposit Insurance Corporation. They warn of grave dangers, most of which are still hidden from view.

In this book, I describe these dangers in detail. I show how, at virtually any time in the not-so-distant future, you may wake up one morning to discover:

- Your savings account, Certificate of Deposit, checking account or money market account—at your local commercial bank, savings bank or S&L—is effectively frozen beyond your reach, precisely when you need your money the most.

- Your Ginnie Mae, tax-exempt bond or long-term corporate bond is either worthless because of an unexpected default or is drastically lower in value due to higher interest rates.

- Your house, vacation home or rental properties are increasingly costly to maintain, difficult to rent, impossible to sell or sinking in value.

- Your job—or the job of your spouse—is threatened by business failures and sinking markets both in the United States and abroad.

- Worst of all, the government's ability to come to the rescue is virtually gone.

A growing minority of Americans have already experienced one or more of these financial catastrophes. In 1983, thousands of investors in Washington Public Power Supply System were wiped out as their supposedly "guaranteed" bonds fell to a small fraction of their original value. In 1985, hundreds of thousands of savers in the states of Ohio and Maryland were locked out of their savings and loans. In 1987, Americans holding stocks and mutual funds suffered a crash which was, by all measures, twice as bad as the 1929 disaster. And in 1988, middle class suburban residents of Denver, Colorado watched in utter horror as the value of their homes plummeted to as low as 30 cents on the dollar. But these events are merely a foreshadowing of what's still to come.

There is urgent need for an investment strategy that will help you survive the Money Panic, that provides the best of all possible worlds—safety, protection and profit. It is with this in mind that I present to you, in the first chapters of this book, my *Delta Strategy*, a plan for savers and investors which is equally valid before, during or after the Money Panic.

With the Delta Strategy firmly in mind, you will be ready to read the final chapters of this book which describe the final outcome as I see it and which give you invaluable clues regarding the best *time* to make critical investment moves. And, with the Delta Strategy firmly in place for at least a portion of your funds, you will be ready for the actual Money Panic, no matter how it may differ from my forecasts.

Is there still hope for this country? The answer to that question is yes, especially if a substantial number of Americans do achieve safety and liquidity in time. Towards that end, the message of this book is: Don't panic. Make rational choices *now*—not only for your own direct benefit but for the future well-being of the entire nation.

With minor exceptions, there will be no widespread social chaos or revolution. The Money Panic is an intense but beneficial house-cleaning process that helps correct imbalances and distortions deeply embedded in the structure of society. Despite the upheaval and unhappiness, it is also an opportunity to stop, reorganize and adjust our economy to the real needs of the future.

The purpose of this book is to contribute, if only in a small way, to this opportunity. By predicting a crisis, I am not yelling "fire" in a crowded cinema. I am uncovering very real financial hazards lurking behind the still strong-looking façade of business and banking.

What will the Money Panic be like? How will it end? How can each one of us survive and profit during this difficult era? In the latter sections of this book we will search for the answers. We will travel twenty years into the future and look back on history from a fresh perspective—first to search for the roots of the panic, and then to examine its consequences.

The Money Panic is a period of unusually rapid movement—intense economic and political change which can only accelerate as we move deeper into the crisis. This book, however, is imobile and fixed—locked into one time and place. Therefore, there is an urgent need for you to receive the very latest data with my current views regarding upcoming changes in the financial markets and how to profit from them. Towards this end, I have established a regular mechanism whereby you can receive a free update of this book directly from my firm, Weiss Research, Inc. (For more information, see page 317.)

Although I will often use the past tense for many events taking place today, as well as those which I believe will occur in the future, I have no crystal ball. As time goes by, and you compare the real events with those predicted in this book, you will inevitably find some that match well and others that do not. No one can predict the future with precision. You will also discover, however, that my forecast of a major financial crisis is based on extensive analysis, giving you the knowledge you will need to protect yourself and your family from the impending disaster.

Book I

RISK-FREE INVESTING

1

—

The Banking Peril

The time is now; the place, your local bank. You walk in to make a deposit. Out of the corner of your eye, you notice the security guard leaning against one of the counters, staring blankly into space. The faithful TV camera pans the bank, recording anything unusual. As you step up to the teller, you glance at the FDIC sign:

"DEPOSITS INSURED UP TO $100,000. FEDERAL DEPOSIT INSURANCE CORPORATION"

By the time you've made your deposit, you're assured that nothing can go wrong, that it's backed by the bank, by the police and by all the authority and power of the government.

But is it really? The fact is that the insurance fund which covers bank deposits has little more than *one cent* in reserves for each dollar at the banks. In normal times, it might suffice. But in a crisis, it would not.

Approximately 200 commercial banks are failing in the United States every year, a shocking 20 times more than the average rate during the 1970s. At the same time, nearly 1,500 banks are on the government's confidential list of problem banks, up from less than 200 in 1981. And most frightening of all, these disasters have taken place in an environment of relatively low interest rates, low inflation and prolonged economic prosperity.

What will happen during the next recession? How many banks will fail when borrowers default on their payments to the banks in increasing numbers? And even if a recession can be postponed still further, what will take place if interest rates surge again, causing big losses in the banks' investments?

3

No one in Washington or on Wall Street has the answers. Most are afraid to even ask the questions. Rather, they are relying on the federal government to guarantee the deposits of every American. In recent months, as the crisis has spread, Congress has tried to calm the fears of savers by pledging to back up all deposits no matter what. But making a promise in times of prosperity is one thing. Keeping that promise during a financial crisis or an economic depression is another!

Merely to clean up the mess now recognized at the savings and loan associations could cost a budget-busting $100 billion, *even assuming continued good times.* To bail-out the depositors of *both* S&Ls *and* commercial banks during a recession could cost many times more. Will there be enough money? If there isn't, will the government be able or willing to print more, risking the destruction of the entire economy?

The time has come for you to get the true facts about your bank and, if necessary, take concrete action to protect yourself.

Four Big Mistakes

If the recent rash of bank and S&L failures could be explained away by citing some isolated event, there would not be as much cause for concern. Unfortunately, however, it is the direct result of four cardinal errors that the banks have committed:

- First, most banks have borrowed money from sources that are very volatile and that have a greater tendency to pull out without notice.
- Second, they have failed to keep enough money on hand to protect themselves against that possibility—to fulfill the demands of depositors who might want to make large withdrawals.
- Third, they have taken greater risks when investing your money than at almost any other time in the twentieth century.
- And worst of all, they have depleted their capital to the point where they don't have enough cushion to fall back on in the case of big losses.

The good news is that some exceptional institutions have *not* made these mistakes and are still strong.

The *better* news is that there is such a thing as do-it-your-self-banking—a solid, alternative method for keeping your money safe, earning a good yield and still retaining immediate access to it. But first, you are probably wondering how and why the banks got themselves into their current predicament.

Graphs 1 & 2. Bank Failures And Problem Banks

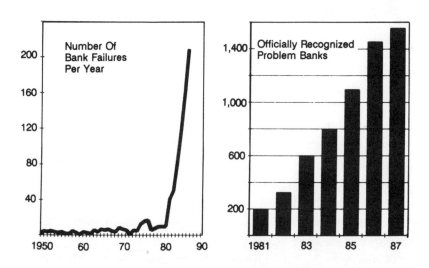

The graph on the left shows the dramatic surge in the number of bank failures in the United States beginning in 1980. The graph on the right shows the number of banks which have yet to fail but which are officially recognized as "problem banks." Bear in mind that once a bank fails, it is removed from the list of problem banks. Therefore a more complete picture of the crisis would require adding together the numbers from both of these graphs. Furthermore, our own analysis of the data reveals that the authorities are underestimating the number of problem banks by as many as 1,000 institutions. Data: Federal Reserve, FDIC.

Mistake #1. The Banks Got Hooked On Hot Money

In order for most banks to keep stockholders happy, they had to grow; and in order to grow they had to attract more depositors. In the old days, this was accomplished simply by building a solid reputation and establishing a close relationship with the local community.

In the 1970s and '80s, however, all that was changed. Many banks sought new methods of raising deposits and invented different *kinds* of deposits which had never existed before. They used expensive advertizing campaigns, enlisted the help of specialized "deposit brokers," and, most dangerous of all, offered higher yields than they could afford. In response, a growing group of depositors jumped frequently from place to place in a never-ending search for the highest possible return. *Hot money was born.*

As *Business Week* once described it, hot money includes "hot Certificates of Deposit that have been broker solicited and will go to the highest bidder, hotter short-term funds with maturities anywhere from a few days to a few months, and the hottest of all—federal funds."

To understand why all this is dangerous, let's follow closely the activities of a typical city banker in charge of the day-to-day inflows of deposits and other borrowings.

One of his chief sources of funds is large deposits of $100,000 or more. The concept is very simple. He prints up Certificates of Deposit (CDs) and sells them to investors.

If this could be exclusively a long-term transaction, things might be a lot easier. But it isn't. Typically, most of the CDs he sells are for no more than 90 days. So he's constantly worried about getting investors to renew. Moreover, often the investor doesn't have to wait the 90 days. He can sell his CDs, almost like a stock, for whatever price he can get in the open market. And, although this doesn't result in a withdrawal right away, the net affect is the same: When everyone is selling the *older* CDs, it makes it very difficult for the banker to sell his new ones.

The banker's next major source of hot money is "commercial paper"—short-term IOUs. Much like the CDs, he prints up certificates and gets investors to buy them. But there are a couple of wrinkles that distinguish these IOUs from the CDs. First of all, the duration is much shorter—typically 30 days instead of 90.

Moreover, technically speaking, a bank is not supposed to sell these IOUs in the first place. To get around this restriction, a separate corporation—the bank holding company—does it and then feeds the money back into the bank. These "backdoor" deposits are perfectly legal, but they are not subject to the same reserve requirements as actual deposits. In a crisis, investors could dump them in the open market, making it hard to borrow enough to pay off maturing IOUs.

The third place the city banker goes to borrow money is other banks, usually for just 24 hours. In the afternoon, when the bank is closed to the public, he calls around for the best deals. The next day, he has to do it all over again. According to Lester Gable, former vice-president of the Minneapolis Fed, these "federal funds" are potentially dangerous because "any reverse flow will very likely produce chaotic effects today or tomorrow. Fed funds are now being traded like marbles, and some day banks might be lending funds to the wrong banks at the wrong time."

Keeping all these balls in the air simultaneously is not an easy job even in normal times. During an economic crisis, just one or two failures could turn the banking system into a house of cards.

For depositors, the moral of this story is clear. First, the very term "making a deposit" is misleading. What you are really doing is *loaning money to your banks to invest as they please.*

Second, there are other, larger and more alert depositors ahead of you. You won't see them in the bank's lobby. Nor will you ever know who they are. But they are there nonetheless. And if there is any sign of trouble, they could take out whatever cash the banks have available, leaving you holding the bag. How much does the hot money represent? At many large city banks, it's often more than 50% of the total deposits, a stark contrast to the early 1960s when these new sources were virtually nonexistent.

Times have changed indeed!

Mistake #2. Not Enough Cash On Hand

The banks would probably be able to handle unusual demands by depositors as long as they could keep enough of the money "liquid"—in a form that they could readily access. In other words, it should not be locked up in brick and mortar, or invested in assets which take time to sell, but rather kept in cash or securities such as U.S. Treasury bills that can be converted into cash within 24 hours.

It's not so much the total that counts, but rather the *relative amount*. Whether you're evaluating your own financial situation or the safety of banks, this is the key question: "How much cash is on hand to back up each dollar of current debts?"

For example, if you or your family have $10,000 in debts due within the next twelve months, it would be a good idea to keep at least that much in cash savings to cover them. You should be able to handle 100% of your current debts without necessarily counting on any more income.

Similarly, banks need cash on hand to meet the demands of depositors, especially in bad times when people are out of work and need to draw on their savings. It would be too much to ask them to keep 100% of the money in cash because then they couldn't do any business. But I feel that 50% is a reasonable figure.

Here's a hypothetical example. Let's say, you're the first depositor in a brand new bank and you open your account with $100,000. The banker takes your money and loans out $70,000 to a commercial real estate developer, keeping the remaining $30,000 in cash and Treasury bills. If you decide you want your money back, he can come up with the $30,000 almost immediately. But the other $70,000 is now locked up in other investments—he has only 30 cents in cash or equivalent for every dollar in deposits. This is his "liquidity ratio."

Unfortunately, aside from some exceptional institutions I will tell you about shortly, the liquidity ratio of most banks is dangerously low. Back in 1976, the average large bank (defined as those that report weekly to the Federal Reserve) routinely kept at least 42 cents in cash or equivalent for each dollar of deposits and other short-term debts. In the late 1980s, they have no more than 32 cents, with many banks far below the national average. As can be seen in Table 1, a few large American banks have 40% in cash or equivalent readily available for every dollar left on deposit. But the majority are well under that level—some are even below the very dangerous 20% level!

Mistake #3. Too Many Bad Loans

When a banker can't collect on a loan for 90 days or more, it's officially considered a bad loan.

Bankers make mistakes from time to time, lending money out to consumers or businesses that, for some unexpected reason, cannot pay it back. As long as the bad loans are kept to a small percentage, however, they're acceptable. The real problem arises when banks aggressively seek to earn higher-than-normal yields and therefore consistently take larger-than-usual risks.

Unfortunately, this is precisely what many institutions have done in the 1980s. The commercial banks made massive loans to less developed nations, charging rates which were much higher than the equivalent rates paid by domestic borrowers. They lent substantial sums to real estate developers and got deeply entangled in the Texas oil boom. More recently, they have been full participants in the speculative merger mania which has swept Wall Street. The end result is that bad loans afflict banks throughout America, especially the large city banks that control most of the nation's deposits.

In fact, *there are quite a few large banks today that have more bad loans on their books than they have in equity* ... which leads to their next big mistake.

Mistake #4. Not Enough Cushion To Fall Back On

Perhaps the most obvious—and widely discussed—problem at the banks is low equity.

To better understand how this works, think for a moment about your own finances. If you have a home valued at $100,000 with an unpaid balance on your mortgage of $80,000, the equity in your home is $20,000. Your "equity ratio" is 20%. If, however, you get a new appraisal and it turns out your home is worth only $80,000, your remaining equity will be zero!

Table 1. How Safe Are America's Largest Banks?

Bank Name	Equity Ratio (%)	Liquid. Ratio (%)	Bad Loans (% of eq.)	Safety Index (Pts)
American Security Bk NA	6.0	38.3	21.3	-34
Ameritrust Co NA	6.3	28.9	30.4	-32
Amsouth Bk Birmingham NA	7.2	32.2	9.3	-39
Arizona Bk	5.9	17.7	18.1	-161
Banco Popular De Puerto R	5.6	49.0	6.0	-26
Bancohio NB	7.0	28.3	10.7	-10
Bank Of America NT&SA	3.6	28.7	108.9	-76
Bank Of California NA	6.1	17.3	40.9	-86
Bank Of Hawaii	5.8	42.8	7.9	34
Bank Of New England Na	4.8	20.5	43.9	-148
Bank Of New York	5.1	31.9	27.0	-16
Barnett Bk Of South FL NA	5.0	29.7	18.5	-17
Boatmens NB Of St Louis	7.0	43.2	10.4	40
Bowery Svg Bk	6.1	33.9	3.8	74
California First Bk	5.9	24.7	24.1	-66
Central Fidelity Bk	5.9	29.1	9.6	-50
Chase Lincoln First Bk NA	6.5	11.2	13.0	-82
Chase Manhattan Bk NA	4.7	33.1	86.7	-35
Chemical Bk	3.3	33.3	100.8	-37
Citibank Na	5.1	28.5	74.9	-52
Citibank NY St	7.9	33.3	2.3	-58
Citizens & Southern NB	5.9	31.8	8.3	-74
Comerica Bk	5.2	40.8	12.5	24
Connecticut NB	5.6	34.6	9.8	-59
Crestar Bk	5.1	19.8	9.7	-116
Dollardry Dock Svg Bk Of	3.5	26.8	10.1	23
Equitable Bk NA	5.8	48.7	6.5	14
European American Bk	5.3	41.9	36.4	-41
Fidelity Bk NA	4.2	39.7	25.9	-38
First Alabama Bk	9.4	41.4	4.0	23
First Bk NA	4.9	41.6	58.4	-109
First Fidelity Bk NA NJ	5.0	35.4	21.1	-10
First Florida Bk NA	7.0	30.7	4.5	26
First Interstate Bk AZ NA	5.9	27.7	35.9	-44
First Interstate Bk CA	3.5	30.0	75.0	-94
First Interstate Bk Or NA	5.5	39.4	26.6	29
First Intrst Bk NA	4.0	33.9	97.4	-101
First NB Of Atlanta	6.1	34.9	7.2	-57

Table 1 Continued

Bank Name	Equity Ratio (%)	Liquid. Ratio (%)	Bad Loans (% of eq.)	Safety Index (Pts)
First NB Of Boston	4.6	24.9	86.5	-108
First NB Of Chicago	2.5	30.4	93.6	-103
First NB Of Maryland	5.7	37.7	7.7	4
First Pennsylvania Bk NA	5.0	35.7	76.6	-35
First Tenn Bk NA	5.6	37.3	12.5	28
First Union NB FL	5.9	52.1	10.1	58
First Union NB NC	5.6	39.0	5.6	33
First Union NB Of Georgia	5.3	44.6	19.9	26
Fleet NB	5.9	25.6	14.9	-104
Florida NB	6.1	38.1	25.7	1
Goldome Svg Bk	3.4	34.9	19.1	-53
Hibernia NB New Orleans	5.7	29.1	15.6	-102
Howard Svg Bk	7.3	12.5	10.3	-18
Huntington NB	5.9	30.2	9.6	-4
Indiana NB	5.8	30.9	12.5	-28
Israel Discount Bk Of NY	5.1	75.8	3.7	102
Manufacturers NB	5.1	35.1	18.3	-49
Marine Midland Bk NA	2.3	16.3	147.2	-148
Maryland NB	4.8	30.6	11.0	-77
Mbank Dallas NA	3.4	20.9	163.4	-209
Mbank Houston NA	3.9	27.9	133.8	-120
Mellon Bk NA	2.6	33.0	150.3	-108
Mercantile Bk NA	6.5	27.4	48.3	-140
Meridian Bank	7.0	31.1	7.5	18
Meritor Savings Bk	4.4	50.7	24.2	-22
Michigan NB, Framington	6.1	29.0	11.6	-36
Midlantic NB	6.1	21.5	21.4	-58
National Bk Of Detroit	5.3	46.9	8.0	29
National City Bk	5.7	40.1	19.4	-61
National Westminster Bk U	3.6	24.7	70.9	-126
NCNB NB Of Florida	5.9	42.5	16.0	25
NCNB NB Of NC	5.5	38.4	11.5	-63
Norstar Bk Of Upstate NY	7.7	37.7	5.4	50
Norwest Bk MN NA	4.6	40.7	34.0	-62
Peoples Bk	6.5	14.7	15.5	21
Philadelphia NB	5.7	34.1	5.7	40
Pittsburgh NB	4.0	48.2	35.0	-76
Provident NB	6.1	38.8	4.5	-35
Rainier NB	6.5	23.4	15.0	-73

Table 1 Continued

Bank Name	Equity Ratio (%)	Liquid. Ratio (%)	Bad Loans (% of eq.)	Safety Index (Pts)
Republic NB Of NY	8.3	80.3	5.6	56
Riggs NB Of Washington DC	4.2	47.0	8.5	66
Sanwa Bk California	6.5	25.7	13.5	-82
Seattlefirst NB	5.3	17.5	72.5	-92
Security Pacific NB	4.0	29.0	74.0	-110
Shawmut Bk NA	5.7	35.7	18.8	-83
Signet Bk, VA	4.8	40.0	8.3	-51
Society NB	6.1	38.6	9.7	40
South Carolina NB	6.8	25.9	7.2	-57
Southeast Bk NA	4.9	32.3	23.9	-49
Sovran Bk NA	5.9	29.0	2.5	-67
Texas Commerce Bk NA	5.3	40.3	87.8	-72
Trust Co Bk	7.6	34.2	2.9	26
Union Bk	6.8	26.9	30.0	-116
United Jersey Bk	5.6	30.8	13.0	-6
United States NB	6.7	35.1	9.5	-55
Valley NB Of Arizona	5.3	27.9	59.1	-64
Washington MSB	5.7	43.2	9.0	27
Wells Fargo Bk NA	5.5	16.0	50.0	-139

Similarly, let's say a bank has $100 million in assets (loans, investments, building, etc.) and $95 million in borrowings from depositors like you or from other institutions. Their equity is $5 million and their equity ratio is 5%. If the authorities step in one day and say that, due to bad loans, the assets are now worth only $95 million, all of the equity is wiped out and the bank is, in effect, broke.

In other words, as long as your bank has plenty of equity to back it up, it would at least have a cushion to fall back on, and might be able to withstand some losses. Unfortunately, the actual data reveals the worst of all possible worlds—insufficient capital *plus* too many bad loans in the same time and place.

Bank of America is among the banks that have been hit especially hard, with 108.9 cents in bad loans for every dollar of equity. Chemical Bank is in a very similar predicament with 100.8%. Marine Midland, MBank Dallas and Mellon Bank are even worse with bad loan ratios of 147.2%, 163.4% and 150.3% respectively. (See Table 1.)

Where Are The Safe Banks?

What do you do about all this? Is there a safe bank in your state or do you have to look outside your own state to find one? What is it that makes a bank safe? To find the answers my firm, Weiss Research, purchased the Federal Reserve's entire data-bank covering 14,000 commercial banks, entered the critical information into a computer and generated a Safety Index for each, based upon a composite of the indicators discussed here. Here are some of my thoughts as I examined the data:

The FDIC says there are some 1,500 problem banks. (They don't give out the names.) But, I wonder how many problem banks there really are; 2,491 by our Index—that's 59% more than the FDIC tally. The FDIC probably doesn't expect the kind of economic decline we're anticipating, so their standards aren't quite as strict.

But nearly all of the problem banks seem to be on the big side; and all the stronger banks are small. This means that, in terms of where the deposits are, the crisis is much worse than it appears. *The problem banks control most of the bank assets in the*

United States: $1.7 trillion vs. only $1.5 trillion held by the relatively safer banks!

In simple language, if you're a depositor, the chances are 6 out of 10 that you're at a weak bank!

Of the largest banks in the U.S., only a very small minority had more than 7 cents in equity for each dollar of assets, the level which I believe could mark the threshold between possible disaster and survival. And among the weakest of the large banks, you could find some of today's most commonly known household names—Chemical Bank, Bank of America, First National Bank of Chicago and Chase Manhattan.

If you examine some of the banks in Table 1 which have the worst Safety Index, you will see where they have gone wrong and will be able to better understand how our Index works.

Arizona State Bank, for example, has a very poor Safety Index of a *negative* 161, among the worst in the nation (see page 22 for details). If you check their liquidity ratio, you will see why. They have only 17.7 cents in liquid assets for every dollar of deposits and other liabilities. That's less than half of what we would consider to be the acceptable minimum. Since Arizona State is not a money center bank, their exposure to bad loans is not quite as bad as it could be. But this alone is not enough to compensate for their poor liquidity.

The Bank of New England is also weak. In this case, though, the institution's low rating cannot be traced to one single indicator. Rather it's due to a combination of several different factors. They have only 4.8 cents in equity for every dollar of assets. Meanwhile, for every dollar of deposits, they keep only 20.5 cents on hand. Their bad loan ratio is also pretty large, especially for a regional bank. If they had to write them all off, it would wipe out a sizable chunk of their capital—43.9%. According to our formula, all this adds up to a Safety Index of a minus 148.

Table 1 demonstrates the sorry fact that *most* of America's largest banks have low equity and liquidity ratios. A substantial number have very large amounts of bad loans. And, as might be expected, nearly all will be hard pressed during an economic crisis.

What about the rest of the 14,000 commercial banks in the United States? Using the Fed's statistics, I grouped them into six categories, ranging from the weakest to the strongest. Then I put together a profile for the extreme categories. And, finally, I ran through the list and picked out the banks which most closely match the averages in each group. Rather than cite their names, however, I have given them descriptive titles.

Over-The-Brink BankCorp

I paid a visit to the first bank on our list—Over-The-Brink Bankcorp. Ironically, I saw nothing in its outward appearance that indicated any sign of trouble. The main office was in one of the city's most prestigious buildings. There were attractive fountains in front. Employees were busy and well dressed.

But the numbers were horrendous. The bank had only three cents in equity for every dollar of assets. In other words, a 4% loss in their investment and loan portfolio would have wiped them out. Unfortunately, they already had much more than that in bad loans!

So why were they still operating? I wondered to myself. Probably because no federal examiners have had the time or energy to check them thoroughly. Yes, it is known on the Street that they have troubles. But the press has been talking about bank troubles for so long that no one is paying much attention any more—not even the federal authorities.

This complacent attitude is probably the only reason Over-The-Brink BankCorp is still operating. If depositors and other creditors asked for their money, this bank would have less than 20 cents on the dollar available in cash or equivalent. Yet over 40% of their deposits comes from "hot-money depositors"—sources that would indeed demand their funds in a crisis!

I stopped for a moment to put these two facts together. All it takes is for one half of the hot-money depositors to move out and all the cash will be gone!

If this had been a small, obscure bank, I might have understood it. But it was a well-known bank with offices all over the state and penetration into other states through the acquisition of failed savings and loans by its holding company.

How many more of these over-the-brink banks are there? 262—that doesn't sound like much, but it is! It means that, instead of 200 or so banks failing this year, there could have been at least double that number. The only reason they have stayed open is that the authorities don't have the time to close them down or, worse yet, the authorities don't *want* to close them down. They're simply too big.

These 262 over-the-brink banks control a sizable chunk of the nation's commercial bank deposits—over $383 billion or 13% of the deposits of all commercial banks. For people who live in a large metropolitan area, the chances are high that their money is in, or passes through, one of them. Furthermore, in the next category on my list—the near-the-brink banks—there are *385*, most of which could go under at any time, especially if the economy weakens or interest rates go up.

None of these were counted among the 200 that failed last year. This means the number of bank failures could *easily* multiply *three or four times* in a normal recession.

Let's now examine a bank in the best category.

Strong Bank, Inc.

Unlike most banks, Strong Bank, Inc. is located in an older, simpler building; has no branches and has few employees. In fact, it seems to lack all the outward signs one normally associates with success. While it has only $116 million in assets, it has impressive numbers as far as I'm concerned: more than 13 cents in equity for every dollar of assets, 70% of depositors' money in cash and liquid investments, and only 1% of its equity tied up in bad loans. Adding this all up, our computer gives it a Safety Index of +129, which is among the best.

I called the president of the bank to ask him why he had followed this path. "It was all quite basic," he replied. "There isn't any point to making a loan if someone can't pay it back. A bad loan would not only hurt the bank, it would also destroy the individual borrower."

"What is your lending policy?"

"We simply don't make any of those energy loans which got so many people into trouble around here. To do the job right, you'd have to set up an engineering department within the bank. Instead, we stick mainly with our consumer business. And we don't even accept a Certificate of Deposit unless a customer does other business with us, such as a checking account."

Considering how much money big banks are spending to raise deposits, this last statement was truly amazing. "You mean, you wouldn't sell me a CD even if I wanted one?" I queried.

"It depends. We'd certainly like to get to know you first. Besides, I'm not sure you'd find our rates all that attractive."

"Are you turning a profit?"

He chuckled. "I'm glad you asked! Since we're in a depressed area, most bank analysts automatically assume that we're having the same troubles as everyone else. But we stick to old-fashioned banking practices and we're actually doing very well *despite* the real estate collapse in this town."

After hanging up, my first thought was to find out how many of these strong banks there actually are in America. Right at the top of my list I found them. Great equity ratios! That's what I call a cushion! Look at that liquidity ratio. Why, over half of their money is in cash. Hot money, zero. Bad loans, zero! How many of those gems are there scattered across the country? Only 103?!

"This is terrible," I said aloud to no one in particular.

"What's wrong?" responded my father, Irving Weiss, who happened to be walking by my office.

"Their assets total a meager $2.6 billion!"

"Whose assets?"

"The assets of the 103 strong banks I just found! Could this be a misprint? This report says that if you add up *all* the assets of *all* the strong banks in the country, it comes to only $2.6 billion. That's less than the total assets of a medium-sized regional bank. BankAmerica alone must have over $70 billion. What a shame!

I had another nagging thought. I tried to shove it out of my mind, but it returned to haunt me: There are so many rotten apples in the barrel and those apples are so huge that, once we get into a real panic, all banks will be affected to some degree.

But no matter what, the strong banks should be better equipped to withstand a crisis. Furthermore, even in the worst of circumstances, you will still need a strong bank for everyday checking and other business transactions. And if you buy U.S. Treasury bills, according to the Fed's new rules, you require a bank account for the Fed to transfer interest payments and other payouts. The next question is: How do you find one?

2

How To Find A Strong Bank

Until recently, the only people who were concerned about bank safety were the institutional investors who buy Certificates of Deposit that are larger than the $100,000 federal insurance limit. But now a growing minority of individuals around the nation are also becoming more safety conscious ... and for good reason. New bank and S&L failures are in the headlines nearly every day.

Therefore, whether you have a few thousand or a few *hundred* thousand dollars in your account, the facts are telling you that the time to move is now. Don't count on the Federal Government to give you your money back in case of a banking crisis. Rather, do your own homework to make sure your bank is safe. If it isn't, find the safest one in your state.

If nothing happens right away, remember that it is better to be safe than sorry, even if that means being premature or a bit too careful in the earlier stages of the banking crisis. Fortunately, as of this writing, there *are* ways to escape disaster.

Do not fall for the idea that it is somehow unpatriotic or irresponsible to talk about a banking crisis. *It is the bankers who have taken the risks—not the public or the press that finds out about them—who have shown a lack of financial and social responsibility.*

True facts have a way of making themselves known no matter what. So the sooner you and others find about them— and the sooner you can escape to a safe haven—the better it will be for everyone concerned, especially yourself. In the long run, if you protect your money now and reinvest it in worthy projects after the crisis is passed, you will actually be doing the nation a service.

Therefore, you can act without hesitation and with a clean conscience. Wherever possible, *move your savings out of banks and S&Ls entirely to Treasury securities or to a money fund which invests exclusively in Treasuries.* At the same time, for those funds you leave in the banking system, try to do business with the strongest banks in your area. Here are some basic steps to follow.

Step 1: Determine Whether You're Dealing With A Bank Or A Savings And Loan Association

Although there are many fundamental differences in their finances and structure, the critical technical distinction between an S&L and a bank is this: Banks report to the Federal Reserve and are usually insured by the Federal Deposit Insurance Corporation (FDIC). Savings and loans, on the other hand, report to the Federal Home Loan Bank and are usually (but not always) insured by the Federal Savings and Loan Insurance Corporation (FSLIC).

If it's a bank, use the guidelines in this chapter. If it's a savings and loan, refer to the next chapter.

Step 2: Ask The Right Questions

Acquire your bank's latest financial statements. Try to find the answers to the short list of questions outlined below. If their statements aren't clear, enlist the assistance of your own accountant or a bank officer.

Question #1. How many cents does your bank have in stockholders' equity for every dollar of assets?

This gives you the *equity ratio*—the amount of actual capital backup the bank has in the event of losses.

I feel that a bank should have at least 8%, sometimes even more. For a point of comparison, we have calculated this ratio for the nation's largest banks as of the latest data. (See Table 1.)

What about your bank? Does it have a high equity ratio? Do check it out for yourself. It's not difficult, and it won't take too much of your time.

Question #2. How many cents does your bank have in cash and equivalent to cover each dollar of deposits, short-term borrowings and other debts? In other words, what's their liquidity ratio?

We feel that your bank should have a liquidity ratio of at least 40%. Most banks don't. And if you've got your money at a savings and loan, you'll be lucky if they keep 10-15% of your money on hand ... which is one reason why we consider commercial banks to be, on average, safer than S&Ls.

Among the nation's largest banks, there are no more than a handful that have acceptable liquidity ratios and could withstand the kind of acute money demands we foresee. It all goes to prove that size alone is not a good indicator of a bank's underlying financial strength.

Question #3: For each dollar of equity, how many cents does the bank have in bad loans?

Let's say your bank has an equity of $5 million. If it has $500,000 in loans which are 90 days overdue, that represents 10 cents for every dollar of equity, a danger signal. To be safe, it should be less than 2 cents.

Step 3: Evaluate The Answers

Once you have most of the answers to your questions, the next task is to interpret them properly. In the accompanying evaluation table (pages 28 through 31), find the range which corresponds to that of your bank and read carefully the descriptions we provide for each.

Bear in mind that our guidelines are conservative. Most bank analysts would be satisfied with much lower standards. However, this is largely due to the fact that most are unwilling to recognize the possibility of a major recession—let alone a financial panic.

Step 4: Find A Relatively Strong Bank

Every three months our computer asks the questions described above—plus many more—for all of the 14,000 commercial banks in the United States, producing a Safety Index for each. Of course, no single indicator can be perfect, but we find that it accurately weeds out the weakest banks. It is also the best way we know to recognize the best banks.

Table 2. The Strongest Banks In America

State	City	Bank Name
Alabama	York	Bank Of York
Alaska	Anchorage	First NB Of Anchorage
Arizona	Phoenix	Metropolitan Bk
Arkansas	Huntsville	First NB Of Huntsville
California	Sacramento	Merchants NB
Colorado	Springfield	Baca St Bk
Connecticut	Putnam	Citizens NB
Delaware	Harrington	Peoples Bk
D. of Columbia	Washington	National Capital Bk Of Wa.
Florida	Belle Glade	Bank Of Belle Glade
Georgia	Chickamauga	Bank Of Chickamauga
★ Hawaii	Honolulu	City Bk
Idaho	Idaho Falls	Bank Of Commerce
Illinois	Oneida	Anderson St Bk
Indiana	Rockville	Rockville NB
Iowa	Washington	Washington St Bk
Kansas	Wichita	Union Blvd NB
Kentucky	Irvington	First St Bk
Louisianna	De Ridder	National Bk Of Commerce
Maine	Lewiston	Androscoggin Svg Bk
Maryland	Frostburg	Fidelity Bk
Massachusettes	Reading	Massbank For Svg
Michigan	Hastings	National Bk Of Hastings
Minnesota	Canby	National Bk Of Canby
Mississippi	Raymond	Merchants & Planters Bk
Missouri	Hannibal	Farmers & Merchants Bk
Montana	Absarokee	Yellowstone Bk
Nebraska	Hooper	First NB Of Hooper
Nevada	Ely	First NB Of Ely
New Hampshire	Portsmouth	Portsmouth Svg Bk
New Jersey	Trenton	Trenton Svg Fund Soc
New Mexico	Portales	Portales NB
New York	White Plains	Great Western Svg Bk
North Carolina	Newland	Avery County Bk
North Dakota	Napoleon	Stock Growers Bk
Ohio	Blanchester	First NB Blanchester

Use this table to find the strongest bank in your state. You will see that all have high equity and liquidity ratios as well as very few bad loans, if any. In addition, I show their total assets to give you an idea of their relative size. It is difficult, however, to find banks which are both large and liquid. Therefore, it is

Table 2 Continued

Total Assets ($Mil)	Equity Ratio (%)	Liquid. Ratio (%)	Bad Loans (%)	Safety Index (Pts)
32	17.0	90.7	4.8	158
877	16.5	76.3	3.0	102
70	76.0	65.7	0.0	116
53	10.5	80.5	2.0	171
63	15.2	101.2	0.0	180
31	9.1	85.6	0.0	158
53	12.6	53.2	0.0	157
37	11.5	49.0	0.0	122
90	16.5	62.1	0.0	168
42	11.8	74.4	0.0	182
30	15.7	81.7	0.0	161
401	6.5	42.9	1.8	77
127	12.8	58.6	1.7	126
30	12.6	91.4	0.0	180
50	17.5	74.1	1.1	160
77	11.1	74.0	0.0	173
85	8.7	83.1	0.0	174
70	9.4	60.9	0.0	162
43	9.5	73.2	0.0	138
140	12.7	65.4	0.0	183
32	9.9	63.3	0.8	169
319	24.6	73.9	0.0	201
31	10.8	60.7	0.0	164
27	14.9	98.5	0.0	184
25	10.0	68.1	2.9	121
39	11.6	81.3	0.0	181
12	13.3	82.5	0.0	176
27	15.3	90.7	0.0	186
22	36.2	120.6	0.0	195
252	12.8	67.9	0.0	186
233	10.0	62.5	0.5	177
46	12.2	73.5	5.1	142
28	19.8	112.9	0.0	200
29	22.1	86.0	0.0	168
30	14.8	78.6	0.0	164
33	14.9	88.0	0.0	165

necessary to include many smaller banks in this list. Also, do not be disappointed if you sometimes find it difficult to gain access to the smaller banks. Data: Federal Reserve's "Call & Income" tapes. (See pages 28-31 for definition of indicators.)

Table 2 Continued

State	City	Bank Name
Oklahoma	Lindsay	American Exch Bk
Oregon	Canby	First NB Of Oregon
Pennsylvania	Kittanning	Farmers NB Of Kittanning
Rhode Island	West Warwick	Centreville Svg Bk
South Carolina	Walhalla	Blue Ridge Bk Of Walhalla
South Dakota	Freeman	First NB Of Freeman
Tennessee	New Tazewell	Citizens Bk
Texas	Palestine	Royal NB Of Palestine
Utah	Lewiston	Lewiston St Bk
* Vermont	Middlebury	National Bk Of Middlebury
Virginia	Monterey	First & Citizens Bk
Washington	Vancouver	First Independent Bk
West Virginia	Union	Bank Of Monroe
Wisconsin	Cuba City	Cuba City St Bk
Wyoming	Burns	Farmers St Bk

Table 2 shows the strongest banks in each state based upon our Safety Index. Simply look up your state and select the one listed. If an asterisk is next to the name, it means that, even though the bank is the strongest in that state, it may not be quite strong enough to withstand a major depression.

Step 5: Make The Big Move

Now that you have accurate information, it is time to start shifting your funds. There is no single mathematical formula or computer program, no matter how sophisticated, which can consider all of the parameters that ultimately determine the safety of a depository institution. Therefore, before making a final decision regarding your funds, you may wish to check the accuracy of your analysis with an accountant or someone who has banking experience.

Once you have determined that your bank is indeed unsafe, then move promptly and without hesitation. Shift to a strong bank and to Treasury securities (see Chapter 8).

Table 2 Continued

Total Assets ($Mil)	Equity Ratio (%)	Liquid. Ratio (%)	Bad Loans (%)	Safety Index (Pts)
25	14.3	89.3	0.8	155
37	9.7	61.2	0.0	131
49	16.1	102.1	1.0	188
211	17.1	73.3	0.0	194
30	11.8	67.1	0.0	171
33	10.2	90.2	0.8	176
60	9.2	69.5	0.0	155
44	11.8	65.1	0.0	167
32	13.4	63.4	1.7	154
52	8.7	30.5	1.5	84
25	15.8	65.2	0.0	163
338	14.3	87.3	0.5	154
29	13.1	78.1	0.0	173
32	9.4	76.0	0.0	188
16	8.5	82.0	1.4	134

Interest Penalties For Early Withdrawal

What should you do if you have CDs or time deposits which have not yet matured? First, you must determine whether or not we are in a full-fledged money panic. Just because you see news of big S&L and bank failures does not, in itself, mean that the crisis has already reached the point when you must push the panic buttons.

How can you know? There aren't any fail-proof devices. However, one indicator which has proven very reliable in the past is the ratio between the 90-day CD rate and the 3-month Treasury bill rate.

To figure it out yourself, here's what to do:

1. On any Thursday, between 9:30 AM and 4:00 PM Central Time, simply call (314) 444-8589. That is the number for the St. Louis Federal Reserve Bank which provides a free hotline—a recorded message with all the interest rate data you need to keep track of what's happening in the money markets.

2. Write down the numbers for the 3-month T-bill rate and the 90-day CD rate. For future reference, also take note of the other interest rates.

3. Then divide the CD rate by the T-bill rate. For example, if the CD rate is 9% and the T-bill rate is 6%, the result would be 1.5%. This is the CD/T-bill ratio.

Graph 3. The Crisis Indicator

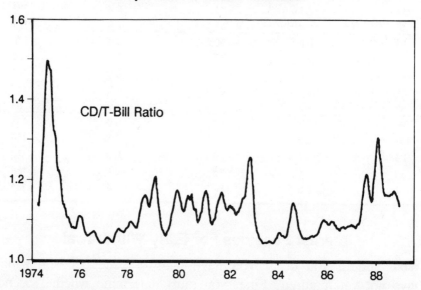

When there is a loss of confidence in the banking system, banks have to pay a higher premium over the rate paid by the Treasury Department to overcome the resistance of depositors. Therefore, the best way to monitor the confidence crisis is by comparing the 3-month T-bill rate with the 90-day CD rate as done in this graph. Bear in mind, however, that this graph does not necessarily give advance warning of a future crisis. It merely reflects the current crisis in the present time frame. Data: Federal Reserve.

As long as it stays under 1.3%, you should be able to wait until the maturity of your CD. But if it rises significantly above that level, we recommend you move without further hesitation. Clearly, there can be no hard and fast rules on when to stay and when to move. Your decision will depend as much on your state of mind as upon the state of the economy.

However, given the grave dangers all around us, my best advice is to err on the side of caution—to accept the interest penalty and protect your principal. Remember, in the stock market, the Crash of 1987 hit without warning and with no time to get out. Once the bubble burst, the mad dash for the exits was so powerful, it threatened the very structure of the market itself. *In the banking system, the rush for the exits could be even worse!* So do not let an early-withdrawal penalty on your interest stand between you and your principal. Two months later, you may kick yourself and wonder why you acted in haste. Then, two months plus one day later, you could wake up and thank your lucky stars that you didn't wait.

Simply look at the penalty in the same way that you view an insurance premium. If there's never an accident or major disaster, all the better. But if that disaster occurs, the little extra insurance will have paid for itself many times over.

If you want to check the safety of your own bank, simply follow the instructions on the following pages. Otherwise turn to page 32.

How To Check The Safety Of Your Own Bank

First, you must determine whether you are dealing with a commercial bank or a savings and loan. Banks report to -- and are regulated by -- the Federal Reserve Board and are usually members of the FDIC. Savings and loans come under the Federal Home Loan Bank and are usually insured by the FSLIC. If it is the latter, refer to the next chapter. Second, request their latest balance sheet and use it to find the information you need to answer the questions below. If there are various balance sheets for the same bank, use the one that has the largest total assets. Next, with a few simple calculations, you should be able to come up with the ratios I use in this book. Finally, evaluate your answers using the descriptions below.

When you compare your own results with those shown in this book, there may be some minor differences due to the fact that the data tapes sent to us by the Fed are based on the "Call And Income" reports which do not include other subsidiaries.

Question #1. How much does the bank have in stockholders' equity for every dollar of assets?

The information you need for this question will be very easy to find right in the balance sheet. You only have to divide the Stockholders' Equity by the Total Assets, multiplying the result by 100 to get a percent. And, if you go no further, it will at least give you a general idea of the bank's relative strength. It can be calculated with this simple formula:

equity ratio = stockholders' equity ÷ total assets × 100

Here are the basic ranges and their significance:

10% or more   *Strong.* Most likely this is a small, conservative country bank.

8 to 9.9%   *Still good but not as conservative.* Even some of the best known conservative banks such as J.P. Morgan and Republic of New York have lower equity ratios.

6 to 8%   *Good in normal times but possibly not good enough during a major banking crisis.* This is the area that regulators are now shooting for as a long-range goal in the shoring up of the banking system. It is doubtful, however, whether this goal can be achieved without a thorough housecleaning of bad debts.

4 to 5.9%   *Average.* Unfortunately, in today's environment of a weak banking system coupled to major economic dangers ahead, "average" implies "not good enough"! Most likely this is the category your bank will fall into

simply because the overwhelming majority of banks, especially in the big money centers, are within this range.

4% or less   *Weaker than average.* This bank is vulnerable to a severe recession and could come under great pressure during the Money Panic.

Question #2. How many cents does the bank have in cash and equivalent to cover each dollar of all deposits, short-term borrowings and other liabilities?

This ratio could take a bit more time to calculate. The items needed for this question are all contained in the balance sheet, but could be more difficult to weed out due to some differences in the precise nomenclature used from bank to bank. If so, do not hesitate to ask for the assistance of a bank officer. The formula is:

liquidity ratio = cash and equivalent ÷ current liabilities × 100

To get the "cash and equivalent," you have to add up as many as six items: (1) Cash And Due From Banks, (2) Interest Bearing Deposits Placed with Banks, (3) Federal Funds Sold and Securities Purchased Under Resale Agreements, (4) Other Money Market Investments (if any), (5) Trading Account Assets, and (6) Investment Securities. (Warning: Some of these may be split up into two separate entries or combined into one.) The easiest way to get the "current liabilities" is to find Total Liabilities and then subtract from it all long-term debt items. These could include "Long-Term Notes and Debentures" or "Long-Term Debt Qualifying As Primary Capital" or "Other Long-Term Debt." Once you get the number, here's what it means:

75% or more   *Unusually strong.* Virtually nonexistent among large city banks, and very rare among the small banks. This institution is obviously flush with cash.

50% - 74.9%   *Strong.* Since your bank has over half of its deposits and borrowings in liquid or immediately marketable assets, we believe that it is in relatively good shape, assuming no major banking disaster. It is only in the event of a nationwide calamity, when it is possible that the stronger banks could be dragged down along with the weaker ones, that you will need to be concerned. Until such time, your money is safe. But don't rely on this ratio alone.

40 to 49.9%   *Better than average for city banks, but average for country banks.* This is normally sufficient. But in the Money Panic, it may not be enough. I feel that a bank

should have over 50% liquidity in order to withstand the pressures ahead.

35 to 39.9%   *Relative to most large city banks, this is actually on the high side.* But in the Money Panic, it may not be enough.

30 to 34.9%   *Average for city banks and below average for country banks.* This is the range within which most large city banks now fall. But again, just because others are in the same boat doesn't make it acceptable.

29.9% or less   *Weak even according to the very liberal standards commonly accepted today.* As a rule of thumb, the 30% level can be viewed as a critical threshold below which there could be grave dangers abound.

Question #3. For each dollar of equity, how many cents does the bank have in bad loans?

The critical information you need to answer this question is the total amount of "nonaccruing" or "nonperforming" loans. This may appear in a footnote or special table of the bank's annual report. Or it may not appear at all. However, every Federal Reserve member bank must report this figure to the Fed and that is considered public information. Therefore, if you try hard enough, you will find someone at the bank's headquarters who can give you the information. Once you have the data, the formula is simple:

bad loan ratio = nonaccruing loans ÷ stockholders' equity × 100

None   *Excellent.* Clearly this is the ideal situation -- no past-due loans at all. It is possible that they are being hidden via a variety of mechanisms. But, for the most part, we must take the data literally.

0.9% or less   *Good.* Giving the bank the benefit of the doubt, we must recognize that no one is perfect. There are always bound to be some mistakes made even in the very best of banks. The key is to keep it to a minimum level as is the case here.

1 to 9.9%   *Average.* Again, "average" should not be comforting. Although the percentages may still appear small, the fact is they could be understated. So watch out.

10 to 19.9%   *Bad.* Now we're starting to get into the high range for this indicator, a bad sign. The fact that 13% of the

nation's banks are in this category is no comfort. Rather, we advise extreme caution.

20 to 29.9%   *Very bad.* This is the worst 10 percentile of the entire banking industry. When you consider that the industry as a whole is in bad shape, you can begin to see the grave risks you are taking when dealing with this bank.

30% or more   *In trouble.* If your bank is in this position, it is in deep trouble. The fact that it has been in this predicament for many years with no apparent consequences is merely a testimony to the complacency of depositors. It should not be construed as a sign that this number is, for some reason, unimportant.

Question #4. Is your bank safe or not? This is obviously the ultimate question, which we seek to answer via our Safety Index. The Safety Index combines all of the above ratios, plus many others, into an overall evaluation. Although it is not possible for you to calculate it yourself, we provide the meaningful ranges here to help you interpret the tables in this book.

100 or more   *Exceptionally Strong.* Only 5% of the nation's banks are in this group.

50 to 100   *Good.* This is generally acceptable in most cases. However, since we cannot guarantee that our formula is picking up all the possible problems and contingencies, we prefer to err on the side of caution.

50 to -50   *Average.* A total of 64% of the nation's banks fall within this range. Above zero is obviously better than below zero. But, there is no magic importance to the zero line.

-50 to -200   *Poor.* These are the low banks on the totem pole. Although some may appear to be doing well in terms of profitability, this doesn't mean they are safe places to keep your money.

-200 or less   *Extremely weak.* These could be disasters waiting to happen.

Warning: No single indicator or formula can encompass all the complexities of banking. Therefore, use our Safety Index as a general guide -- not as the ultimate answer. Also, bear in mind that there is no significant difference between, a bank with, say, a Safety Index of -100 and another with an Index of -120.

3

The Sick S&Ls

Richard Dexter, the Chief Economist of a major financial institution, has been in a coma caused by a head injury in 1984. Like a modern Rip Van Winkle, he finally regains consciousness and asks to be brought up to date. Mary Ann Brown, the firm's 36-year old Comptroller, comes to his hospital room to "debrief him."

The bright and cheerful Comptroller greets the bedridden economist but barely manages to mask her surprise when she sees the man's shriveled appearance. Nevertheless, he is anxious to learn what has transpired during his missing years. Not knowing exactly where to start, she summarizes some headlines from the financial press. Savings & loans are being decimated by loan losses. Commercial banks have suffered huge declines in their regular operations, most of which have been covered up by one-shot profits in their speculative bond and foreign-exchange trading.

"I see," Dexter says, nodding sadly. "So I guess it didn't happen."

"What didn't happen?"

"The big growth in the money supply! The big expansion of credit. The big interest rate decline. You know, that's what I predicted. Those were the things I saw coming in 1984, the things I staked my reputation on." The economist sighs deeply and then continues: "From what you're telling me, none of my forecasts materialized. Otherwise I'm sure these problems would not exist. The economy would be home free by now, not mired down in all this garbage!"

"Calm down," she says reassuringly. "It happened just like you said it would. The Fed pumped in a lot of money. Interest rates fell and bond markets enjoyed a big rally."

"No kidding!" says Dexter, greatly cheered. "But then why all the news about failures and declining profits and God knows what else?"

"That's the 64-billion-dollar question, the one that burns everyone's brain, but no one knows how to answer. In the years you were unconscious, we jumped for joy over the decline in interest rates. Hardly a day went by without some economist mentioning the big boost this would give to banks and S&Ls in trouble. Now here we are at the appointed time and place when the big boost was supposed to arrive, but it's nowhere in sight."

"Do me a favor, will you?" he asks.

"Sure. You name it."

"Get me some more info on that S&L thing."

"For your forecasting model?"

"The heck with my model! What I'm worried about is my money, which I've got in ..." Dexter's eyes go blank, reminding her that it hasn't been long since he regained consciousness. "Now I remember, the Beverly Hills ... never mind, just bring all the latest you've got on the thrifts, OK?"

"No problem," she says, anxious to help.

The next day, the Comptroller phones Dexter at the hospital. "Brace yourself!" she says. "When it comes to the S&Ls, you ain't heard nothing yet!"

"You mean the old, low-yielding mortgages they're stuck with, their big borrowings from the Federal Home Loan Bank, their low capital? Heck! That's old news!"

"No, I'm talking about the commercial real estate debacle! The junk bonds! The deliberate violations of the law and wholesale cover-up operations at the highest levels."

"How bad is it?"

"Here. Listen to some of these."

She cites four of the largest failures: *Western Savings Association, Dallas.* $2 billion in assets. Accused of speculative lending, regulatory violations including deficient or nonexistent real estate appraisals, inadequate loan documents, inaccurate accounting and shoddy record keeping. Third largest takeover in history!

Central Savings & Loan Association, San Diego. $2.2 billion. Second largest takeover ever.

Sunrise Savings & Loan, Boynton Beach, Florida. At $1.5 billion, they were the fourth largest. They were taken over by the Federal Home Loan Bank Board but the Board finally had to close them down.

"Here's where you come in," she says. "The Beverly Hills Savings & Loan Association's $2.9 billion easily made it one of the biggest takeovers of all time."

"Oh no! That's where my money ..."

"Yup," she answers with great sympathy. "Those guys really went to town with *everyone's* money. You know what they did? Here's just an example. It seems they made an outright investment in an apartment complex, became actual partners in the deal. Then, when the thing went sour and nosedived in value, they turned around and apparently doctored the thing up to make it look like a loan which they recorded at full face value.

"Record keeping was another problem. When new managers walked in, they discovered that the records of a $1 billion portfolio of construction loans were kept only on a single floppy disk in a personal computer in the office of an aide to the thrift's president. This is typical. Whenever an insolvent S&L is taken over, managers are consistently shocked at what they find—such a back-office mess that just figuring out how bad things are is a challenge in itself. Often the only place you can find any information at all is inside the heads of the people who were there, and once they've walked out the door, it's gone forever."

"That can happen to the best of firms. What else is new?" he queries.

"What's new is that Uncle Sam is nearly out of money to bankroll all this nonsense."

"Typical government operation!"

"Yes, but what I'm going to tell you next is not what you'd normally associate with 'typical.'" She asks Dexter to hold on for a moment, puts down the receiver and picks up some news clippings. "Until recently, regulators tended to be lax. They winked at what they euphemistically called 'more liberal accounting treatments.' They figured that was a good way to help the ailing thrift industry. Now, that concept has gone in the trash."

Dexter nods nervously. "I think I know what you're getting at, but ..."

"Let me explain it this way," says Mary Ann. "When I was a kid and my dad had a lot of money, he was pretty lenient. But when he didn't have it, he suddenly turned strict. With the government authorities, I can see how the same thing might happen. Let's say I'm an official at the Federal Savings & Loan Insurance Corporation, and let's say you're the chief executive of a thrift in trouble. As long as I had plenty of dough to spread around, my attitude was: 'OK, little boy, you can cheat and lie once in a while. Nobody's perfect!' Now I'm saying: 'You SOB, look what you've done to me!' So guess what the regulators do?!"

"What?"

"They sue the managers and directors personally!" she says softly.

"You're kidding. How can they do that? I've heard of private citizens suing insurance companies, but never of Federal insurance companies suing the S&Ls. Why?"

"It gets the regulators off the hook. They don't have to fork over as much cash. And, boy oh boy, when they sue they really go for it! That's when the real dirt comes out! Sunrise, the Boynton Beach S&L, is a case in point. The FSLIC sued 27 of its former officers, directors and attorneys for more than $250 million. They allege a 'flagrant pattern of unsafe and unsound lending practices, negligence and a breach of fiduciary duty.'"

"Was it really that bad?" Dexter sputters.

"Nope. It was worse! Sunrise officials made numerous bad loans based on inflated and otherwise improper appraisals, without securing collateral. The suit says that pay incentives and bonuses to Sunrise's executives encouraged a high volume of loans without regard to their feasibility. Under its accounting method, Sunrise immediately recorded the loan fees as income for the thrift.

"One developer whose properties were going bad," she continues, "drew down his $500,000 line of credit at Sunrise to make interest payments. Then the S&L approved checks on his NOW account when funds were unavailable, creating about $3 million in overdrafts! In another instance, Sunrise's board approved the purchase of real estate on which the thrift already held a lien, for $5 million more than the developer had recently paid for it, to provide him 'with funds to pay off other Sunrise loans,' the suit says."

"I get the point," he replies. "How often does the FSLIC take such drastic action? Once in a blue moon, I'd imagine."

"Actually, it's becoming standard practice. According to the *Wall Street Journal*, 'the FSLIC, facing a rising number of thrift failures, has been increasingly filing such suits against former officials of such institutions in an effort to bolster its financial strength. Currently, thirty-one suits are pending, including thirteen filed this year.'"

The bedridden economist thinks for a moment before commenting. "If I were Sunrise I'd say to the FSLIC: 'You were the ones who told me it was OK to do this in the first place.'"

"Tough!" is their reply. Besides, what really counts is the green stuff! Just a short time ago, the FSLIC had $6 billion in reserves. Now they're almost down to $1 billion. Within the next few years, they are projected to fall deep into minus territory."

"WHAT?!" This time Dexter is truly surprised. "What do you mean 'deep into minus territory'?"

"This AP wire story explains it: 'The Federal Savings and Loan Insurance Corp. could need as much as $30 billion to deal with hundreds of insolvent S&Ls in coming years.' That's how much they themselves estimate they might need just to bail out the trouble spots they already know about. That doesn't include the institutions which are more adept at covering things up, or the ones that are borderline. What's most wrong with their estimate, though, is not the amount; it's the timing. Rather than 'a few years,' I think it could turn out to be a few *quarters.*"

"So Congress will provide more money, that's all!"

"The first time around, probably. The second time, maybe. The third time, fat chance! Already, even on the first go-around, the Senators are resistant. The Chairman of the House Banking

Committee has told the savings and loan industry they first have to get their act together. If they don't clean up their problems, they won't get any dough."

"Congress can't let the FSLIC fail, can it?"

"Listen to the Chairman's own words: 'It is all well and good to pump more money into the insurance fund, but unless we get to the cause of the disease, it is a bottomless pit.'"

"I've heard enough!" Dexter says dejectedly. "Please let me off this phone so I can call Beverly Hills and get my money out before it's too late!" He hangs up and she goes back to her accounting work.

A scant fifteen minutes later, he calls back, with a certain sense of I-told-you-so satisfaction. "I knew that name wasn't quite right. I didn't have my money in the Beverly Hill Federal Savings & Loan after all! It's the Columbia Savings & Loan, also of Beverly Hills, California."

She pauses for a moment and says, "Oh, really? Congratulations! You may some day become the proud owner of one of the largest pools of junk bonds ever! In fact, Columbia is notorious for having $2.3 billion or a whopping 28% of their assets in junk bonds. In fact, the legal counsel of the Federal Home Loan Bank Board says that the problem is nationwide and 'rather than wait for any kind of disaster to occur'—as if one hadn't occurred already—they want to take some action to try to perhaps head off ..."

Dexter curses and hangs up on her again, this time in the middle of her sentence. She knows he's not being rude—he simply needs the line for one more phone call.

The Rule, Not The Exception

How typical are these *S&Ls*? How widespread are these dangers? To find the answers, we again went to the source: We purchased the complete data tapes on all federally insured savings and loans from the Federal Home Loan Bank. Then, as we did for the commercial banks, we pumped their data into our mainframe computer, extracted a series of critical ratios, and grouped the S&Ls into categories.

Table 3. How Safe Are The Largest S&Ls?

Savings & Loan Name	Equity Ratio (%)	Liquid. Ratio (%)	Repos. Assets (% of equity)	Safet Inde (Pts
American Svg Bk FSB (N.Y.)	8.8	6.9	17.1	-163
American S&L (Stockton, CA)	-0.4	5.4	0.0	-40!
Amerifirst Bank (Miami)	4.7	5.9	35.9	-19(
Anchor Svg Bk (Northport, NY)	7.3	6.2	1.1	-11!
Atlantic F.F.(Bala Cynwid, PA)	6.1	4.4	12.1	-24!
B. Franklin S&L (Portland)	4.6	6.1	9.6	-26(
Bright Banc S (Dallas)	-1.7	6.8	0.0	-43(
California F S&L (L.A.)	4.9	5.3	15.2	-27!
Carteret Svg (Newark)	5.4	6.9	7.2	-22
Centrust Svg Bk (Miami)	4.9	5.5	3.6	-23
Citicorp Savings (S.F., CA)	13.0	5.5	0.1	-4!
City Federal (Bedminster, NJ)	3.1	4.0	34.3	-30!
Coast S&L (L.A.)	8.7	4.7	4.5	-18!
Columbia S&L (Beverly Hills)	6.4	7.2	2.1	-14!
Commercial F S&L (Omaha)	3.0	4.3	46.5	-28!
Crossland Svg (Brooklyn)	9.2	5.7	0.5	-13!
Dime Savings Bank of NY	6.2	8.8	4.1	-18!
Empire of Am. (Buffalo, NY)	2.5	5.5	60.5	-29!
First FS&L of Rochester	1.9	8.0	8.0	-28
First Fed. of MI (Detroit)	4.4	4.5	1.4	-24
First Nationwide (S.F., CA)	4.9	5.3	9.8	-28
Florida FS&L (St. Pete., FL)	2.8	6.2	35.6	-28
Franklin Svg (Ottawa, KS)	5.6	2.3	1.5	-22
Gibraltar Svg (Houston)	3.1	3.7	147.6	-2!
Gibraltar Svg (Bev. Hills)	3.0	4.4	31.0	-3(
Glendale FS&L	5.6	5.5	6.4	-2!
Great Western (Bev. Hills)	4.5	4.8	17.2	-2!
Gt. Am. 1st Svg (San Diego)	6.0	3.2	19.7	-2!
Home F S&L (San Diego)	7.2	4.9	21.3	-2!
Home Savings of Am. (L.A.)	5.5	8.4	11.0	-2!
Homestead Svg F S&L (S.F.)	3.7	6.7	18.4	-3!
Imperial Svg (San Diego)	3.8	4.0	11.1	-3
Lincoln S&L (L.A.)	5.5	9.5	29.7	-2
Merabank Fed. Svg (Phoenix)	7.8	4.7	16.4	-2
Northeast Svg (Hartford)	4.4	4.6	2.5	-2
Pacific 1st Fed. (Tacoma, WA)	4.9	4.4	10.9	-2
Perpetual Svg Bk (McLean, VA)	7.0	5.7	6.4	-2
San Francisco F S&L	4.7	4.8	11.5	-2
Santa Barbara S&L	2.7	3.0	6.6	-2
Seamens Bank For S (N.Y.)	3.9	2.0	28.5	-2

Table 3 Continued

Savings & Loan Name	Equity Ratio (%)	Liquid. Ratio (%)	Repos. Assets (% of equity)	Safety Index (Pts)
Sears Svg Bk (Glendale, CA)	5.3	4.7	32.8	-286
Standard Fed Bk (Troy, MI)	6.6	9.9	0.7	-133
TCF Bkng & Svg (Minneapolis)	3.2	4.5	26.3	-269
Talman Home FS&L (Chicago)	31.0	24.4	1.0	52
Talman Home S&L (Chicago)	4.9	4.4	14.0	-199
Transohio Svg (Cleveland)	5.0	3.5	15.0	-257
United Svg of Texas (Houston)	0.7	5.7	702.1	-333
University Svg (Houston)	2.9	4.3	281.1	-312
Western S&L (Phoenix)	3.7	10.9	65.3	-227
World S&L (Oakland)	5.9	9.5	3.9	-200

The largest savings & loans in America are, on average, in much worse shape than the largest banks. Compare, for example, their equity and liquidity ratios with those of the banks on page 10-12. The ratios shown here mean essentially the same as they do for the banks. However, the "normal ranges" are quite different, especially with respect to the liquidity ratio. Among banks, it is rarely below 25%. Among S&Ls, it is rarely *above* 15%. Data: FHLB (See pgs. 45-46 for a definition of the indicators.)

We did find some thrifts where sound practices were followed, but the overall totals showed a very sharp deterioration in the industry as a whole.

Over half of the S&Ls have less than 5 cents in equity for every dollar of total assets. In other words, it wouldn't take more than a 5% loss in their loans and investments (their assets) to wipe out their capital and close their doors. Furthermore, over 22% of the S&Ls have only three cents in equity for every dollar of assets. Even in the best of times, this is a precarious position.

To make matters worse, very few S&Ls keep money in readily available cash. In fact, *85% of the savings and loans have less than 25 cents on hand for every dollar of deposits and other borrowings!*

The sorry truth is that, the majority of savings and loans— 1,762—are weak. Only 1,410 are in relatively *less bad* financial shape.

Furthermore, the unsafe savings and loans control over 79% of the S&L deposits. In other words, if you have your money in a savings and loan, the chances are over three out of four that they are unsafe.

Study carefully Table 3, which shows the lamentable financial condition of the largest S&Ls in America (pages 38 and 39). Again, as was the case with the banks, we notice a distinct pattern wherein the biggest tend to be the worst! So when an institution advertises in big letters at their front door "Over $10 billion in assets," it should immediately raise the eyebrows of savers. Unfortunately, it doesn't.

Most Americans pay little attention to the fact that two of the largest thrifts in the country have equity which is *below zero*.

They ignore the fact that, of the 50 largest S&Ls in the country, only four have more than 8 cents in equity for each dollar of assets.

Furthermore, savers don't seem to mind the fact that some Houston S&Ls are up to their ears in repossessed assets: For every dollar of equity on its books; Gibraltar Savings has $1.48 of repossessed assets; University Savings has $2.81 in repossessed assets; and for United Savings, the figure is $7.02, primarily because their equity has been virtually wiped out.

In fact, it is safe to say that, among the 50 largest S&Ls, only *one* is reasonably sound: The Talman Home Federal Savings & Loan of Chicago has a very respectable 31 cents in equity for each dollar of assets. It has 24 cents in reserves and cash on hand to meet each dollar of deposits—quite high for an S&L. And it has only one cent in repossessed assets per dollar of equity. Consequently, it is the only one that has got a positive rating from our computer program which combines these and other measures of the thrifts' financial health. (For a detailed description of these indicators, see pages 45 and 46.)

The General Accounting Office, Congress' auditing agency, has estimated it would cost about $35 billion to resolve the cases of the more than 500 insolvent institutions. Private analysts put the price tag at $50 billion or more. Our statistics indicate a figure in excess of $100 billion!

Nevertheless, the charade continues, unabated and unchecked. And the American saver is taking little or no action to protect himself from the shenanigans until it is much too late.

Most don't realize that you *can* take action right now to protect yourself from the S&L crisis.

Check The Safety Of Your S&L

If you are concerned about the safety of your money in a commercial bank, you should be even more concerned about the safety of the average S&L. Although there are exceptions, as a rule, we find that:

1. The equity ratio of most S&Ls is significantly lower than that of most commercial banks.

2. Their liquidity ratio is consistently *much* lower. Some of this is due to the difference in the nature of their business and their methods of accounting. But not all of it!

3. Unlike the banks, S&Ls rely heavily on advances from the Federal Home Loan Bank to keep them afloat.

4. Perhaps most important, the FSLIC—the federal insurance company that covers your deposits at the S&Ls—is far weaker than its counterpart in the commercial banking sector, the FDIC. Therefore, in a widespread banking crisis, the chances of a failure by the FSLIC are greater than those of the FDIC.

To determine the relative safety of trusting a particular S&L with your funds, the questions you should ask are similar to—but not exactly the same as—those we asked in the previous chapter:

Question #1: How much stockholders' equity does the S&L have for every dollar of assets?

This is the same equity ratio that we used for the commercial banks—the "capital cushion" that the S&L has to fall back on in times of trouble. It is the best indicator of the S&L's capacity to withstand loan losses.

Some people believe that an S&L doesn't need as much capital as a commercial bank of the same size. We disagree. Both have accepted the responsibility for your funds. Both should be subject to the same basic safety rule: A minimum of nine to ten cents in equity for each dollar of total assets. Finding one with a strong equity position isn't easy, though. In fact, there are several hundred in the United States today that have *negative equity—defacto* bankruptcy.

Table 4. The Strongest S&Ls In America

State	City	Name
Illinois	Chicago	East Side S&L
Louisianna	New Orleans	Guaranty Svg & Homestead
Louisiana	New Orleans	Union S&L
Maryland	Baltimore	Fraternity FS&L
New Hampshire	Salem	Salem Coop Bk
New York	Brooklyn	Atlas S&L
New York	Lynbrook	Jamaica Savings Bank
North Carolina	Roxboro	Roxboro S&L
North Carolina	China Grove	Rowan FS&L
Pennsylvania	Strabane	Slovenian S&L Of Canonsbu

This table was originally designed to help you find the safest S&Ls in each state of the U.S. Unfortunately, there simply are no safe S&Ls in most of the states of the union! However, we have come up with 10 which do have good

Question #2: How many cents does the S&L have in cash and equivalent to cover each dollar of total deposits, short-term borrowings and other liabilities?

It is this ratio which could be the most important during a run on deposits. It is also in this ratio that we see the greatest contrast between S&Ls and commercial banks. Nearly *all* the S&Ls in our database have a liquidity ratio of 35% or less! All are in dangerous territory according to this barometer. And over 10% of the S&Ls are in even more extreme difficulties, with a liquidity ratio of 4.9% or less.

Question #3: For each dollar in equity, how much does the S&L hold in repossessed assets?

No S&L wants to get stuck with repossessed assets. They're difficult to sell even in the best of times. These items do have some value, however, and they are recorded on the balance sheet. Clearly, the greater percentage of repossessed assets, the greater the chances that they have more bad loans still on the books.

Table 4 Continued

Total Assets ($Mil)	Equity Ratio (%)	Liquid. Ratio (%)	Repos. Assets (%)	Safety Index (Pts)
67	14.0	59.5	0.0	219
85	18.4	40.8	0.2	199
63	18.6	53.4	0.7	198
53	13.9	39.5	0.0	192
110	10.2	41.4	0.0	199
47	15.0	66.8	0.0	216
1399	13.7	68.6	0.0	190
66	10.0	47.4	0.0	211
34	12.1	34.1	0.0	181
64	9.7	36.9	0.0	190

financial ratios – solid proof that it *is* possible to follow sound banking practices in this industry. Data: FHLB. (See pgs. 45-46 for definition of the indicators.)

Once you have the answers to your questions, use the evaluation tables at the end of this chapter to get a better grasp as to where your S&L stands.

Your Strategy

The number of strong banks is small. The number of strong S&Ls is even smaller. However, by scanning all 3,000 S&Ls in the country, our computer has been able to come up with a handful that are in relatively good shape. You will note, however, that all of them are in the Northeast. They maintain top-notch equity ratios, keep excellent liquidity on hand and have virtually no bad assets on their books.

They have earned top ratings from us—near 200. Take East Side S&L in Chicago, for instance: 14 cents in equity for every dollar of assets; almost 60 cents in cash or equivalent on hand to cover each dollar of deposits; zero in repossessed assets. And look at Atlas S&L of Brooklyn, New York, or the Jamaica Savings Bank in Lynbrook, New York! If only the rest of the thrift industry had followed the examples of these shining stars, how much grief and loss could have been avoided!

As we saw with the banks, the truly unfortunate aspect of all this is that the bad apples in the barrel spoil the few good ones. If there are going to be panic withdrawals from the thrifts, how many savers are going to stop and ask about these balance sheets? How many are going to notice that these ten should be spared from the withdrawal madness?

Our best advice is to avoid S&Ls entirely. Move most of your funds to Treasury bills (or a money fund that invests exclusively in T-bills) and do all your banking with a *strong* commercial bank.

The question is not whether the public is going to start pulling their money out, but how soon they will begin. As of this writing, most people have taken the bad news about the S&Ls without flinching, probably because short-term rates have been relatively low. In the Money Panic, however, it won't take much to wake up the complacent savers of America. It could be a sharp stock market crash, a decline in the economy, or a temporary upsurge in interest rates. No one can say for sure.

What we do know is that once a run on the thrifts—and the banks—gets under way, it could be too late for you to make your move. You must be well prepared *ahead of time*, or one day you may find yourself in line at your bank's locked front door.

Unfortunately, however, banks and S&Ls aren't the only institutions in trouble.

How To Check The Safety Of Your Own S&L

First, read carefully the boxed section in the previous chapter "How To Check The Safety Of Your Bank." The procedures to follow here are quite similar.

Question #1. How much does the S&L have in stockholders' equity for every dollar of assets? (For the formula, see previous chapter.)

10% or more   *Excellent.* Actually, there is a small group of S&Ls that do fall into this category.

7 to 9.9%   *Better than average.* Make sure, however, that the other ratios confirm this.

4 to 6.9%   *Average.* This is, in my view, a very poor equity position. The fact that the biggest proportion of the nation's S&Ls fall into this range is no consolation.

3.9% or less   *Below average.*

Question #2. How many cents does the bank have in "regulatory liquidity" (cash and equivalent) to cover each dollar of all deposits, short-term borrowings and other liabilities?

The formula and items used will be almost the same as that for banks. However, there may be no long-term debt items to speak of.

35% or more   *Rare and probably very strong for an S&L.* There are less than 150 S&Ls in this group. However, you cannot rely on this measure alone.

20 to 34.9%   *Better than average.* This is actually still high for an S&L but not necessarily strong enough in a major crisis.

10 to 19.9%   *Average but weak in a crisis.* Over 1000 S&Ls are in this range. But again, just because there are many others in the same boat doesn't make it acceptable.

5 to 9.9%   *Very weak.* Unfortunately, this is the category which has the most S&Ls -- nearly 1200. In other words, they have less than 10 cents available on hand to meet every dollar of withdrawal. The reason there are so many is because that authorities have established an average monthly balance of 5% as their statuatory miniumum. Their view is that if an S&L's liquidity is too high, it can adversely affect their profitablity, which in turn will hurt them in the long run. My view is that if they can't turn a profit and keep their depositors' money safe at the same time, they should cut their costs.

Under 5%   *Probably taking big risks.* This S&L could be in trouble. Again, the fact that there are many -- over 300 -- in the same boat is no consolation.

Question #3. For each dollar in equity, how much does the S&L hold in repossessed assets?

The item "repossessed assets" is often found in the balance sheets under more euphemistic sounding terms such as "Property Acquired In Settlement Of Loans" or "Real Estate Held For Sale Or Development, Less Accumulated Provision For Estimated Losses." Here again, make sure you get help to properly identify these items. The formula is:

$$\text{repossessed assets ratio} = \text{repossessed assets} \div \text{stockholders' equity} \times 100$$

None   *Good.* Unfortunately only 20% of the nation's S&Ls are in this group. But if yours is among them, it is a good sign. Make sure that the other ratios corroborate this.

0.9% or less   *Acceptable.*

1 to 4.9%   *Average but not good.*

5 to 9.9%   *Below average.* If you recognize that delinquency rates are bound to go up sharply in the years ahead, you will realize that an S&L with an already-high repossessed asset ratio is in for some hard times.

10% or more   *Weak.* This S&L is already in difficulty even before the economy goes into a decline.

Question #4. Is the S&L safe or not? (See explanation and warnings on the bottom of page 275.)

200 or more   *Relatively strong.*

100 to 200   *Above average.*

-100 to 100   *Average, which means weak.*

-100 or less   *Extremely weak.*

4
—

The Hidden Crash

Well before the Crash of '87, while doing some research for my *Money & Markets* newsletter, I was visited by Ben Jackson, an old family friend.

"Where's the fire?" was his first question. "Where's the disastrous panic you warn about in your newsletters?" At the time, the stock market was still booming and the bond market had yet to take its big plunge. So it was natural for even the most faithful subscribers to have doubts about our view of the future.

In response, I displayed a series of graphs on my computer.

"Let's start with the consumer," I said. "To keep the economy going, every effort has been made to lure people deeper into debt. As a result, the financial fitness of the average American has fallen to pieces. In the first graph [page 49], we ask the question: How many dollars does the consumer make in personal income for each dollar of consumer debt outstanding?"

"What's the answer?"

"The answer," I replied, "is that until 1982 he earned enough income to cover each dollar of consumer debt. But starting in 1983, a major transformation set in. Credit buying went wild while income barely grew. As a result, this measure plummeted from its peak in 1982 to an all-time low in the last quarter of 1986. We're not just living beyond our means; we've jumped off the deep end!"

Jackson gestured, pointing at the next graph on the screen (not shown on page 49). I responded: "That's the Federal budget deficit, ballooning to new peaks."

"So what else is new?"

I couldn't blame him for being skeptical. The deficit was an issue that had been bandied about so often for so many years, it almost lost all meaning. "Bear with me for a moment. Look at this graph of the deficit—just get a mental image of its pattern. Got it?"

"Sure. But ... "

"OK. Now here's the trade deficit. Again, step back from the trees and look at the forest. Put aside the political issues and just view this as a barometer of America's economic performance relative to other nations. Again, try to grasp, in one glance, the overall picture of what's happening here."

"Yes, that's easy enough, but what exactly is it?"

"All it's showing is the difference between our imports and our exports. For decades, it was invariably a surplus. Here also, just like the consumer, the collapse has been extremely rapid. Most economists blame it on the dollar. What they overlook is that the consumers' spending binge (which you just saw in the previous graph) is the true culprit. Americans are simply buying too much and not selling enough! Most important, economists have failed to recognize that *all of these are directly related.*"

"OK. What's next?"

"This graph is the financial health of corporate America."

"How do you measure that?"

"There are many ways. This chart focuses on the *consequence* of too much debt: bankruptcy. It shows the total number of liabilities tied up in corporate failures every month. See how the pattern is the same as the other graphs? Not much change until the early 1980s, then boom! A collapse greater than anything ever witnessed during so-called 'good times.'

"The big question remains unanswered: if this is what has happened without a 'recession,' what will befall us when a real economic decline gets going?"

"I don't know. You tell me."

Graphs 4-7. The Hidden Crash

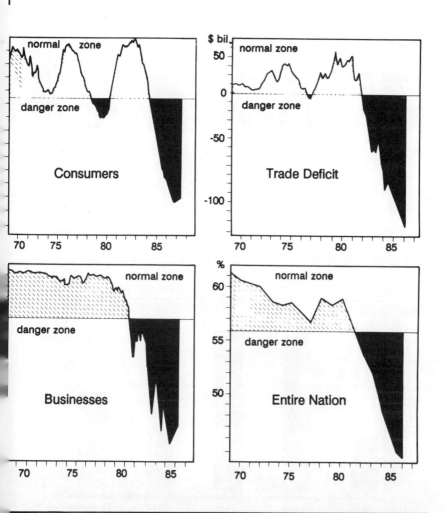

In the weeks and months following Black Monday, Washington and Wall reet managed to convice the public—and themselves—that the Crash of '87 as not caused by any fundamental change in the economy, but was merely a action to speculative excesses limited to Wall Street. Few realized that this as the same theory proposed after the 1929 crash. And fewer still were aware the "Hidden Crash" depicted in these graphs. It encompassed every aspect of onomic life: The average citizen had suffered a huge drop in the amount of oney he earned (personal income) for each dollar of consumer debt he held p left). Businesses had suffered wave after wave of bankruptcies involving ger and larger amounts of liabilities (bottom left, 6-month moving average). e U.S. trade balance plunged into the greatest deficits of all time (top right). d the U.S. as a whole accumulated the largest debts ever relative to the onomy's size (bottom right). Data: Federal Reserve, Dept. of Commerce, n & Bradstreet.

Graphs 8 & 9. The Worst Liquidity In The 20th Century

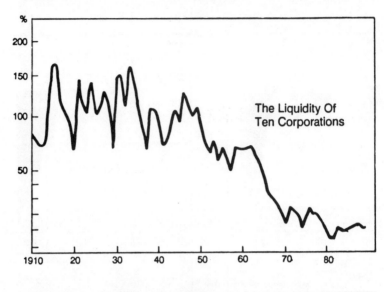

The Liquidity Of Ten Corporations

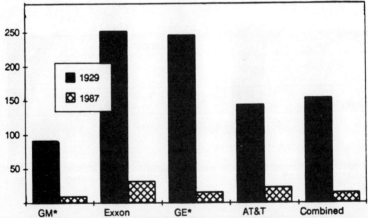

* includes captive finance subsidiaries

These graphs answer the question: "How much cash and equivalent was available to cover each dollar of debts coming due within 12 months in 1929 vs. 1987?" It is generally assumed that, in the late 1920s, our nation's financial health was significantly worse than it was in the late 1980s. However, the facts prove otherwise. In 1929, the corporate giants had far greater liquid resources in proportion to their current debts than in the 1980s. Data: Corporate reports.

"A catastrophe. A sudden implosion! That's why the authorities have done everything possible to stop even the slightest recession. That's why they've been pumping in money like mad, driving the stock market sky-high despite the relative weakness of corporate profits."

I reminded Jackson of the story of the "bicycle market" used to describe the 1929 crash. As long as the bull market kept moving, it was OK. Once it stopped, it had to fall. The same applied today to the economy as a whole.

"Any more?" Jackson asked.

"Let me skip to the most important one, the one that shows the entire picture in a nutshell."

"Which is ...?"

"All debts. The grand total." I pushed a key and the last chart appeared on the screen. "This graph is the clincher. It provides an overview of the entire debt problem. The question it answers is: how many dollars are in our Gross National Product (GNP) to cover each dollar of all debts outstanding today? Again, it confirms the same pattern. It collapsed in the early 1980s and has been falling ever since."

"Wait a minute," Jackson bellowed. "They all look the same—like a man jogging on a plateau and then suddenly running off a cliff."

But that was exactly the point! Every sector examined invariably led to the same conclusion: The country was moving along normally until the early 1980s when the first wave of the crisis hit. We recovered temporarily. Then, sometime during the middle of the decade we reached the end of the line. We crossed an invisible threshold beyond which a major disintegration took place. Debts burgeoned. Cash became scarce. Everyone became vulnerable!

It is primarily because of this *hidden* crash—not because of the stock market debacle—that a Money Panic will occur.

Worse Than 1929?

Will it be as bad as 1929? Will it be worse? In the years ahead, it is inevitable that many analysts will draw parallels between the events of the late twentieth century and those of the 1930s.

But far more important are the vast differences between the Great Depression and the Money Panic.

Back then, the debt pyramid centered on brokerage loans, with as little as ten percent margin on stocks. This time, the debt pyramid has spread to every sector of the economy, leaving most of the nation on average margins of 10 percent or *less.*

Before the 1929 crisis, a sample of the largest U.S. corporations held a minimum of 70 cents in cash or equivalent for every dollar of debt due within one year. In the late 1980s, they were down to 10 to 15 cents. Not enough cash! Too much debt!

Comparing the financial health of key individual corporations shows an even starker contrast. At the time of the 1929 stock market crash, General Motors had 92 cents in cash assets for every dollar of current debts. In the late 1980s, they had little more than 10 cents. The figures for other top firms are even more dramatic: Exxon, $2.52 in 1929 as opposed to only 32 cents in 1987; and General Electric, $2.46 in 1929 but merely 16 cents in 1987.

Why such a contrast? One reason is that in the 1920s most executives had been through a major panic earlier in the decade when they were caught with huge inventories, big short-term debts and scarce cash. By the time 1929 came along, they were better prepared for disaster. But in the 1980s, executives have assumed that, no matter what, they could always count on the short-term credit markets for extra cash whenever they needed it. And they have relied on the government to keep those money markets liquid. With this rationale, they have allowed their available cash resources to fall to the lowest levels of the twentieth century.

What is most surprising of all is how few people are aware of these facts. In fact, most economists deny the relevance of the 1929 experience. Strangely enough, however, whenever they can find a *positive* comparison, suddenly these crashes are invoked again as relevant.

This is especially true when it comes to any discussion about the banks. The press and the financial literature repeatedly refer to the weakness of the banking system in the 1930s compared to its "relative strength" in the 1980s. Unfortunately, none of this is supported by the facts. Every indicator proves that *when the stock market crashed in October 1987, the U.S. banking system was even weaker than it was in 1929.*

Here's the proof: As of year-end 1929, all Federal Reserve member banks had $17 billion of cash and liquid investments. On the other side of the ledger, they owed $40 billion to their depositors. Divide the cash by the deposits, and you find they have 42.5 cents in cash available for every dollar on deposit.

Now compare this to the 1987 figures: As of December 31, 1987, all reporting member banks had $382 billion in cash and liquid investments. That sounds like a lot untill you see the liabilities side. In addition to the $836 billion they owed to ordinary depositors, they had other short-term borrowings of $250 billion. So their total short-term debts were $1,086 billion. Dividing the cash by the deposits and debts, you find they had only 35 cents available to back up each dollar—significantly weaker than the already-weak 1929 situation! And, by 1989, the situation was even worse!

Failing where it really counts—in the hard-nosed statistical comparisons—some bankers of the 1980s have resorted to abstract concepts which cannot be refuted statistically. They insist that they don't need as much liquidity or equity as in the 1920s because of "the emergence of the highly liquid money markets" which they feel can be tapped for cash at any time.

It is indeed true that our market system has evolved and the banks have been given borrowing privileges that 1920s bankers could never have dreamed possible. Trouble is, no one asks the simple questions: "What are these money markets? Where does their money come from?" Obviously, it is *not* created out of thin air. The funds have to come from other banks and other financial institutions. Therefore, all they have accomplished is to *spread* the risk, not eliminate it. The money markets have cushioned individual institutions, but not the system as a whole. And, despite this cushion, there are *still* record numbers of bank failures even before a recession. What will happen if the liquidity of the money markets themselves is damaged?

"Impossible!" cry the Pollyannas of the 1980s. Their memory is short and self-serving. They have conveniently forgotten February 1980, when the government bond market—the largest and most liquid market in the world—literally shut down. Surely they couldn't have forgotten October 19 and 20, 1987, when liquidity disappeared among the specialists of the stock exchange, creating a veritable black hole into which prices fell uncontrollably. The fact is, they have forgotten!

They should realize that if it could happen in the world's two largest markets, it could also happen in the markets for bank Certificates of Deposit, foreign currencies and even the overnight loans that banks make to each other. Indeed, as you will see later in this book, *market gridlock could strike all those markets precisely when the banks need that money the most!*

And, never forget these facts: Back in 1929, the United States Government had $1.50 in gold and foreign-exchange reserves to cover every dollar of foreign debt. In the late 1980s, those reserves are down to 8 cents.

In 1929, the United States was the world's biggest creditor, with a well-entrenched trade surplus. In the late 1980s, it is the largest debtor, with a chronic and huge trade deficit.

In 1929, the federal budget was in surplus, giving policy makers some latitude to combat the crisis. In the late 1980s, the continuous dependence on the huge influx of borrowed funds—both from U.S. and foreign investors—has crippled the government's room to maneuver.

In short, both the Congress and the Federal Reserve have far fewer alternatives today than in the 1930s. Rather than depend upon Uncle Sam—or anyone else—to bail out the economy, you must find a safe haven which can stand on its own. It is towards that end that I have devised the Delta Strategy.

5

The Delta Strategy

The majority of Americans have yet to suffer the consequences of these debt problems. There is still time to protect what you own.

Congress and the Chairman of the Federal Reserve say that they will not permit the failure of any banks anywhere. They pump money into the economy and help to stimulate sharp rallies in the financial markets plus temporary blips of inflation.

Yet savings and loans fail daily, farms are in disarray, the number of bank failures is the largest since the Great Depression, and periodic shocks rock Wall Street.

Welcome to the *schizophrenic economy*, which delivers to your doorstep each morning the greatest dangers and the greatest opportunities of a lifetime.

How do you escape the dangers and profit from the opportunities? How do you guarantee that your hard-earned savings will always be protected against the ravages of crisis, regardless of what shape that crisis takes? At the same time, how do you increase the yield on your cash and the profits from your assets? Whether or not you accept the predictions of this book, I believe the best solution is the Delta Strategy.

The Delta Strategy is not a complex master plan that only a genius can follow. Nor is it merely a stopgap solution to get you through a temporary period of uncertainty. The Delta

Strategy is a simple set of rules any disciplined investor can follow to achieve three, well-defined goals: Safety, protection and profit.

Your first goal is *safety*, an ironclad guarantee that your hard-earned savings will be 100% inviolate and available to you when you need them. Your second goal is *protection*, a hedge against unprecedented events which will catch nearly everyone, including the so-called "experts," by surprise. Last but not least, your third goal is *profit*.

In other words, you should have the opportunity to profit from major moves in the markets while still keeping your capital 100% intact. These three goals—*safety, protection and profit*—fit neatly together to form the three sides of a Delta triangle; and this triangle will serve as a solid base for all your investment strategies during and after the Money Panic.

Leave No Stone Unturned

The survivors of the Money Panic will not be high-flying speculators. Nor will they be those who simply stick their heads in the sand and ignore the changes around them. Rather, the most outstanding characteristics of the survivors will be moderation, assertiveness, the courage to buck the crowd and the patience to stick with one's beliefs.

Once you reach a decision, carry it out thoroughly and persistently. Once you resolve to run for cover, to protect your hard-earned savings and investments, leave no stone unturned. Seek to clean out or protect every single item that could conceivably be vulnerable to the events ahead.

Beware of "Guaranteed" Investments

If you've ever been interested in buying a mutual fund or getting into an investment plan of some sort, I'm sure you've read or heard this catch phrase: *Past success is no guarantee of future performance.* In other words, a high batting average last year doesn't necessarily imply an equally good average this year.

This warning appears everywhere—in prospectuses, in the contracts with money managers and even in television ads.

Why? Sometimes in the pursuit of fairness, but usually because the Securities and Exchange Commission mandates such warnings to help protect the public.

It is truly unfortunate that the Federal Reserve doesn't enforce some similar rule for supposedly safe, income-oriented investments such as bank CDs or government agency bonds. Otherwise, you'd see this equally important warning for all the so-called "guaranteed" investments in America:

WARNING: A PAST RECORD OF SAFETY IS NO GUARANTEE THAT YOUR MONEY WILL BE SAFE IN THE FUTURE.

For reasons explained in Book III, this warning should appear in ads for CDs, life insurance, tax-exempt bonds, Government agency bonds and many money funds—just to mention a few. But it doesn't. Every day in the financial world you hear salespeople telling you that "no one has ever lost a dime" in this or that investment. As it turns out, in most cases, past performance is totally irrelevant. We are entering a new era with entirely new conditions—the first real test for many savings vehicles.

The rule of thumb is this: The money you invest belongs to *you*. Therefore what a broker, an insurance company or a bank does with your money is your business. You have the absolute right to find out all the details—from your banker, your mutual fund or whomever is making investment decisions on your behalf. If they do not give you the information you want, then you have the right to pull out, immediately!

A better procedure, however, is to do your research *before* getting involved. Before buying *anything*, check thoroughly to see what will be done with your money.

You wouldn't buy a $15,000 automobile or a $150,000 home sight unseen. You wouldn't want to sign a long-term contract with a firm you know nothing about. So why not apply the same rules and discipline to examining the actual content of the CDs, bonds or money funds you buy?

What are you getting into? Will the door always be open to get your money back when you need it? Ask these and other hard-nosed questions about each and every important item in your financial plan. Let's begin with your home.

6
—

Protect Your Home

For the average American family, the biggest financial dangers come from the area closest to home—the house itself!

In the days immediately following the 1987 stock market crash, some real estate salespeople tried to convince potential investors of a newly minted theory: "Now that stocks have taken a beating," they argued, "investors must put their money in something tangible, the best of which is real estate. Real estate isn't just paper. It's down-to-earth value which you can sink your teeth into."

In this theory, money coming out of the stock market was supposed to drive up the price of homes, land and other properties. The same rationale was applied to bonds, precious metals and other investments that didn't crash as fast as stocks. There was one fatal fallacy. It wasn't true that the money was "coming out of the stock market." It had evaporated into thin air as paper profits went up in smoke.

In any event, *the real problem is not the stock market. It's debt. Before long, the debt disaster will pull the rug out from under the real estate industry.*

At times, salespeople, anxious to somehow drum up business despite the desperate times, try this tack. "The silver lining in the stock market crash," they declare, "is that interest rates are going to go down ... which means that real estate values will soon rise." This also could turn out to be a trap. Yes, interest rates can fall during a recession. But *real* interest rates (adjusted for inflation) will remain high.

The actual numbers tell the story: In 1970, if you bought a home and took out a mortgage, your net interest cost, after subtracting the appreciation in your home, was about 2%. This was already pretty cheap. But in 1974, it turned even cheaper: you actually profited from the mortgage to the tune of 2% per year! By 1981, however, the net cost of carrying a mortgage surged to nearly 8%!

Throughout the 1980s, interest costs have been high; and mortgage payments, big. But rents are low. So the net cash flow from most income property has stayed negative. Consequently, investors and speculators, who in previous decades bid up real estate prices, have been largely absent.

Nevertheless, most Americans cling to their properties. This is partially because of the deeply entrenched American dream of owning a home. But it is mostly due to the widespread belief that, over the long haul, real estate prices can only go up. Indeed, over the preceding decades, despite recessions, most areas in the country had enjoyed stupendous price appreciation—the Northeastern seaboard, Southern California, South Florida.

What most people do not realize is that there are also exceptional periods when many of their cherished beliefs can be shattered. During the 1930s, home and land prices dropped sharply and, for 20 years thereafter, prices failed to recover from those lows. Therefore, except for those who had both the financial ability and the nearly infinite patience to wait half a lifetime, real estate owners took big beatings. In the 1990s, it could happen again.

In the 28 years after World War II, mortgage debt on the family home grew at an annual rate of $14 billion. During the next fifteen years, it grew at the unbelievable rate of $106 billion a year, or over *seven times faster*.

As long as these debts are covered by an equally rapid appreciation in the value of the homes, everything is fine. But as soon as housing prices begin to soften, a hidden time bomb is set to go off.

If family earnings had kept pace with the current $2 trillion mortgage debt on 1-4 family homes, then there might be no great problem. But how many families are there that have had a

700% rise in income over the previous fifteen years? Certainly not the average homeowner! And even among those who did enjoy such increases, how many would be able to sustain those incomes in a recession?

For a sneak preview of what could be in store for the home values in nearly all regions, all one has to do is visit Denver, Colorado. In 1987, a depressed economy precipitated widespread mortgage defaults; the government agency, HUD, repossessed 1500 homes in August 1988—more than the total for all of 1985. Everyone was dumping in unison for whatever they could get. Result: Prices nosedived to as low as 30% of their purchase price, a decline of 70%. Perhaps most devastating of all, sharpshooting homeowners quickly latched on to the idea of defaulting on their own homes immediately before purchasing the much lower-priced dwellings, thus further compounding the crisis.

Nevertheless, homeowners and real estate investors in high-growth regions believe they are immune to these trends. They are wrong. It is precisely those areas which have enjoyed the strongest real estate growth before the crash, the South and the Northeast, that could take the biggest beating during the Money Panic.

The problem will be the same everywhere—an excess supply of unsold homes, condos and office space, coupled with sharp declines in sales. It doesn't take more than a normal cyclical fall in the economy—5% to 10%—to bring about the chain reaction of home abandonments, reneging of debt and widespread bankruptcies. Added to the already out-of-control S&L crisis, the housing panic could become unstoppable.

For those who depend on their homes as their sole reservoir of savings, the impact is bound to be devastating. But those who keep their money in cash and wait patiently for the bottom will be greatly rewarded.

To join that minority, watch real interest rates carefully each month. (For more details on real interest rates and what they mean, see Chapter 23.) It won't be until real interest rates have fallen sharply from their lofty heights that you should invest in real estate. In the meantime, follow this simple rule: Sell, sell, sell! Restrict your ownership to those properties which you absolutely need to maintain your lifestyle. And, if you have the flexibility to do so, reevaluate your current lifestyle to determine whether or not you would be equally content in a rented property.

In the decades ahead, renting will be relatively cheap. Ownership, on the other hand, will be very expensive—not only in terms of the interest expense, but because of the potentially large losses you can incur in your principal.

Do not fall into the trap most American now find themselves in: Their home is their largest asset, far exceeding their stocks and bonds. Many even view their homes as the primary source of retirement funds and capital appreciation. When they discover that real estate prices have not only gone down ... but are *staying* down, they are bound to feel an urgency to cut spending and increase savings.

The end result is a vicious circle wherein a falling economy depresses real estate and lower real estate values depress the economy *still further.*

Be careful not to get caught in this dilemma. Many Americans are simply unable to sell even if they want to. They have gone so deeply into debt and property values in their area have fallen so sharply that, by the time they list their homes for sale, it is too late. They are shocked to discover that the money they could get out of it is less than the money they owe.

To protect your home, you should take the following steps:

1. Reduce as much as possible—and as soon as possible—the debt which you currently owe. First work on the second mortgages or home-equity loans with the highest interest rates. Then move on to the other mortgage debts. If it isn't possible to pay up a portion, do everything you can to refinance at better terms.

2. If you can find an alternate place to live, definitely think about selling. Consider the fact that putting your home on the market doesn't cost you anything; and even if you are pleasantly surprised and get the price you want, you are not obligated to sell if you change your mind. Also consider how much interest you can earn on the proceeds and how much interest you *won't*

be paying on the mortgage. The combination of these two should easily cover the rental.

3. Later, after a substantial decline in property values, you can reinvest your cash into a better piece of property at a better price.

You have moved out of your bank or S&L. You have converted most of your financial or real assets into cash. The next question is: Where do you put it for maximum safety and yield?

7

"Money Markets"

One phenomenon of the late twentieth century that never ceases to amaze me is the mass movement of funds by millions of American savers without a complete understanding about what they are buying. The "money market" is a case in point.

The money markets represent a special segment of the debt markets—where *short-term* debts are bought and sold. These include U.S. Treasury bills, bank Certificates of Deposit, short-term IOUs issued by corporations, and overnight borrowings between banks.

Unfortunately, most people are uninterested in the real meaning of the term, with little concern for the vast differences that separate one type of "money market" from another. This is due to no fault of their own—rather, the publicity campaigns by commercial banks and S&Ls cause the confusion. They customarily use catch phrases purposely designed to blur the differences between one type of investment and another.

The term "money market" itself, as it is used by the banks, is a misnomer. The banks have opened millions of accounts and have taken in billions in savings with an instrument they called "Money Market Accounts" (MMAs). However, if you put your money into one of these accounts, it is not invested in the nation's money markets per se. Instead, it is simply added to the banks' or S&Ls' general pool of funds, which is then invested in long-term mortgages, mortgage-backed securities and consumer loans. The only reason it's called a "Money Market Account" is because its rate of interest is competitive with money market rates and because it is available for immediate withdrawal. In terms of the actual *content* of your investment—what is being done with your money—it is no different from any other bank deposit.

Money Market Certificates (MMCs) are similar. In substance, they are no different from other deposits, except for the fact that you have to lock up your money for a period of time. Again, the term "money market" is misleading.

Some bank officers may try to convince you that their certificates are "better than United State Treasury bills." Some even give you the false impression that you are, in effect, buying T-bills through the bank, which of course is absolutely not true. The MMCs are *not* T-bills. They are plain, ordinary bank deposits.

Unfortunately, millions of savers fall for this argument. They don't realize that the risks of owning bank CDs far outweigh the meager rewards. Let's say that, for example, an investor shifted from Treasury bills into CDs. What would he have gained? What risks would he have incurred?

In the three years before the Crash of '87, bank CDs yielded an average of 7.15%. Meanwhile, the average yield on T-bills was 6.55%. Some savers felt that this was enough to justify the risks. Not true. The danger of a bank or FDIC failure was greater than any equivalent period in recent history. So, a slight reduction in interest was a small price to pay for absolute safety.

During a panic, however, the gap between Treasury bill rates and bank CD rates would grow still further. Therefore, the extra yield earned in a bank would be substantial—provided, that is, you could get to your principal when you needed it. In my newsletter, *Money & Markets*, I put it this way:

> Every day, you will forego more income by staying with Treasury bills rather than CDs. In other words, the price you have to pay for safety and liquidity will go *up*. Does this mean that you should abandon them? On the contrary! Safety will cost more because the dangers associated with all other investments will be more intense. The borrowers who pay you extra yields are doing so to compensate you for the added risk you incur. In the process, they will be digging themselves even

deeper into the debt quagmire. *The more desperate they are, the more distance you should put between them and your hard-earned money.*

Some wealthy Americans, instead of switching into Treasury securities, have sought to buy Eurodollar Time Deposits. They don't realize that the Eurodollar CDs are essentially the same as domestic CDs. The only difference is that they are sending their money to a bank overseas.

Like their American counterparts, most foreign banks are deeply involved with questionable long-term loans to less developed countries; they are overdependent upon short-term, hot-money deposits; and they are vulnerable to the collapse of the world's real estate and equity markets. There are some exceptions, but even the stronger foreign banks are threatened by disruptions in the world banking system.

The Money Funds

The greatest mass movement of money in the late twentieth century is none of the above. Rather, it has been in and out of money funds. When you buy a money fund, your money is deposited into bank Certificates of Deposit, invested in corporate IOUs or loaned out to Uncle Sam.

Unlike an ordinary mutual fund, however, the price of each share is fixed at exactly $1.00 and never changes. So when you earn interest, instead of increasing the value of each share, they issue new shares for you.

For example, if you open an account with $2,000, you will start off by owning 2,000 shares. If you earn $100 in interest, you will now own 2,100 shares.

As in the case of the banks, these are loosely labeled "money markets," without due consideration for the actual content of the investment. This is not to say that all Americans have made a poor decision. If selected wisely, money funds can provide maximum yield and complete safety. However, you have to be fully aware of how your money is invested.

Unfortunately, the typical investor's overriding concern is finding the highest-yielding fund. With yield performances changing daily, some investors set up several money fund ac-

Table 5. Recommended Money Funds

Money Fund Name	National No.	Intrastate No.
Alex Brown Government Series	301-321-4444	
Capital Preservation	800-227-8380	800-982-6150 (CA)
Carnegie Government Securities	800-321-2322	216-781-4440
Dreyfus M.M. Instruments - Gov't	800-242-8671	718-895-1206 (NY)
Franklin Federal M.F.	800-247-1753	
Fund for Gov't Investors	800-343-3355	
Mariner U.S.Treasury	212-503-6826	
Merrill Lynch CMA Gov't Securities	800-262-4636	
Merrill Lynch Government	800-225-1576	617-357-1460 (MA)
Merrill Lynch USA Gov't Res.	609-282-2800	
Midwest Income ST Government	800-582-7396	800-543-8721 (OH)
NLR Government Portfolio	212-356-2600	
Neuberger & Berman Gov't M.F.	800-367-0770	
Pacific Horizon Funds/Gov't	800-645-3515	
Paine Webber RMA M.F./U.S. Gov't	800-338-3810	800-432-9607 (FL)
Reserve Fund/Gov't Port.	800-223-5547	
Short Term Income/U.S. Gov't	212-370-1240	collect calls OK
T. Rowe Price U.S. Treas. M.F.	800-638-5660	
Tucker Anthony Gov't Sec. Fund	617-523-3170	800-392-6037 (MA)
U.S. Treasury Securities Fund	800-873-8637	800-824-4653 (TX)

These money funds invest exclusively in U.S. Treasury securities or equivalent. They do not invest in the items which could be vulnerable in the Money Panic such as Certificates of Deposit, the short-term IOUs of corporations, etc. Data: Donoghue Organization.

counts, switching from one to another, depending upon each fund's yield. Usually this is not a good idea. The yield reported by a money fund invariably reflects the *past* which has little bearing on future performance. Furthermore, investors who chase the highest yields are, by definition, also chasing the highest risk.

During the Money Panic, the fractions of a percent some investors have gained will quickly be wiped out in the first default!

Why You Should Use A Treasury-Only Money Fund

If there were to be no crisis, almost any money fund would be OK. You could earn relatively high yields. You could get your money out at a moment's notice. Most important, you are assured of no loss of principal regardless of market fluctuations.

In the Money Panic, however, an entirely new set of circumstances arises. You must distinguish between two basic groups—Treasury-only money funds and nonTreasury money funds. The former, as the name implies, puts 100% of the money in Treasury securities or equivalent, always with maturities of one year or less. The latter owns mostly bank CDs, commercial paper, bankers' acceptances and Eurodollar deposits.

Even in a money panic, the Treasury-only funds are absolutely safe. The nonTreasury funds are not. It's that simple. Once the banking panic and corporate bankruptcy crisis begins, it will naturally spill over into the money funds that hold bank CDs and corporate IOUs.

Table 5 shows the Treasury-only money funds I recommend in the period before and after the panic. All you have to do is call toll free, ask for a prospectus, and send them your check.

When you want to take your money out, you can simply write a check, just like you would in a NOW account at your bank. The only limitation is that there may be a minimum amount for each check, such as $100 or $500 (depending on the fund). You can use these checks to pay your rent, to go on a Caribbean vacation, or to buy appliances for your home. Best of all, until your check clears, your money stays in short-term Treasury securities, earning interest.

Or you can call in for a wire transfer to your checking account. Simply make sure that you give your money fund authorization and bank account numbers ahead of time. If you wish, you can also have the fund send you a check via overnight mail, and if it's a broker-operated fund with an office in your city, you can pick up your check in person the next day.

Table 6. How Safe Are The Money Funds' Custodian Banks

Treasury-Only Money Fund	Custodian Bank
Alex Brown Gov't Series	Provident Natl. Bank
Capital Preservation Fund	State Street B&T Co.
Carnegie Gov't Secur.	Boston Safe Deposit & TC
Dreyfus M.M. Instruments	Bank of New York
Franklin Federal MF	Bank of Amer. NT & SA
Fund for Gov't Investors	Amer. Security Bank NA
Mariner U.S. Treasury	Marine Midland Bank NA
Merrill Lynch Gov't	State Street B&T Co.
Merrill Lynch CMA Gov't Sec	State Street B&T Co.
Merrill Lynch USA Gov't Sec	Bank of New York
Midwest Income ST Gov't	Star Bank of Cincinn.
Neuberger & Berman Gov't	State Street B&T Co.
NLR Gov't Portfolio	Provident Natl. Bank
Pacific Horizon Funds\Gov't	Bank of New York
Paine Webber RMA M.F.\U.S. Gov't	State Street B&T Co.
Reserve Fund/Gov't Port.	Chemical Bank NA
Short Term Income/US Gov't	Bank of New York
T. Rowe Price US Treas MF	State Street B&T Co.
Tucker Anthony Gov't Sec.	State Street B&T Co.
U.S. Treas. Sec. Fund	Frost Nat. Bk. San Ant.

The safety of the bank which acts as a custodian for your money fund ould not emerge as a critical issue even during the Money Panic. The reason that the banks' custodial functions are completely separate from regular posits. However, in order to avoid any possible interruption of service, me money funds have gone the extra mile to use only the strongest banks.

To find out about your money fund, first look it up in the list above to find ich bank it uses. Then check the safety of that bank in the table below. ata: The various money funds, Federal Reserve. (For a definition of the asures used in the bottom table, see pp. 28-31.)

me of Custodian Bank	Equity Ratio	Liquid. Ratio	Bad Loans	Safety Index
ner. Security Bank NA	6.1	38.3	21.3	-34
nk of Amer. NT & SA	3.6	28.7	108.9	-76
nk of New York	5.2	31.9	27.1	-16
nk One Columbus NA	6.0	24.7	21.3	-128
ston Safe Deposit & TC	5.7	68.5	2.1	96
emical Bank NA	3.3	33.3	100.8	-37
ost Nat. Bk. San Ant.	5.6	53.3	20.1	20
arine Midland Bank NA	2.3	16.4	147.3	-148
ovident Natl. Bank	6.2	38.9	4.5	-35
ar Bank of Cincinnati	7.3	30.4	4.0	-29
ate Street B&T Co.	6.4	71.8	3.6	91

Can Your Treasury-Only Money Fund
Survive The Worst Case Scenario?

What happens during a banking crisis? No matter what, the Treasury bills are safe.

The Treasury bills themselves are kept absolutely secure in the Treasury Department's computers in Virginia. All the records are thoroughly backed up multiple times in multiple ways. Even if every private institution in the country were closed, those T-bills would still be there.

Furthermore, a record of ownership of the T-bills is kept by a commercial bank on behalf of the money fund. This is the "custodian bank." After reading the chapters on the banks, you may wonder why I view this as a strong point. The reason is that the banks' custodial services are entirely separate from their regular banking business. Indeed, even if the bank is "closed" due to bankruptcy, that side of the business will probably stay open.

The only potential problem with all this comes down to the question of getting your checks cashed. Would people accept your money fund checks during a banking holiday? The answer is probably yes, but the fact is no one can be absolutely sure. With this in mind, we have checked into the safety of the banks used by the Treasury-only money funds. (See page 69.)

Remember, no matter what happens during the most acute stages of the crisis, the most important fact is that the underlying security you have invested in—T-bills—will remain intact. The U.S. Treasury Department must continue to borrow.

To retain that borrowing ability, it must pay off its existing obligations promptly. If investors are unwilling to buy Treasury bills at a given rate, the rate will automatically go up, gobbling up the funds invested in passbook savings, CDs, NOW accounts, stocks, real estate, plant and equipment, or even longer-term Treasury issues themselves. *Thus, money funds that invest solely in short-term Treasury securities will be able to meet their commitments to shareholders without delay, even in the worst-case scenario.*

Some of the money funds recommended also buy repurchase agreements or "repos." However, I do *not* view this as a problem. Here's why: Say you are a money fund manager and your job is to decide what to buy for your portfolio, and say you want to turn over the entire portfolio within an average of 30 days. Sometimes you can buy enough T-bills that are already two months old and have only one month left to go. But these aren't always available at a reasonable rate. That's where repos come in. In effect, you find a banker or a government security dealer who has Treasury securities in his portfolio and you say: "I'll buy your Treasuries with the agreement that I can sell them back to you exactly one month from now at a slightly higher price."

Another way of looking at it is this: When you do a repo, you are simply loaning money to a financial institution for a short time. However, unlike the average saver who deposits money in a bank, you are making no pretense of trusting the institution with your money. Rather, you take back solid collateral: U.S. Government securities. If they default and don't give you your money back, you simply sell the securities and recoup your funds with no loss.

It's too bad the millions of savers in America don't take this attitude. If they did, they might save many billions in losses and over a decade of suffering.

Back in 1984, the turning point when the debt shock hit and the Fed launched its massive money-pumping operation, there was much debate about the safety of repos. Some institutions were careless. They accepted the borrower's word that he owned the government securities he said he had. And they didn't pay enough attention to declines in their market value.

The fact is that the repos are safe, as long as the proper precautions are taken. A money fund that runs a tight ship makes sure the collateral is exclusively direct Treasury obligations, not agency bonds. They require actual delivery of the Treasury obligations to their custodian bank. Then they monitor the market value on a daily basis to confirm that the collateral is always worth the value of the repo.

As of this writing, it is our understanding that the funds listed in Table 5 do take these precautions. However, before investing in money funds that use repos, it can't hurt to double-check that this is indeed their policy at all times.

Do-It-Yourself Banking

Follow these steps carefully. You will earn more interest, make your life easier and, sleep well at night!

Step #1. Order from your money fund a full set of checks. (Unless you specifically request a checkbook, many money funds send you no more than a half-dozen drafts.) If you use pegboard checks or computer checks, you can arrange for the printing yourself but make sure you follow the money fund's specifications.

Step #2. Choose the safest bank in your area and use it to deposit all income, dividend or salary checks. Wire-transfer as much as possible to the money fund as soon as possible.

Step #3. Pay all bills over $100 (including rent, mortgage payments, bills from suppliers, etc.) with money-fund checks. With the exception of some banks, virtually everyone will accept them without question.

Step #4. Instruct your money fund to return your cancelled checks to you. If you don't, most will hold them, making it difficult to reconcile your monthly statements.

Step #5. Send your money fund a letter for their files listing all the banks, brokerage firms or credit unions (along with the account numbers) to which you may wish to transfer funds. This will occasionally be necessary for purchases or investments in case you need immediate cash.

The advantages of money-fund checking are many. You earn interest on funds that otherwise would sit in a noninterest-bearing checking account. You can earn as much as two extra weeks of interest from the "float"—the delays between the time you issue a check and when it clears. And, most important, assuming you have followed our guidelines in selecting a money fund, you will know that your savings are completely secure.

If you run a business with an active cash flow, daily wire transfers—combined with thorough use of money-fund checking—can increase the yield on your cash balances by several percentage points. In fact, when real interest rates are high, or when their business turns sour, many of our clients earn an inflation-adjusted yield that outstrips their normal profit margins.

For a substantial portion of cash, however, there is no better investment than Treasury securities bought directly from the U.S. Treasury Department.

8

How To Buy U.S. Treasury Securities

There is really only one place to put your money: Treasury securities, whether bought directly from the Federal Reserve to through a money fund. They are the safest investment in the world. And if you buy Treasury securities which mature in less than one year—T-bills—you incur almost zero risk of a loss in their market value.

Most Treasury securities have one other safety aspect which most investors don't understand or appreciate: The Treasury Department does not give you an actual T-bill certificate. Rather, it just records the transaction in its computers and sends you a receipt.

When I first learned about this change in the rules, I didn't like the idea. Somehow, I felt more comfortable with a physical piece of paper than an electromagnetic signal recorded on a disk in some obscure government office. But over time, I not only got used to it, I have come to prefer it over the old method.

Previously, there was always a concern that the T-bill certificate could be stolen, damaged by fire or misplaced in some way. Now, those concerns are gone. Furthermore, no matter how beautifully engraved, the reality is that the old certificates were nothing more than paper. And if it's paper that I want, I can make plenty of it. I get my Treasury-bill receipts or my broker's statements. I make multiple copies and store them at my home and at my office. I can even keep them in a safety deposit box at the trust company I use. And even if all my records are destroyed, I still can get duplicates from their original source. So all told, the present system is a lot more secure than ever before.

How Safe Is Uncle Sam?

When you buy Treasury securities, you are loaning money to the United States Treasury. So it is only natural that many savers ask: "If the government's finances are so botched up, why do you recommend entrusting your money to that same government?"

The reason is simple. Everything is relative in nature and economics. Despite the huge budget deficits and mismanagement, *relative* to all other investments you could make, the U.S. Government is still the most powerful and stable entity in the world—economically, politically and militarily.

Gold has enjoyed periodic surges in value, but it has also fallen sharply when least expected. T-bills have not.

Real estate is subject to boom and bust cycles. T-bills are not.

Commodities, bank deposits and rare coins have—at one time or another in the great economic cycles—fallen prey to the all-encompassing wrath of deflation. T-bills have not.

Some savers ask: "What if the U.S. dollar itself—the money in which T-bills are denominated—comes under attack?"

Unless you plan to spend your money abroad, the declining value of the dollar vis-à-vis the foreign currencies is more a theoretical problem than a practical one. Let's suppose, for example, that you decide to buy large amounts of those currencies, and they fall in value. You will be subject to real and direct losses in your principal. Now let's say you own only dollars and the dollar falls. You suffer no direct loss in dollar terms. This is why I recommend primarily U.S. Treasuries for U.S. residents, Japanese Treasuries for Japanese residents and so on, with only limited investments in overseas Treasuries for diversification.

How far would the dollar have to decline before it became a more direct threat? While there can be no definite answer, one can generally rely on this basic principle: As long as the T-bill rate is equal to, or greater than, the inflation rate, the dollar will remain viable. When the T-bill rate falls below the inflation rate, it signals danger. Since T-bill rates are now well *above* inflation—and should continue to stay well above it for many years—we expect the dollar to remain viable despite intermediate setbacks. Therefore, Treasury securities are clearly the very best investments possible in today's world.

When you buy Treasury securities, you have three choices: Treasury *bills* which mature in one year or less, Treasury *notes* which have a life of one to ten years, and Treasury *bonds* which are issued with maturities from ten to thirty years.

Treasury Bills

Until interest rates reach a peak, Treasury bills should be the mainstay of your cash investments. They are the true "liquid gold" of the world today. You can buy them for three months, six months or one year, giving you the opportunity to ride interest rates up when they're rising and lock in the current rate for a full year when they're declining.

In virtually every other investment, brokers or bankers have a typical sales pitch; for T-bills, there is none. In fact, many money market salespeople will try to talk you *out* of buying Treasury bills because they can't make much money selling them. Also, beware of some bank or S&L employees who may try to sell you six-month Money Market Certificates as if they were T-bills. Only a *U.S. Treasury bill* is a T-bill, and only a Treasury bill offers these advantages:

Advantage #1. Safety. T-bills are the last safe haven in an unsafe world. During the Money Panic, when banks close and bluechip corporations fail, Treasury bills will remain.

Advantage #2. A discount check up front. In effect, you receive your interest at the time of purchase. For example, a $10,000 one-year T-bill at 8% actually costs $9,200. You receive the difference of $800 (the discount) deposited directly to your bank account. That gives you another $800 to invest or use any way you wish. (The same holds true for a three-month T-bill or a six-month T-bill.) When the T-bill matures, you receive the entire $10,000, no matter what. Technically speaking, your $800 discount check is not really the interest. Rather, it is more correct to say that the true amount of your initial investment is the $9,200 from which you will earn, over the year's time, $800, for a total yield of 8.75%.

Advantage #3. Liquidity. You don't have to wait until maturity to get your money back. If you want to sell your Treasury bills early, you can do so in what is called "the secondary market."

If you bought your bills through your broker or banker, just call him and have him sell them for you. If you bought them directly from the Fed, obtain Form PD4633 from your local Federal Reserve branch. Fill it out and turn it over along with your T-bill receipt to your broker or commercial bank. They will sell it for you in the secondary market. (Warning: If you buy your T-bills from the Fed, this procedure can take a couple of weeks.)

Advantage #4. The equivalent of cash. T-bills are considered as good as cash and can usually be used as collateral. If you're investing in the futures markets or if you're buying and selling other kinds of securities, you can often put up your Treasury bills while continuing to earn the interest. You need not tie up interest-free cash.

Where And How To Buy T-Bills

There are four methods available, each with advantages and disadvantages. As to which is the safest, the differences between these methods are hairsplitting. No matter where you buy T-bills, you are completely safe. The Treasury Department stands behind all T-bills, no matter how or through whom they are bought. The one possible risk arises if and when there is a back-office crisis at the brokerage or bank that handles your T-bills. Before we discuss that issue, however, let's look at each method of buying T-bills.

Method #1. Direct from the Treasury or Fed. You can buy directly from the U.S. Treasury Department by going to your nearest U.S. Federal Reserve branch (see Table 7). Here are the steps to follow:

Table 7. Federal Reserve Banks and Branches

Atlanta	404-521-8500	Little Rock	501-372-5451
Baltimore	301-576-3300	Los Angeles	213-683-2300
Birmingham	205-252-3141	Miami	305-591-2065
Boston	617-973-3000	Minneapolis	612-340-2051
Buffalo	716-849-5046	Nashville	615-259-4006
Charlotte	704-336-7100	New Orleans	504-586-1505
Chicago	312-786-1110	New York	212-720-5823
Cincinnati	513-721-4787	Oklahoma	405-270-8400
Cleveland	216-579-2000	Omaha	402-221-5500
Dallas	214-651-6177	Philadelphia	215-574-6580
Denver	303-572-2300	Pittsburgh	412-261-7864
Detroit	313-961-6880	Portland	503-221-5900
El Paso	915-544-4730	Richmond	804-696-8000
Helena	406-442-3860	S. Lake City	801-355-3131
Houston	713-659-4433	San Antonio	512-224-2141
Jacksonville	904-632-1000	San Francisco	415-882-9490

Even in the worst possible banking crisis, there is one bank in your region which will not close its doors—the Federal Reserve bank or branch. What most people don't realize is that the average citizen can open an individual account with the U.S. Treasury Department through the local Federal Reserve bank. However, under the Fed's new rules, you will still need a regular bank account for the transfer of funds to and from your account at the Treasury Department. Data: Federal Reserve.

Step 1. If you do not have one already, open a checking account with the strongest possible commercial bank in your state.

Step 2. Acquire from the bank their "direct deposit information" including their "routing number" (ABA identifying number) and their complete name.

Step 3. Write to: U.S. Treasury Department, Bureau of the Public Debt, Washington, D.C. 20239-3703 or call them at 202-287-4113. Ask them for "Tender for 13-week Treasury Bill" form (PD 5176-1). Also have them send you their five explanatory booklets on: Reinvestment, Registration Options, Features, Account Information, and Direct Deposit. You won't have to wade through all of them, but they're free, and the more you know, the better.

Step 4. Complete the form, using the same name on your bank checking account. Also, this is where you will need to fill in the "direct deposit information" which you acquired from your bank in step 2 above.

Step 5. Return the completed form and payment to the Treasury Department. If you wish to deal with your local Federal Reserve banks, you may.

However, if you want to buy the T-bills in person, on or before the day of public auction, simply bring a cashier's check for the full amount desired. ($10,000 is the minimum, with increments of $5,000.) At a teller's window, as in a bank, you state that you are buying at the average bid price.

Soon after that, you will receive your "discount" (the difference between the $10,000 and the actual auction price). Then, about five to seven days before your T-bill matures, you will receive a notice in the mail asking you to choose either a "rollover" or a payout to you.

There are several inconveniences in using this method, especially if you do not live in a major city. You need to obtain a cashier's check in advance at your bank, then spend time waiting in line. (You can overcome some of these problems by dealing with the Fed via first class or registered mail.) More significant disadvantages are the red tape and possible delays in transferring your T-bills to your broker or bank if you want to use them in another transaction.

Nevertheless, if you won't need the money until your T-bill matures and if a secretary or accountant will handle the small amount of paperwork, you should use this method for at least a portion of your T-bills. You will have an individual account at the U.S. Treasury and there will be no intermediary between you and your T-bills.

Method #2. Through your broker. Have your broker buy the Treasury bills on your behalf at the regular auction. With this method, you receive the discount immediately upon purchase.

The charge for this service is usually $25 to $50 per order, regardless of the amount up to $1,000,000. You have the obvious convenience of giving buy and sell instructions over the phone, using the T-bills as margin, or transferring them to other accounts with other brokers or banks. In this sense, a Treasury bill bought through a broker is more liquid than a T-bill purchased from the Fed.

Method #3. Through your bank. Go through the Bond Department of your commercial bank or through your personal bank representative. The bank may charge a bit more for this service than a broker, but the advantages and disadvantages are the same.

Method #4. Through a Treasury-only money fund. You can buy your T-bills through a Treasury-only money fund. The advantages are many: You can start with a much lower minimum investment than the $10,000 required by the Fed. You can add or subtract from your investment in very small increments rather than $5,000. You can request automatic reinvestment of your interest, a convenience the Treasury does not offer. And you can write checks against your T-bills which continue to earn interest until the checks clear.

The disadvantage is simple—the money funds normally charge a fee of 1/2%. If the T-bill yields are low, say 5%, this represents one-tenth of your income—a relatively big chunk. If T-bill rates are high, the 1/2% charge is easily absorbed and well worth the services provided.

Which method should you use? Here's what we recommend:

1. If you have less than $10,000, a Treasury-only money fund is your only choice.

2. If you have from $10,000 to $200,000 and do not invest with a broker, you can split your investments into two parts:

a. funds needed regularly for spending or imminent purchases to be placed in a Treasury-only money fund, and

b. funds which are not needed immediately to be invested in T-bills purchased directly from the Treasury Department.

3. Finally, if you have more than $200,000, or if you have an active account with a broker, you can use several of the above methods.

The Secondary Market

Normally, you will be buying your T-bills at the Treasury's regular Monday auction, at the average price for investors under the $1,000,000 limit.

But you can also buy older T-bills on the secondary market. The advantage is this: At the auction you are limited to either three-month or six-month T-bills and, less frequently, one-year bills. In the secondary market, a full array of T-bills is available, with maturities from one week to one year.

Check the *Wall Street Journal* for the most recent listing (in the section titled in the "Treasury Issues, U.S. Treasury Bills.") Or you can probably find a similar table in the financial pages of your local newspaper.

But read the note at the bottom of the T-bill listing carefully: "The actual price you receive will vary, depending upon the size of your lot and market fluctuations." Therein lies the disadvantage of the secondary market: Unless you are a very large investor, your transactions will be considered a "small lot" or "retail business."

As a result, your price will be higher than the market price, giving you a yield which is lower than that quoted in the newspapers. If you avoid the secondary market and use the regular auction, you get the average price, regardless of how large or small your order is.

Are My T-Bills Safe At The Bank Or Broker?

These days, it is normal for investors to ask, "What happens if my brokerage firm or bank fails?" Unless you're dealing with a fly-by-night operation that violates Federal laws, your T-bills are safe. However, at the brokerage firm, they are typically kept in the "street name"—in the *broker's* name. In other words, if you call the Fed to inquire about "your" T-bills, you will find they have no record of your account.

Nevertheless, even if the brokerage firm or bank loses every dime they own due to poor management, foreign-loan defaults or other causes, the worst that could happen is that you might have to endure some red tape to locate and pursue your T-bills.

So make sure to keep all your statements in a safe place. As long as you have proof of ownership, all Treasury securities will be honored by the U.S. Treasury Department. (For more details on this issue, see Chapter 10.)

U.S. Treasury Notes And Bonds
(T-Notes and T-Bonds)

A Treasury note or bond is the first cousin of a Treasury bill. When you buy one, you have an *absolute guarantee* that your principal and interest will be paid. This is far better than the "full faith and credit" guarantees of other government securities such as Ginnie Maes.

However, there are some very important differences between a T-note or T-bond and a T-bill. First, the maturity date is much further away, as long as 30 years. While the government guarantees your $10,000 30-year T-bond will be worth $10,000 when it matures, what happens to the market price any time before the due date is entirely your problem.

Most people believe that bond prices don't fluctuate very much, but they're wrong. If you hold a 30-year T-bond until maturity, your principal is fine. If, however, you need or want that money in the interim, you may have to sell your T-bond at a loss. Or, if you're fortunate, you may be able to sell it for a profit.

An extreme example occurred in late 1979. If you bought a typical 20-year bond in mid-August and sold it in late February of 1980, you'd have incurred a 32% loss in six months, wiping out eight times the interest income earned. If you bought that same bond in early April 1980 and sold it in early June, you'd have earned a *profit* of about 26% in just two months (156% annually). Clearly, long-term bonds can be as volatile as many stocks. The best time to buy T-bonds, therefore, is when the prices are at their lowest and their yields are at a peak.

The other differences from T-bills are minor. First, you receive an interest payment every six months, not one lump sum paid in advance. Second, instead of a money fund, you will be using a Treasury-bond mutual fund. However, please do not confuse a bond fund with a money fund. Money funds cannot and do not buy Treasury securities which have more than one year left before maturity. Bond mutual funds, on the other hand, can buy any maturity they choose—10 years, 20 years or even longer. Therefore, as with the bonds themselves, you incur the risk of a price decline. Third, the auctions are far less frequent or regular. Each auction will involve different amounts and maturities, depending on the Fed's evaluation of market conditions. Because of the wider variety of bonds available in the secondary market and the greater flexibility for getting in and out, the best method for buying T-notes and T-bonds is through your broker.

How much of your funds should you invest in T-bonds and when should you buy them? I deal directly with this question in Chapter 32, especially on page 282.

9

Save Your Business

To understand the urgency of immediate action, you need not subscribe to a large number of investment letters. Nor do you have to be an "expert" on the economy. You must, however, accept some simple logic:

1. The stock market crash in 1929 led to the Great Depression.

2. The crash of '87 was much worse than the '29 crash.

3. Therefore, it is conceivable that the next depression could also be worse than the 1930s in many ways. And, even if it isn't, there are abundant reasons to believe that the next recession will be far more severe than most of us have experienced.

This leaves you only one course of action in your business: Raise cash, cut expenses, and get out when you can!

It may be difficult to convince associates and family members of this conclusion. You will probably run into fierce resistance when it comes to the idea of selling the family business or home. Your associates will cite the protection of the government, the temporary declines in certain interest rates, the cooperation among Western nations. They will find a myriad of reasons, some of which appear quite plausible, why your region or your industry is an exception or even "stands to benefit from a recession."

Never Too Late

If you live in one of the already depressed regions of the country or if, by the time you read this book, the entire economy has already fallen sharply, some people may use this argument: "I told you to do this a long time ago, but you wouldn't listen to me. Now it's too late, so let's stay put." The fact is it's *never* too late. And in a depression, what appears to be "the worst it could ever get" can be just the beginning of a still deeper decline.

In your business, your problem will no longer be to convince your associates that something must be done. Rather, it will be to reconcile yourself to the fact that you cannot get as much out of your business as you think it's worth. Your associates will say "we can't sell now" or "there's bound to be a recovery sooner or later." *Don't let them talk you out of concrete and swift action.*

Nor can you rely on forecasts made by the consensus of economists. They have rarely been successful in predicting recessions, let alone a depression! Their primary expertise is telling you what has *already* taken place, what businesspeople like yourself are *already* experiencing on the front line.

Beware also of the built-in tendency among most economists to prematurely predict an end to the decline. It's a trap which businesses could fall into again and again at each step down the precipice.

Above all, watch out for the "silver lining" syndrome—pundits trying to outdo each other in locating "the positive side of the crisis."

For instance, they often stumble on interest rates. They don't realize that major changes have taken place in the way interest rates behave. You can avoid this confusion by taking these precautions:

First, don't rely upon the widely publicized prime rate. Make sure the actual rates *you* yourself have to pay on business and personal loans are also coming down.

Second, compare short-term vs. long-term rates. Towards this end, the information on other interest rates which you have collected from the St. Louis Federal Reserve will now come in handy (see page 26). The Fed may artificially lower the rates it can control (the short-term ones), but it will have only limited success with rates it cannot control (the long-term ones).

Third, verify that *real* interest rates (after subtracting inflation or deflation) are coming down. If, for example, the prime rate is down to 7%, it may look good on the surface. But if, at the same time, the consumer price index is *down* to a *minus* 3 percent, the *real* prime rate—the difference between the two— is actually 10%, or near a historic record!

Finally, watch to see how long the rates actually *stay down.* To have an impact on your business, it's not enough for the government to knock rates down only to have them bounce right back up. They have to stabilize at the lower levels.

Only if and when these four conditions are met, can you look at low interest rates as a potentially positive force.

Most important, do not let your decisions be influenced by an emotional attachment to your business. This is no time for fear *or* complacency. This is a time for a rational, step-by-step strategy that will protect you from the crisis.

The collapse of the bond markets, the dollar and the stock market *are not false alarms.* Yes, there may be intermediate recoveries that last for months, and, the stock market can surge for a while—but that does not change in the least, the fundamental dangers at hand. If anything, it only makes the nation *more* vulnerable to a sharp decline and *more* subject to financial upheaval. No matter what size or type of businesses you are involved in, the ten-point program outlined below should be implemented.

1. Begin Immediately

Unless you take action, excessive debts will wind up eroding your assets, creating cash shortages, and causing disintegration of management morale. You will find yourself in a vicious circle wherein sales declines lead to discouragement, which in turn lead to more sales declines.

If you see signs of this happening you are probably not alone; such experiences are typical of the Money Panic. The good news is that, although you may sometimes feel trapped, in reality, if you collect your wits and adjust to the new conditions, you *can* escape intact.

First and foremost, you must improve *executive awareness*. Brief your associates and your middle management regarding the dangers described in this book and keep them up to date. Make it clear that this is a true emergency—a once-in-a-lifetime economic war—which demands extraordinary management efforts.

Dissuade them of the notion that their recent failures might be their own fault and redirect their energies towards coming to grips with the crisis. Give them the latitude and encouragement to come up with innovative cost-cutting measures.

At the same time, however, you must make sure you have complete control over your cash management. Do you have systems in place which guarantee that all excess cash balances are moved promptly to safe havens? Are you taking full advantage of the "float" on your checks? Has there been a tendency of late for inventories to get out of hand, eating into your cash position? If so, it may be time to take a hard look at sales incentives, consumer survey tests and new marketing methods.

In this environment, the old rules of thumb must be reversed. You should scrutinize every aspect of your business to root out the psychology developed in the inflationary boom and adapt to the new world of deflationary bust.

2. Take Personal Control Over Personnel

It's far too easy to assume that your old guidelines are good enough or that the personnel department is doing the right thing on its own. Instead, make sure that the personnel department is under the direct control of top management. Take a critical, even exaggerated posture and force a total re-examination of the personnel process.

Don't refill jobs as they open up. Work with plant or warehouse foremen to gather up scattered jobs and locations. And do not hesitate to lay off those who are idled. In the short term, they may feel that you are being unfair. But in the long run, it will do them a lot more good if you survive the crisis and hire them back than if your business goes under.

How long has it been since you've asked yourself the following type of questions: Is my human resources manager really doing his utmost to find idle employees? Is he meeting with, and being critical of, plant, warehouse or store managers? If so, is he discovering that supervisors are putting a protective shield over employees who do not pull their own weight?

Have you been on top of these and other management work-problem areas yourself? If not, why not? Too busy? Don't let anything or anyone stand between you and what you must do to survive.

3. Make Deflation Work For You Instead Of Against You

If you are still experiencing rising costs despite the deflation in other areas, it may be possible that your industry is unique. More likely, however, it's because your purchasing manager is locked into old buying channels and methods. After so many decades of inflation, few indeed are versed in the methods of handling deflation.

Check a futures market chart on the products or materials which are related to those you buy. Are the prices going down? If so, you should be able to shake out substantial discounts from your suppliers. Undertake a complete review of all possible sources—domestic and foreign—and ferret out the ones which are in better synch with the real market.

Do you have a standard practices manual which is oriented towards deflation? In other words, does it stimulate your purchasing people to seek competitive bids on a continuing basis? If not, put one together as soon as possible.

How much effort are your purchasing agents or managers putting into negotiations with existing suppliers to improve discounts and services—to get allowances for provable goof-ups?

Are they taking full advantage of the current deflationary environment to get suppliers to lower prices for goods and services? If so, reinforce these tendencies. If not, get them on the right track as soon as possible. Tell them to be creative about finding and substituting other, lower-cost materials. Make sure they are influential in discussing cost-saving ideas with the production or sales staff.

4. Collect What's Yours!

In the Money Panic, the control of accounts receivable will be the bellwether of business cash flow and one of the major determining factors in corporate survival.

Even if your firm is relatively large and has a sophisticated credit manager or comptroller, a drastic slowdown in payments can wreak havoc with current assets. And if you have a small business, in which collecting from customers is just another one of the many duties of the owner/manager, the potential for damage is even more severe.

In a declining economy, don't let your customers get the notion that payment slowdowns are a good source of interest-free cash. If you haven't done so already, institute substantial cash discounts for early payment and severe penalties for late payment. Send out a chart to all your customers showing them, in simple and blatant terms, exactly how much they will be earning, on an annualized basis, by paying their bills ahead of time—and how much they'll be losing by delaying their payments. If you're offering a 1% discount for a two-week early payment, that's an annual yield of 26% *without* compounding! They can't beat that anywhere! Now, more than ever, you cannot allow passivity or inadequate managers to deter you from being paid on the terms and conditions agreed upon.

Here are a series of further steps you can take right now to move your receivables into cash position:

Step 1. 10 days late. Notify the customer (politely), that his current orders are standing on your shipping dock, awaiting his overdue payment. Do not ship until paid.

Step 2. 20 days late. Write two strong form letters (with invoices) mailed one week apart, reminding the customer of the overdue status. Each letter develops stronger language, the second stating that "necessary action will be taken."

Step 3. 30 days late. Your urgent phone calls begin. The minimum goal is to arrange for partial payment immediately with short-range terms for the balance. At the same time, try to find out the customer's cash/credit situation. If he appears to be near a critical stage, discuss a one-time reduction in the amount due, if paid within three days. While you're collecting your money, clear up any of the claims or disagreements that can develop in all business relationships. And compromise! Usually you will find that it's the hard times—and not so much the personalities—which are the true cause of any trouble or ill will.

Step 4. 45 days late. Unless there are very special circumstances, the account is in dangerous waters. While alerting your customer, do not hesitate to contact professional collection services or consider legal action (even if that's expensive). In any event—whenever you draw the line, do not allow the program to exceed 60-90 days from invoice date! By then, the account could be out the door, and the key thrown away!

Admittedly, collecting receivables is unpopular, occasionally dangerous, and sometimes oddly embarrassing. But remember: You're asking for your own money! It takes adequate, persuasive behavior to request payment. If you can't handle it, refer it to a self-confident employee, your spouse, or your accountant—but don't neglect it! In 1987, there were 61,235 bankruptcies in the United States—seven times more than in 1979. Do not join the many creditors who will be stuck holding the bag.

5. Slash Inventories

Whenever economists hear that business inventories are falling, their immediate response is that the stage is set for a "rise in industrial production to replenish stocks." This is supposed to mean that the time is now ripe for you to start rebuilding your inventory as well. They fail to consider certain basic facts of life: (1) Old rules of thumb regarding inventory-to-sales ratios are no longer valid, and (2) in the Money Panic, credit sales can fall dramatically.

Carefully examine (a) what *each* item costs you in terms of the interest on cash you're not earning plus the interest on financing that you are paying; (b) how much cash you can raise if you act immediately to discount the merchandise versus how much cash you may lose if you wait for price levels to fall further; (c) which inventory items you keep on hand for your own use—packing supplies, etc.—that you can redeem for cash.

Retrain inventory-control personnel and accountants. Are they fully aware of the new deflationary trends? Have they completely incorporated this new orientation into their handling of parts, materials, work in process and finished goods? If you're a manufacturer, have you fully investigated the cost-saving possibilities of the Japanese methods of taking delivery for new materials and parts only as they're used? The same holds true for wholesale/distribution operations. If you and/or your purchasing agent have made a mistake, face up to it and unload!

In short, if you haven't done so already, shift your thinking from inflation to deflation—making across-the-board changes in immediate strategies and long-range planning.

6. Convert Assets To Cash

How do you make solid profits during the Money Panic? Investing in high technology, manufacturing a new product and making substantial inroads into your market? No—you'll do a lot better by sitting back and lending all your money to Uncle Sam for three months at a time! Even if interest rates decline, it could take years for business yields to recoup to the level of Treasury yields.

Here are four ways to cash in on your surplus equipment, machinery, plant facilities, vehicles and even land you don't intend to use:

1. *Direct advertising sales*: Begin by writing strong, attractive ads in the business classified section of your local newspapers. As necessary, expand to major cities and eventually to your industrial trade journal or *Wall Street Journal* classifieds.

2. *Personal contact:* Get in touch with any local firms you feel may have use for surplus equipment. Don't hesitate to trade off discounts for cash up front, writing off the losses if necessary.

3. *Auctions*: Contact "auctioneers" or "liquidators" through the Yellow Pages in nearby major cities. Be sure to verify their reputation and seek those of many years' experience who will work with you on a 3-10% commission depending upon the volume and desirability of the surplus items you wish to sell.

The auctioneer will inventory your "package," which can also include plant and land and give you approximate estimates of prices they might bring at auction. If the items are significant in type or value, you should require that the auctioneer promote the sale on a regional or national basis, using mail brochures or media advertising. (Note: Always place a "contractual reserve" as the lowest price you will accept for specialized equipment or inventories.)

4. *Export:* If you have time, advertise in export publications, or use the *Wall Street Journal* for rapid results, as well as newspapers in export cities such as New York, Boston, Baltimore, Miami, New Orleans, Los Angeles or San Francisco. Stick with a first class export bank to handle and assure incoming letters of credit. Then work with reputable freight-forwarder customs brokers who will handle all documentation and paper work at a reasonable fee.

7. Maximize Yield

Once you've taken aggressive action to build up the cash in your business, the next logical step is to do everything within reason to maximize interest income.

Amazingly, many businesspeople are still locked into the old habit of letting relatively large cash balances sit in noninterest-bearing checking accounts. Not only are the banks cashing in on the "free money" by taking full advantage of the Fed Funds market but, despite new legislation to make banks reduce the "float," your money will still be held up. Make the float work to your advantage without risk by following the steps in Chapter 7 for interest-bearing "checking accounts" with a Treasury-only money fund. (Read carefully page 72.)

Have your bookkeeper produce a Daily Cash Report with columnar headings such as: "Cash Receipts," "Bank Account," "Money Funds," "Cash Disbursements," "Invoices Payable," "Fixed Monthly Overhead," etc. This will enable you to determine your cash flow at a glance, giving you flash warnings regarding excess cash sitting around in your bank as well as unexpected changes in fixed overhead, current payables, etc.

Stay on top of the situation so that there is no delay in wire-transferring cash balances to the money fund as soon as they are available. Negotiate with your bank to shorten their hold time on checks. With the latest changes in legislation, you have the law on your side.

Make sure also that all bills over $100, including rent, debt payments, bills from suppliers, even the U.S. post office, are being paid with your money-fund checks. If you see any non-money-fund checks being used, find out why.

The advantages of this method are indisputable: You earn interest on funds that otherwise might be sitting in a noninterest-bearing checking account; you earn as much as an extra two weeks of interest due to the float (between delays in depositing and clearing your checks); and assuming you have been careful in the selection of a sound money fund, you can feel comfortable that your cash is virtually 100% safe.

8. Trim The Product Line

Research and development of new technology and products are the backbone of a vibrant and growing economy. But the long-term future of the nation will not be adversely affected by a temporary respite from the rush to be "bigger and better," in order to rebuild liquidity. In fact, those businesses that step into the forefront of this retrenchment could also be the leaders of the ensuing recovery.

The dilemma of our times demands that cash be treated with royal respect. Therefore slow-moving raw materials, "in-process" parts or finished goods on the rack must come under scrutiny. A major reassessment of specific product sales history is a must. It's time to eliminate those products that have been carried in stock out of sentiment or for minor demand by special customers. (Many of the following steps apply to distributors as well; for a smaller operation, the same rules apply on a do-it-yourself basis.)

1. Require your sales management team to furnish comparative two-year sales figures on related product lines. Select the profitable ones, and clean house on the slow-movers by special discount offers, etc. One tried-and-true method is to offer current late-model merchandise at a 10% discount if ordered with a specific quantity of older goods to be eliminated from the line.

2. Review your current inventory levels at each material production stage, and scrap raw materials in lines selected to

become obsolete. Finish all goods "in process" if more than 50% complete and add to the promotion pile.

3. Review your print and advertising schedules to be sure all newly-cancelled products are eliminated from your current schedules, catalogs, promotion bulletins and price sheets.

4. Issue clear directions to the marketing-sales staff to dispose of "surplus" on hand and make the best deals possible in accordance with top management decisions.

5. Move the labor force from depleted areas to other stations, or make the unhappy choice of group layoffs. To avoid difficulties, deal with the union in the early planning stages.

6. Cut back on R&D, thereby saving design, drafting and engineering time. Concentrate the efforts of your creative staff on improvement of existing product.

7. If you are using large and expensive-to-maintain computers, reevaluate their cost as compared to smaller but faster networks of personal computers which are cheaper to maintain and where the software is also far less expensive.

8. Finally, require weekly reports on the progress of the program, and be sure your managers do a thorough job of elimination.

For retailers, the obvious course would be to run "Reduced Price" sales and "Jumble Counters" to clear the shelves of old, dust-collecting, merchandise.

The ultimate goal, however, is the same: Cash!

9. If The Price Is Right, Sell Your Business

With business failures at record highs and with many bluechip corporations already overleveraged, many businesspeople prefer to fight rather than sell. "It's a buyer's market," they say, "so why should I sell now?" The reason is quite simple: Price deflation has barely begun! If you decide to sell, I suggest you follow these steps:

Step 1. The Confidential Method: Your best choice is to sell through a reputable business brokerage network. The professional broker will analyze your business and what it's worth, advise on optimal strategies, and work directly with your attorney and accountant. The good broker will market you to serious buyers under a code number, describing the type of business, location, etc., and will qualify buyers to acquire and operate the business. Finally, he will aid the buyer and seller to structure a creative, tax-advantaged financing plan, and nurse the deal along to closing when he gets his 5% to 10% commission—all in complete confidence.

You can find business brokers through bank officers, attorneys, accountants, or in the Yellow Pages under "Business Brokers."

Step 2. The Open Marketplace: If there is no need for confidentiality, you can advertise in local and regional newspapers, using headlined ads not less than 2 inches by 1 column. Describe your business in this order: (1) Type of product or service, (2) physical facilities, (3) advantages of location to markets (sunbelt, railroad, seaport, major truck artery, etc.), (4) sales volume, (5) number of employees, (6) years of operation, (7) distribution area, (8) reason for sale, (9) financing and (10) potential for growth. Include at least the name of the person to contact, phone and city/state.

Step 3. Offering To Competitors: This may be your last choice—or your first choice depending on your relationship with other firms in your industry or field. Usually, a larger corporation (which may have felt your impact in the marketplace) would be the logical target for merger or complete acquisition.

Whichever route you choose to travel, you'll save lots of time by conducting the interviews at the highest level of integrity and excellence. Any worthy buyer will spot (and expect) weaknesses. So be frank and discuss your known problems and their solutions honestly.

At the same time, spruce up your offices, physical plant, equipment, grounds and vehicles. Emphasize to your potential buyer any steps you may have already taken to streamline your operations in preparation for the ongoing recession—the good liquidity, lack of burdensome inventories, receivables or plant and equipment.

Most important, don't wait too long for a top bid—if you can get cash up front and a quick closing.

10. Watch Out For The Other Guy

Even though you have taken every precaution possible to drive safely through the turbulent times ahead, the damage which can result from the reckless spending and borrowing done by others is incalculable. In the days before and during the Money Panic, you can take nothing for granted. If you thoroughly and objectively analyze the personal and business transactions you make on a regular basis, you will uncover hidden dangers. Ask yourself these questions:

Question #1. "What will I do if one of my main suppliers goes under?" In the bygone days of shortages and inflation, you worried about getting delivery on time. Now you may not get delivery at all—due to a forced shutdown of your manufacturer or distributor.

The best way to keep track of your suppliers' financial status is by asking point-blank what their liquidity is. Divide their cash, government securities and other readily marketable investments by their current bills and promissory notes coming due within the next 12 months. As long as the ratio is above 50%, you have nothing to worry about for now. Anything below 10% could be big trouble. And those in between require periodic monitoring.

Also try to find out how much progress they are making along the lines recommended in this chapter.

Question #2. "How can I protect myself against the bankruptcy of my largest customers?" Unfortunately, this is largely beyond your control. However, it calls for some foresight on your part to promptly sell off receivables to banks. Deep discounts for cash payment upon delivery are another alternative.

Question #3. "Suppose trucking or other transportation facilities are disrupted?" By that time, you should be sitting on a hoard of interest-earning cash while your company goes into what I call "planned hibernation." Although most of your operations may be temporarily in deep freeze, your cash will continue to be working at full capacity to earn considerably more than you could earn from your normal operations.

Unfortunately, events can move so quickly that it may not be feasible to effectively monitor the finances of everyone you do business with. No matter how big or how stable they may appear, you need a large number of diverse back-up suppliers for all essential goods and services.

You have chosen the right investments. You have safeguarded your home, your cash and your business. But have you done everything possible to protect your financial future? Not yet.

10

Use A Strong Broker

You must ensure that there are no weak links between you and your money, no institution or intermediary that will somehow throw a monkey wrench into your financial future. You must make sure that your broker will not go under. If you have a substantial amount of your money with a stock broker, just how safe is it? What safeguards are in place in case of a major default? What protection do you have against fraud within the brokerage house?

Fortunately, the news is not all bad: *The overall safeguards for brokerage firms are more solid than those for banks and S&Ls.* This doesn't mean that a bank CD bought through your broker is any safer. Rather, the likelihood of losing money on a CD— or any other investment—*due specifically to a failure by the broker* is far less.

When you deposit your funds in a bank or thrift account, they take your money and "run with it." They loan it out to consumers and businesses, plus a wide range of investments over which you have no say whatsoever. They are your debtor; you are their creditor. But when you put your money into a brokerage account, it's untouchable. They can't invest it elsewhere. It must stay put in the securities that you specify. They are merely your custodian; you are their customer—nothing more.

In short, you are financially entangled with your banker. With your broker, however, you have an arms-length relationship. Even if the worst-case scenario comes to pass, and major brokerage houses run into tough times, you will get your money back—*eventually*.

That last word may be the hiccup that keeps you from sleeping nights. Just how long it would take before you finally see your assets in the Money Panic is difficult to pin down. And just what those securities would be worth when you finally are able to liquidate them is even more difficult to estimate. Therefore, the need to analyze your brokerage firm is just as great as the need to check the safety of your own bank or thrift. Ironically, in the 1980s, investors who had an account with a smaller firm got their money back relatively quickly. Those with accounts in larger firms had to wait significantly longer. This presents a definite dilemma. The large, well-capitalized firms were generally safer and less likely to go under, but when they did fail, they were more of a mess to clean up.

However, to retreat from Wall Street entirely would be to deny yourself countless profit opportunities and vast facilities for the purchase of many of the securities recommended in this book. There *are* concrete steps you can take to avoid trouble:

Step 1. Make sure your broker is a member of the Securities Investors Protection Corporation (SIPC). Since the overwhelming majority are, there should be no problem on this score. However, if he fails this very basic test, something is definitely unusual or wrong.

Step 2. Find out what additional insurance the firm may have. If there is no additional coverage, if you don't have an independent manager who is monitoring your broker's safety on a regular basis, and if you have more than $500,000 in your account, *transfer the amount over $500,000 to another firm.*

Step 3. Find out how much capital the broker has. Although officials at the SEC may not agree, I firmly maintain that if a brokerage firm has enough of its own capital (called either net worth or stockholders' equity) in relation to debt which it piles up, then the cushion against failure is greater—a good sign for customers.

I call this measure "the broker's equity ratio," similar to— but not the same as—the equity ratio of the banks. It answers the question: *For every dollar of total debts, how much does the broker have in stockholders' equity?*

Table 8. How Safe Is Your Broker?

Broker Name	Equity ($mil.)	Total Liab. ($mil.)	Equity/ Debt (%)
Bear Stearns	939	24,308	3.9
Charles Schwab & Co.	155	2,105	7.4
Dean Witter	786	14,024	5.6
First Boston	1,134	40,929	2.8
Goldman Sachs	2,572	47,365	5.4
Kidder Peabody	350	20,600	1.7
Merrill Lynch	3,400	56,500	6.0
Morgan Stanley	1,461	39,070	3.7
Paine Webber	1,096	11,864	9.2
Prudential Bache	978	17,060	5.7
Salomon, Inc.	3,607	71,275	5.1
Shearson, Lehman, Hutton	1,860	77,800	2.4

Although there are other, more thorough measures of the strength of a brokerage firm, this one will still give you a rough idea. All else being equal, we prefer a large firm with an equity ratio of at least 5%. Data: Corporate reports.

The formula is simple:

Broker's equity ratio = stockholders' equity ÷ total liabilities × 100

This does not delve into the myriad of complexities associated with brokerage-firm accounting. Nor can you use it as an end-all measure of your broker's strength or a proxy for the more complex formula for "net capital position." But it does allow you to make a quick check.

Almost invariably, a broker with a high equity ratio will be much stronger than a broker with a low equity ratio. There could be some very rare exceptions. But to catch them, a far more extensive analysis—beyond the scope of most investors—would be needed.

Step 4. Regardless of how strong your broker is, don't put all of your eggs in one basket. Place a substantial portion of your keep-safe funds in Treasury securities bought directly from the Federal Reserve.

The Strongest And The Weakest

If you look at the balance sheets of any of the major brokerage houses, the amount of debt is indeed staggering. Merrill Lynch, as of June 30, 1988, had total liabilities of $56.5 billion, with a stockholders' equity of only $3.4 billion. Still, that gives Merrill Lynch a broker's equity ratio of 6.0%, better than many other firms. Salomon Inc., as of the same date, has total liabilities of $71.3 billion and stockholders' equity of $3.6. That gives them an equity ratio of only 5.1%. The worst of the lot is the newly formed giant, Shearson Lehman Hutton, with $77.8 billion in liabilities and $1.86 billion in stockholders' equity, resulting in a startlingly low 2.4% ratio.

These very same firms usually hold alarmingly high inventories of securities. These are *not* the securities belonging to their clients—they're securities they themselves take a position in. Merrill Lynch, for instance, holds a net security inventory of some $7 billion. While some of that amount is in relatively safe money market instruments and government bonds, almost half is in corporate securities and mortgages.

The Hutton balance sheet during its final two years is typical of a firm in trouble. If you want to know what to look for in order to spot potential candidates for defaults, that may be the first place to go. In 1986, it had stockholders' equity of $760 million, with total liabilities of $25,188 million, yielding a weak 3.0% equity ratio. The next year, in its final death throes, equity sank to $320 million and total liabilities to $11,565 million, with a consequent 2.8% ratio.

Some may say their troubles are over. But what has really taken place is that *much of the liabilities accumulated on Wall Street has been concentrated into one firm: Shearson Lehman which has only a 2.4% equity ratio.*

Big Players In For Big Trouble?

What does all this mean for you? In the Money Panic, it may be impossible for some major firms to escape without significant restructuring. Most of these firms are into virtually *everything*, from leveraged buyouts to bridge loans, speculative commodity trading to helping corporate raiders. And some will do almost anything to make hugh profits.

Merrill's balance sheet is relatively strong. But will they take the necessary steps to keep it strong in a panic? For others, already relatively weak, these questions are even more critical.

Calculating The Ratio

How do you go about calculating the equity ratio? It's actually quite simple: Look at the consolidated balance sheet your broker sends to you periodically. As you probably know, underlying every balance sheet is the simple formula: assets = liabilities + equity.

You'll see, then, that the liabilities and equity are listed together, and that their total equals total assets. (It's on the asset side that you'll find what securities your broker owns.)

Sometimes you will see the figures clearly marked as "total liabilities" and "stockholders' equity." That makes your job easier.

More often, although you'll find stockholders' equity easily enough, the total liabilities won't be so obvious. To get it, you'll have to perform the following operation:

First, find the "total liabilities and stockholders' equity" (usually underlined by two lines). Then subtract the stockholders' equity from that figure. The result is the "total liabilities."

Once you have the two figures, simply divide the equity by the liabilities and multiply the result by 100. That's the broker's equity ratio.

Small Versus Large: Which Is Better?

Now that you can calculate the equity ratio, you can begin to resolve the dilemma I raised earlier. However, your primary concern here is not how much you pay in commissions. Oftentimes paying less in commissions can turn out to be a false economy. Rather, you should be far more concerned with the *safety* of your capital.

The first thing you should look for is a high equity ratio, regardless of size. Once you have that, the next question is large versus small. The advantage of going with a larger firm is that *changes in the equity ratio from period to period will tend to be less volatile.* In a small firm, it doesn't take much—a bad mistake by a manager or a default by a large creditor which is beyond their control—to throw their equity ratio out of whack. In a brokerage giant, on the other hand, many different disasters have to converge in one time and place to cause a sharp drop in the equity ratio.

The smaller firms—as well as many of the discount houses—do have one advantage: They make most of their money from commissions. Most do not carry huge inventories of their own securities. Most do not play the takeover game. Consequently, they are less likely to go bankrupt in our worst-case scenario. Charles M. Schwab, Inc., for instance, had a relatively healthy 7.4% equity ratio as of June 1988.

An even stronger discount house is Brown & Company Securities Corporation of Boston. It is an affiliate and owned by Chemical NY bank. The question here is: Will Chemical Bank, the parent, call its loans to its affiliate, Brown & Co., should the bank get into trouble itself? No one can say with certainty. The big pluses for Brown, however, are their 8.7% equity ratio, very small security inventory, and the fact that they keep almost all of it in T-bills.

Be forewarned, however, that when you elect to deal with a discount broker, you will get *no* advice. If you misspeak and say to *sell* when you meant *buy*, you won't get a personal broker who knows you and will say, "Are you certain that's what you want?" Consequently, reliance on your broker and his knowing your strengths and weaknesses may be far more important to you than getting a break on the commission.

Beware Of The Repo Man

After going through all the trouble of checking the safety of your broker, you may sit back one day and ask: "Am I wasting my time? If it's guaranteed by SIPC, what difference does it make?"

For that answer, ask the investors who relied on Beville, Bresler & Schulman of Newark, NJ, a firm that went under in 1985. Like virtually all of the firms that SIPC has liquidated—205 firms in 17 years, with a total of $227 million spent through 1988—Beville, Bresler & Schulman involved fraud. In this case, the firm dealt extensively in "repos," a process in which a broker sells securities with the understanding that they will be repurchased later. This is perfectly legal. But Beville, it turns out, was promising the same securities *simultaneously* five or six times to different institutions.

"In that case," Ted Focht of SIPC says, "some of the clients didn't see their money back until the end of 1987."

SIPC attempts to arrange for "bulk transfers" of accounts if possible. If another healthy brokerage firm can be found to take over the accounts, they are simply switched to it and the customers notified. They then may leave the securities with the new firm or move them elsewhere.

Sometimes, if the books and records are in a state of disarray, or if no other firm wants the accounts because they are so speculative, a bulk transfer cannot be handled. In the case of such chaotic conditions, there can be a difference of opinion between the trustee and the customer as to what securities the customer actually owns. Needless to say, you must save your confirmation slips to prove they're yours. What most people don't realize is that you must do so for all securities they hold on your behalf—including T-bills and other cash equivalents!

SIPC feels that if one of the major firms were to go into default, there would be little problem finding other firms eager to take over bulk transfers. They are making the false assumption, however, that there will be no domino effect where one firm after the other goes under. In that worst-case scenario, who knows what would happen or how long the SIPC would take, with only 35 employees, to untangle the mess and secure payment?

What's In A Street Name?

Most brokers suggest that clients leave the securities in the broker's name ("street name") for the sake of convenient trading. That way, trades can be handled by a simple phone call. You have the option, however, of asking your broker to actually give you the stock certificates in your own name. In that case, you would have to physically deliver the certificates to your broker for trading. That might be inconvenient, but you would be safe in case the brokerage ran into trouble. Otherwise, although the "street name" securities would indeed belong to you legally, you would have to wait for SIPC to untangle the mess and get them back to you.

For the most part, those who trade actively may keep stocks in street name. But as the crisis deepens, this one advantage of holding the certificates could outweigh the many disadvantages.

Living On Margin

Margin accounts are another consideration. By law you are allowed to purchase securities up to 50% on margin. Many investors further leveraged their holdings during the bull market by taking out a home equity loan and investing that on margin, in effect putting their home on the line with their investments and creating a double-leverage effect.

How safe would a margin account be in the case of a brokerage firm's demise? According to SEC regulations passed in 1973, every brokerage firm must keep a segregated fund equal to the net amount owed to customers. In other words, if you take the amount customers owe to the firm and subtract it from the amount the firm owes the customers, you have the net amount the firm must keep segregated. Thus, there ought to be sufficient funds to cover all margin accounts. This is the cushion for your protection—providing the broker is effective in getting the money on undermargined accounts when markets are in a free-fall.

You can see this amount in your broker's balance sheet, usually called something like "cash segregated and securities on deposit for regulatory purposes." In the Merrill Lynch 1988 balance sheet, it amounts to over $2 billion.

As you might expect, I recommend that you avoid highly margined positions. The typical margin agreement permits the broker to close out customer positions for *any* reason deemed necessary for the broker's protection. While that normally is done only for unanswered margin calls, it *could* presumably happen if a brokerage firm were in desperate straits.

The real problem is that, in the event a brokerage cannot pay back the bank for the loan of margined securities, the bank has a superior claim ahead of the client. According to an official at the SEC:

> Numerous court decisions have established that the bank's rights are strong, generally superior even to those of the customer. Although the situation is infrequent, if the broker became unsecured as a result of price activity and was not able to meet the bank's loan terms, the bank has the legal right to sell the customer's pledged securities to protect its loan. Naturally, the customer in this situation will have a difficult time salvaging much equity.

The moral of the story is simple: Put as much distance as possible between your money and the debt problem.

11

Reduce Your Risk To Zero!

Let's assume that you *have* liquidated your stocks, bonds and all assets which might be vulnerable to the crisis.

Now you can proceed to your third goal—profit. But you must do so in such a way as not to jeopardize—even to the slightest degree—the safety of your principal.

It doesn't take long to start. In fact, a few days after you buy your T-bill, you receive the "discount" check which, in effect, represents your interest paid in advance.

Let's say, for the sake of simplicity, that you buy a $20,000 one-year T-bill and that the T-bill rate is 10%. You will receive a check for $2,000. Your principal already has, in effect, yielded one year's worth of interest. It is your harvest, collected in advance. But it is also the seed money that can multiply several times during the next twelve months. Here are the steps you should follow:

Step 1. Divide the next twelve months into four seasons, each three months long, to match the maturity date of your one-year T-bill.

Step 2. To each season, allocate one-fourth of your seed money. In this example, it amounts to $500.

Step 3. With these funds, you will purchase limited risk investments that have high potential for profit: options, strip bonds plus, at the right time, greatly undervalued stocks.

Suppose You're Wrong?

If your investment decision-making is 100% wrong and every last penny of your seed money is lost, despite four successive attempts, *you will still end the year with 100% of your capital intact.* Your Treasury bill will mature. You will collect the money. And that will be the end of the story unless you want to repeat the program for another year.

If you achieve below-average success, you can end the year with an income that is at least equal to the yield on a short-term T-bill alone.

And, if your success is above average, the net yield on your total funds could be several times greater than a T-bill.

Vehicle #1: Options

Suppose you want to invest in the stock market. You think the crash is over but you're not sure. If you buy stocks at the wrong time, you could lose a substantial portion of your investment in another wave of panic selling. If you buy futures contracts without the proper risk control, you could lose even more. Guess right and make a killing; guess wrong, and you get killed.

But suppose you could somehow wait until the outcome, and then, with the benefit of 20-20 hindsight, decide whether or not you wanted to go ahead with the deal? Rather than take any immediate action, you would just sit back and wait to see what happens. If the market goes up, you buy a whole portfolio of stocks at the price it *was* near the bottom of the market, sell it at the current level and take a profit. On the other hand, if the market falls, you take a raincheck. Too good to be true? Nevertheless, this is what options allow you to do—both in declining and rising markets.

The options to buy are *calls.* The options to sell (go short) are *puts.* Until recently, puts and calls were available only on individual stocks. Now you can buy them for general market indexes and for some of the important futures markets. You can buy options on the S&P 100 stocks, Treasury bonds, foreign currencies, gold or silver, plus various stock indices and a number of different agricultural commodities.

Those already familiar with stock options will very easily be able to make the shift to futures options. The mechanism is almost identical. The problem to beware of, however, is liquidity. Make sure the options you buy are traded actively and that there is a large amount outstanding in the hands of investors.

There are two catches associated with options, but both of them are reasonable compared to the opportunities they provide. First, you have a limited amount of time in which the expected market move is to occur. Second, you have to pay a price for the options. The price varies depending upon how much time you have left, and how far you are from where you expect the market to go.

Options also provide advantages that are ideally suited for the Delta Strategy.

First, when you buy an option, unlike buying securities or futures, you are not responsible for any losses in the securities themselves. Let's say you buy a call in the S&P 500 for $250, hoping the market will go up. Instead, to your disappointment, the market crashes causing holders of the actual S&P contracts to suffer huge losses. You need not worry! The most you can lose is the original $250 you paid for the call and not a dime more. This is why your principal, locked up in a Treasury bill, will never be adversely affected.

Second, despite the limited risk, your leverage is almost *un*limited. In other words, you do not suffer from the huge losses that can result from futures trading, but you *can* benefit from the huge profits.

Third, options also give you diversification, either by purchasing options in specific stocks, by buying options on stock indexes, or by using options on futures.

Fourth, if you are careful to select options in the mainstream of trading, you benefit from the large volume of transactions done daily. Bear in mind that this is not true for every option traded. However, you can determine which are the most active ones by looking them up in *Barron's* or by asking your broker. (Note: The *Wall Street Journal* also lists the volume but only for the total of all the different months in each category. You need to know the vital statistics on the *specific* options you buy, and this is published only in *Barron's.*)

The two things you need to learn are the *volume* and *"open interest"* for the particular option you are considering.

The volume, as in stocks, is the number of contracts that change hands on a particular day. As a rule of thumb, we suggest you select options where the daily volume for the specific put or call you want is at least 1,000 contracts.

The open interest is the total number of option contracts owned by everyone at a given time. As a general rule, there should be a minimum of 5,000 contracts.

Vehicle #2. Zero-Coupon And Strip Bonds

When interest rates have peaked, zero-coupon or strip bonds are excellent vehicles for locking in high yields and for making a profit from falling interest rates.

Like savings bonds, they are ideal for your children's college fund or your retirement fund. To see why, first you must understand how they work.

A major brokerage firm like Merrill Lynch will buy a large block of 20-year bonds. They then split the bonds into the components—interest and principal. In the case of its "Principal Type" package, Merrill Lynch collects all the interest and applies it to the eventual redemption of the bonds. In a typical example, you pay, say, $2,000 for a $10,000 bond and your yield to maturity is 10%.

If you put it into an IRA, you pay no tax until the bond is paid off 20 years later and it locks in the equivalent of roughly 10% for the 20 years, collectible at the end of the period.

The difference between the "zeros" and the "strips" is that the former are repackaged and issued by the broker who holds the Treasuries. The question is how readily can you sell them on the secondary market? If interest rates rise, the market value of the bonds will fall and the zero-coupon market could be temporarily inactive.

For this reason, I prefer strip bonds. The concept is identical to that of the zero-coupon bonds. But you have the advantage that you retain direct ownership of the Treasury securities themselves. You thereby eliminate the middleman (the broker) as a principal in the transaction. You pay a small price for this extra measure of safety in that the yield on the strip bond will be slightly less than the yield on the equivalent zero-coupon bond. But it's worth it! Moreover, you can usually count on better liquidity and a wider range of maturities available.

Vehicle #3. Undervalued Stocks

In the Money Panic, many investors will inevitably throw out the baby with the bath water. They will sell companies that have good fundamental values simply because they are scared of events they cannot understand or are in desperate need of the cash to pay bills coming due. This will be your opportunity to pick up major values with a very small investment. You will be surprised how many solid stocks are selling for $2, $3 or $4 per share!

Although probably costing somewhat more, one of the first areas to look at will be the gold shares.

Due to the crosscurrents of deflation and financial crisis, picking the precise bottom in gold and gold shares will be difficult. It is for this reason that, as of this writing, I do *not yet* recommend gold as the mainstay of your portfolio. Unlike the early 1970s, when it was an investment shunned by the establishment, it has now joined the mainstream of investment vehicles along with stocks and bonds. This implies that a shakeout of some kind is possible before the big up move.

Thus the true golden opportunity will come to those who are patient and prudent—patient enough to wait for big dips before buying, and prudent enough not to buy too much too soon.

Making The Delta Strategy Work For You

More important perhaps than *what* to buy is the question of *how much* to buy. In this regard, here are three money-management rules you should follow to ensure the success of your investments allocated to the Delta Strategy:

Rule #1. Never violate the basic premise: Your principal must be preserved for the full duration of the plan. In other words, promise yourself not to sell the T-bill, *no matter what.*

The options market provides incredibly powerful leverage. Be aware that there is a tendency among investors to discontinue the program too soon (before the year ends) or to draw funds out of the principal during the course of the year.

Sometimes, investors will say: "This plan isn't working. Why should I pursue it?" Or they'll say, "It's doing so well, I'll double my ante." Instead, stick with it the full year without adding or subtracting to the funds.

Rule #2. Do not "borrow" funds allocated to a future "season." Sometimes an opportunity looks so good you are tempted to double your normal option purchase. Experience shows that the best performance is achieved by spreading your purchases equally over time. I call this *time-diversification*: Your entire portfolio—when added up over a period of a year—will contain a greater diversity and encompass a broader range of market conditions.

Rule #3. Do not reapply seed money that was allocated to a previous season. Using the $20,000 account example, suppose you bought $500 worth of options in your first season and then sold those options for $1,200. The original $500 should be added to your "untouchable account." However, the net profit of $700 can be added to the seed money for the second season, giving you a total of $1,200 to invest. If you achieve the same results in the second season, you can stash away another $500 and have still more to work with, and so forth.

In options, it is not unusual to achieve two-for-one results, and much higher ratios are also possible. However, the most common outcome is that investors lose the *entire value* of the option. Thus, although the risk on each option is limited, if you keep buying them and they keep expiring worthless, your overall losses can be *un*limited, completely defeating their original purpose. This is why the discipline imposed by the Delta Strategy, especially these last two rules, should be adhered to religiously.

Those who have adhered to the rules have found that they can increase their total yield to 20% or more, without having risked one cent of their principal.

Make Money On The Way Down As Well

Most investors assume you are either *in* the market or *out*. During a bull market, they're in, of course. However, they usually miss the fact that there are equal, or *greater*, opportunities on the way down via short positions.

Even some of the more savvy investors still don't fully grasp how this works. My friend, Jackson, is a good example.

"I know how to make money when the market's going up. But how do you make money when it's going down?" he asked once over dinner.

"Loan me your watch," I responded.

"Huh? It's brand-new, fresh out of the box."

"Come on. Take your watch off and let me borrow it." He grudgingly obeyed.

"Now, how much did you pay for this watch?"

"A hundred bucks!"

"Well, I think it's going down in price. I think the Taiwanese and the Koreans will be dumping these things in such big quantities, you'll be able to pick them up for $20. So here's the deal: Loan me this watch today with the understanding that I will buy you one just like it a few months from today."

"But—"

"Let's assume you go along with the idea. I sell your watch for $100 and put the money in my wallet. When the price falls to $20, I buy another watch and give it to you, replacing the one I borrowed. I have just made a good, honest profit of $80."

"I get it. But how can you do that in the stock market?"

"Simple. You go to your broker who's holding all kinds of stocks in inventory. You borrow the shares from him and sell them at today's price. Later, you buy them back—hopefully at a lower price—and return the shares to him. When you sell borrowed shares, you 'go short' or 'sell short' the stock. When you buy the shares back, you 'cover your shorts.'"

He understood. But to this day, he is still hesitant.

Like Jackson, you probably believe that short positions are somehow riskier than "normal" investments. But Black Monday proved that there are equal risks holding regular positions in stocks. Furthermore, you can buy a *put option* which gives you the *right* to go short when and if it's profitable to do so. It is these put options—and not the outright short positions—which are best adapted to the concept of the Delta Strategy.

History clearly shows the consequences to those who are unprepared and pretend that nothing will change. History also demonstrates that if you can tame the bear market, you can make more profits in one year than you made in the previous thirty years. Most investors, no matter how astute, will miss this opportunity. But if you aim at a more reasonable goal—hedging against losses in your other assets—you could be very pleasantly surprised by the results.

For years you have heard stories such as: "I could have bought that land for $1.00 an acre, and now they're building a shopping center on it!" or "I could kick myself for not buying AT&T when it came out at $2 a share." You are inundated with "bullish-on-America" ads from major brokerage firms. You are thoroughly indoctrinated in the concept "buy low, sell high."

Therefore, when it comes to "selling short" in a down market, you are unprepared, uncertain and unwilling. It somehow seems unfair and risky, as if you were capitalizing on the misfortunes of others.

Or you may have the feeling that going short is somehow unwise or unpatriotic. The fact is that *some of the greatest fortunes have been made in the shortest period of time during great down markets.*

Short selling is an honest, legitimate way to protect your assets or to make a profit. Short sellers provide liquidity to the markets by accepting risks that others are not willing to assume. Short sellers are essential for starting rallies and recoveries. As a matter of fact, all the futures markets of the world would cease to exist if there weren't short sellers. Most important, in a down market, short selling offers much larger potential profits than the most spectacular bull markets.

Try thinking of it this way: If investing in the stock market is like having the best dinner prepared by the greatest chef, would you only eat half and throw the rest away? I doubt it. If you were going to take a trip around the world, would you go halfway and never come home? Of course not. Then why not learn to invest in both sides of the market? Why not embrace the market opportunities that come only once every half century? Just make sure that, no matter how confident you are, you keep your positions modest, with the bulk of your funds firmly grounded in absolutely safe, worry-free havens.

Bernard Baruch was perhaps the greatest and most famous short seller of all time. He was one of the astute few who sold short into the euphoria at the very peak of the 1929 stock market. He was considered crazy, unpatriotic and suffered innumerable derogatory aspersions as a result. But when we look back, we see that, although historians have not recorded the names of his detractors, Mr. Baruch's reputation is considered to be unparalleled to this very day. The reason is obvious: Those who didn't heed his warnings walked around destitute; Bernard Baruch rode home with a fortune.

Timing Your Investment Decisions

Most advisors or brokers will tell you there are only two basic methods of timing your investment decisions. You can use *fundamental* information on interest rates, the economy, corporate earnings. Or you can analyze *technical* patterns such as cycles, chart formations, and other indicators.

Both of these approaches have their validity. But in addition to the more commonly used methods, there is a third system that I believe forges into new ground and, by so doing, provides consistently good results.

This new method is based upon an analysis of *who owns what* in the market.

If a security or commodity is held by strong hands, the likelihood that they will be forced to sell is very small. But if weak hands hold all positions, a sudden wave of panic selling can hit at almost any time.

Thus, your key to timing the market is to track the strong hands versus the weak hands. Know what each group owns in what relative proportions. Most important, follow how this critical "market composition" changes from one month to the next.

Who are the strong players? Who are the weak ones? In the actual markets for stocks or bonds, it is hard to say. But in the *futures* markets, we can track these groups by using the monthly survey published by the Commodity Futures Trading Commission (CFTC).

The strong hands are the *commercials*—those who produce or use the actual products of commodities and who buy and sell futures almost exclusively as a protection against unexpected price changes. The weak hands are the speculators who are in the market strictly to make a profit and are not in the business of producing or selling.

There are some speculators who do extremely well in the markets and make substantial profits. Conversely, there are no doubt some commercials who get caught on the wrong side from time to time. But when taken as a group, there is consistent evidence that the commercials are usually the winners and the speculators are usually the losers.

At Weiss Research, we track who owns what in twenty different markets. And, as you shall see in Chapter 21, it was the sudden rash of selling by the commercials in the stock index futures that gave us advance warning of the Crash of '87. Similarly, concentrated buying or selling by one of these groups has consistently forewarned us of important moves in interest rates and precious metals. (For more information on this forecasting method, see the Weiss Research books, *Winning With The Insiders* and *Timing The Market*.)

Although you may not have time to track all the indicators on your own, you still need to know if you should sell immediately, wait to sell, or not sell at all. Unfortunately, there's no universal answer to these questions. But, in a major down market, it is generally wise to sell half of your stocks immediately, no matter what. Then wait for a rally in the market, whether from the market's current level or from a lower level, before selling the remaining half. If a rally is already taking place, use it to sell your shares on a scale up. Most important, stay in touch with an advisor who meets the requirements of a prudent, balanced manager.

How To Choose An Advisor In A Down Market

In good times, it is easy to choose an advisor who can make money for you. Despite intermediate corrections, markets are going up and the overwhelming majority of advisors have plenty of experience in handling up markets. In bad times, however, it's much more difficult. Advisors with proven experience in handling down markets are few and far between. And although there are many who claim to have lived through the Depression, there are very few indeed who have a *proven track record and actual hands-on experience with a major decline.*

If you find such a person, listen carefully to what he or she has to say. Although the next depression will not be the same as the last one, there *will be* enough similarities to warrant close attention to the experiences of those who have seen it once before.

There is nothing wrong with extreme views. After all, it is the conditions we face—not the people who analyze them— which are so extreme. But make sure that the advisor is flexible, not locked in to one theory or philosophy. You need balance and stability. When markets reach a bottom, allocate your assets over a broad spectrum of top-quality investments. The last person that you want as your advisor is a fanatic so stay away from those who would have you believe in their "absolute truth."

Seek those whose predictions are supported by fact and logic, carefully documented and clearly explained. Your advisor has to be rational, willing to recognize his mistakes when he makes them. Most important, he must have fail-safe strategies to protect you against the possible mistakes he will make—mistakes which otherwise could prove fatal.

Finally, *it is important to maintain contact with your advisor on a regular basis.* What good is it if your advisor gets you into a specific investment, but isn't around to get you out again? The vehicle for contact can be a regular newsletter, a telephone hotline or a personal consultation.

Once you've found an advisor, do not second-guess him. Do not selectively use some of his recommendations but not others. Follow his advice consistently. If you don't feel confident enough to go that far, split your funds into two or more portions, earmarking only one of them for the recommendations of the advisor. And if you can't afford to follow all of the advisor's recommendations, touch base with him to get his "core" recommendations.

If you can't find a good advisor, should you play the market anyway? If you confine yourself to the limitations of the Delta Strategy, yes. But if you want to go beyond the Delta Strategy and risk a substantial portion of your capital, probably not. Looking back over previous crashes, we find that most of the survivors did not trade in and out. Rather, once they achieved maximum safety and liquidity, they simply sat with it, regardless of the market's ups and downs. The big profits came when the markets hit rock bottom and major bargains were available.

You can make money in the same way. When the average cost of a stock goes down, your money is automatically worth more in terms of the number of shares you can buy. And when there occurs a major collapse in real estate as well as other commodities, you will have made substantial gains just by holding Treasury securities or equivalent.

In the interim, *compound interest* with safety—and not necessarily trading profits—should be the underlying key to your success.

As you will see in Chapter 23, the yield you earn on absolutely safe securities should remain well above the inflation rate throughout most of the Money Panic. And, if you follow the suggestions made in Chapter 32 for timing your purchases, it should not be difficult to lock in high yields for many years to come.

With your assets far from the dangers of the debt pyramid, with your money safely protected in T-bills or equivalent and with a clear strategy for profit, you are now prepared for the Money Panic. As you read the chapters which follow, you need not be frightened by the calamitous events described. You can rest easy in the knowledge that your money is secure—or will be secure—just as soon as you put the Delta Strategy into practice.

Where did the Money Panic begin? How will it end? How will it affect the average American in the coming decade? No one has the complete answers to any of these questions. We live in an economic environment which has no precedent, with only limited clues from history which might illuminate our future path.

Therefore, to find the answers, let us take a flight of fancy into the future. From the perspective of a twenty-first century historian, let us look back upon these turbulent times to try and find the true causes and consequences of the Money Panic.

In Book II, "The Past," all material is factual. In Book III, "The Future," most events are fictional.

Book II

THE PAST

12

The Origins Of
The Money Panic

I write to you from a farm near São Paulo, Brazil, in the year 2008.

Two decades ago, in the late 1980s, few could foresee what lay ahead. Even those of us who had arduously studied panics and crashes of the early 1900s were unprepared for the events that followed: the financial panic which spread from the savings and loans to the commercial banks, the turmoil on Wall Street and America's second great depression.

But today, a new millennium is unfolding. We anticipate a brighter future. At the same time, we can look back on those turbulent times of the late twentieth century and see them in a different light. With hindsight, we can finally discern patterns which were only vaguely visible to the observers of that era. What we see is the phenomenon called the Money Panic.

Most twenty-first century economists believe the Money Panic started on Black Monday, October 19, 1987, when the bottom fell out of the stock market and the Dow Jones Industrials cascaded by 508 points. Others, myself included, would argue that it actually began early in the decade with the bond market collapse of 1979-80.

Whichever moment you pick, one thing is certain: The true roots of the Money Panic can be traced to the early stages of the boom. In this section, as we travel quickly from the first midcentury growth pangs to the 1980s collapses, you will see that the Money Panic should not have come as such a great surprise. During the earlier years, a sequence of crises, credit crunches and near-disasters should have served as adequate forewarning to even the most sanguine of observers.

How far back must we go to unearth the true origins of the crash? The best place to begin is 1946 when the euphoria of military victory, and the great cash hoards saved during World War II, launched the longest era of economic prosperity in American history.

Inflation and boom went hand-in-hand; one was part of the other. Turn on the boom, and inflation heated up. Turn off the boom, and inflation temporarily disappeared. Fortunately or unfortunately—depending upon your historical perspective—no one during those four decades between the mid-1940s and the mid-1980s had either the power or the courage to moderate the economic boom. Instead, we plunged headlong into the most intense period of expansion, construction and production ever seen. Like a bulldozer, the giant industrial machine of the Western world rolled forward, mowing down anyone or anything that dared to block its path.

Ostensibly, the executive branch of government determined the course of the economy. Whenever there was a choice between inflation and unemployment, the postwar presidents always chose inflation. All were faced with essentially the same alternatives: sacrifice the present for the future, or sacrifice the future for the present. And with the possible exception of the last two years of the Eisenhower Administration, the politicians invariably chose "prosperity now" and "the hell with what happens after the next election." Push ahead, move on, stimulate more production and growth. Above all, create more debt! What about rampant inflation and the destruction of the dollar? "Well," said they, "you can jump off that bridge when you come to it."

Anyone who was opposed to excessive growth and inflation was weeded out of the decision-making process at all levels of government and business. Conversely, anyone who moved into power had to be, by definition, in favor of economic "progress," "prosperity" and, implicitly, inflation as well. Few leaders thought seriously about the long term. As a result, it was those of us who lived through the last two decades of the century who suffered the consequences.

Truman's economic policies were determined by the public psychology of the immediate postwar era. When he came into office, there was widespread fear of a depression. Consumers, businesspeople and government officials expected some kind of economic slump. The Truman Administration responded to this pessimism with stern antidepression measures—"a pledge on the part of the people voiced through their laws that never again shall any sacrifices be laid on the altar of natural economic forces." In effect, depressions were branded and stamped "illegal, immoral and impossible." Consequently, while there was a minor setback in the winter of 1948-49, the big event was the outpouring of pent-up savings. The Marshall Plan in 1947 and the Korean war in 1950 added another $44 billion in government spending to the private economy. The big postwar boom was on.

The Eisenhower years can best be described as the launching pad for the superboom which was to follow during the Kennedy and Johnson years. At this stage, great battles were fought between the old, waning forces which sought moderation and the new emerging forces pushing towards growth. The moderates wanted to slow economic expansion, preserve the dollar, prevent inflation. They were later labeled the "bad guys," primarily because they lost and were kicked out. The expansionists wanted to push forward, borrow and spend. They became the "good guys," primarily because they won and subsequently wrote the textbooks.

One of the classic midcentury struggles was the battle over Montgomery Ward, the nation's second largest retailer. In the winter of 1954, Louis Wolfson, a Florida junk dealer who had risen to the control of a large industrial concern, mounted an all-out raid on Montgomery Ward.

Sewell Avery, the Chairman, was vulnerable to attack because he had been so conservative and refused to plow profits into construction and expansion. He preferred instead to build up $300 million in cash reserves, and it was this huge bundle of cash that became the prime target of the Wolfson raiders. Wolfson accused management of "hoarding cash," "running a bank with a department store front."

Avery stood for moderation, safety and caution; Wolfson, representing the forces of expansion and rapid growth, wanted Avery out. It was that simple.

At the time, my father, J. Irving Weiss, happened to be one of Avery's business advisors. He decided to help his client by organizing a defense committee—the "Businessman's Committee For Seasoned Management." He enlisted bankers and businessmen including James Kemper, Chairman of the Commerce Trust Company in Kansas City, Walter Paepcke, founder of Aspen, Colorado and Chairman of The Container Corporation of America, former Senator Prentiss Brown of Michigan, and many others. And he won what the *New York Times* called "one of the fiercest battles in the history of corporate finance." But, as you will soon see, he lost the war.

In one sense, the expansionists and the moderates had the same goal: to prevent a recurrence of the tragedy called the Great Depression. But whereas the expansionists sought to cut it off as soon as it appeared, the moderates felt that, in the long term, the only way to prevent a great bust was to prevent a great boom. They believed that *both* extremes should be avoided in order to maintain a pattern of balanced growth and social stability for the remainder of the century.

Whether one subscribed to this philosophy or not depended on the era in which one grew up. During the booms of the '60s and '70s, these values were labeled "poppycock." In the Western and Eastern world of the twenty-first century, they are again in vogue. In short, the moderate philosophy was neither right nor wrong. It was merely untimely—at once outdated and premature. In a system that had already left the Depression far behind, but still had many more years of dynamic expansion ahead, their battle against excessive economic expansion was doomed to fail.

This was certainly the case with Montgomery Ward. Soon after the battle, Sewell Avery resigned and Montgomery Ward went on to eventually exhaust its cash reserves, accumulate huge debts and merge with Container Corporation.

Competing retail operations were expanding. Therefore, Montgomery Ward had to expand. There was really no choice. If they hadn't, they would have been left behind, squeezed out of the marketplace, and eventually taken over by a cashless giant. The push for growth at any and all cost spread quickly throughout the business world. Alcoa, American Motors, Chrysler, C.I.T. Financial, General Dynamics, General Motors, Sears Roebuck, Pan American World Airways and Zenith were just a few in the vanguard. For those companies that resisted the trend, victories by moderates such as the Businessman's Committee for Seasoned Management team were the exceptions.

In 1959, American Telephone and Telegraph, one of the last bastions of financial conservatism, finally knuckled under to new pressures. During the fifties, AT&T management had been reluctant to distribute excess profits to stockholders or to go into debt. Suddenly, it yielded to the changing times. The dividend was raised 10 percent and the common stock was split three for one. More important, it began borrowing in the capital markets to take advantage of the tax deductions that come from a large interest expense. Subsequently, AT&T went on to become the largest private debtor in the world.

Of course these developments of the mid-fifties are well documented in the history books. But the political changes that swept through Washington—the maneuvers that led to double-digit inflation, the dollar collapse and the stock market crash—have never been fully revealed to the American people.

13

The Sound Dollar Committee

Despite the expansionist thrust in the business world, the Governors of the Federal Reserve Board, under William Mc-Chesney Martin, were still sticking to the old school and not issuing large amounts of money and credit.

There then arrived on the scene the first in a long line of businesspeople who, in later Administrations, would make the pilgrimage to Washington and put pressure on the President whenever the going got rough or the Federal Reserve got tough. That's when the problems began for the Fed's conservative policies. Within a span of 125 days, between November 14, 1957, and March 18, 1958, the Fed dropped the discount rate three times and lowered the reserve requirements twice. Government construction projects, more unemployment benefits and liberal amounts of mortgage money were thrown into the pot. When Eisenhower entered his last two years in office, the federal budget looked as if it was going haywire. It was anticipated that the budget deficit would jump to a then-whopping $13 billion.

Eisenhower didn't have to wait two decades to learn that deficits lead to inflation. He didn't have to listen to the exhortations of still-unknown economists who would blame the government's deficits for the Crash of '87. He knew it all too well back in 1959. Years later, when the dollar collapsed or when a panic took place, he didn't want to be blamed by economic historians as the President who doomed future generations. So he set out to balance the budget.

In his State of the Union Address of January 3, 1959, Eisenhower complained about the excessive costs of military hardware and insisted that "we must avoid extremes ... of waste and inflation which could reduce job opportunities, price us out of world markets, shrink the value of savings." To minimize the danger of soaring prices and to keep the economy sound and expanding, he announced that he would submit a balanced budget.

The most conspicuous reaction to Eisenhower's speech came in the form of an unrestrained yawn by the Senate Democratic leader, Lyndon B. Johnson, giving Ike the first warning of a major political attack by the Democratic Congress against the balanced budget.

At the time, the cold war was a hot issue. Congress was being bombarded by signs of Soviet military and economic advances—Mikoyan bragging about Russian GNP and Russian satellites orbiting Earth. It was the Wolfson-Avery debate all over again, but on a far grander scale: Do we yield to the competition or do we invite economic instability? Eisenhower was more concerned about the possible economic instability and felt that, if the dollar should fall, the cold war would be lost anyway.

A flood of economic experts paraded before Congress, testifying that "inflation is not a present danger." The only real dissenter was Federal Reserve Chairman Martin, who warned that "inflammatory material" was everywhere in the economy and could flare up later on. Once again, the forces against excessive expansion and waste were labelled "antiprogress." Once again, the moderates were doomed to defeat.

For the short term, the Democrats did have a point. Despite the business recovery from the 1958 recession, high unemployment lingered. Later, despite the boom that began in the Kennedy years, the U.S. dollar wouldn't suffer a significant collapse until the late 1970s. Eisenhower, however, was worried about the long-term danger and not just the next election. He decided to go over the heads of Congress and appealed directly to the public.

On February 4th, it was announced that Ike was "planning a 'grassroots campaign' to combat spending legislation beyond his budget and would make a strong public appeal in his news conference the next day." In his news conference, he stressed repeatedly the fact that if Congress spent more it would have to tax more. But the appeal failed. The next morning's headlines in the *New York Times* said nothing about it whatsoever: *CON-GRESS VOTES RISES IN HOUSING: DEFIES PRESIDENT.*

As a result, public response was mute. The Administration's grassroots campaign was virtually nonexistent. A week passed, and the American people remained silent: No protests, no editorials, no voter appeals to Congress. Could it be that the public didn't give a damn about the dollar? As it turned out, there were many people who did care. Several weeks later, they raised their voices in the loudest protest against inflation ever recorded in American history.

My father, J. Irving Weiss, followed the budget battle closely in the newspapers, noticed Ike's public appeal, and waited for something to happen. When nothing did, he organized another committee.

With former President Herbert Hoover as Republican co-chairman and presidential advisor Bernard Baruch as Democratic co-chairman, the committee would lobby and advertise for a balanced budget and against inflation. Herbert Hoover was eager to participate. Bernard Baruch, however, despite his initial sympathies, was skeptical. In a final attempt to win his support, my father called Baruch in February 1959.

Baruch was still unwilling to join. "I have come to the conclusion," he said, "that it's not timely. We can't stop their spending until they come to us for help. We really can't do anything until we see the whites of their eyes."

My father tried to convince him. "You may be right, but we decided to start the campaign with a full-page ad in the *Wall Street Journal.* We sent you a copy. Did you receive it?"

"Yes."

"Then you know that it promotes the concept of a sound dollar and the concept of a balanced society and relates the two concepts. So far, the response has been excellent and contributions are already coming in strong."

"Fine, fine! But don't you see? It's all premature. Even if you get a good public response, it's for naught. I can tell you from firsthand personal experience that very few in Washington want to pay any attention to moderate spending and conservative business policies. I have tried but they won't listen. Later, when they come to us for help, when they're in hot water because of these huge budget deficits, *then* we can do something. But not now. It's too early."

"That's my point," My father responded. "We have to nip it in the bud! We can still put your name on the committee, if you're willing. Herbert Hoover has agreed. The results show that the time is now. I'm quite confident of that."

"I'm not! I've tried time and time again to give them this advice. Truman wouldn't listen. Eisenhower wouldn't listen. Now he's changed his mind. But even if your campaign succeeds, I question whether they'll follow through."

Even without Baruch's support, however, the campaign was a resounding success. The ad in *The Wall Street Journal* merely set off the first sparks and was followed by an ad in the *Chicago Tribune*. In a matter of days, the *Tribune* called the Sound Dollar Committee, asking for permission to run a similar campaign at their own expense. The *Los Angeles Times*, the *New York Daily News* and *Reader's Digest* followed suit. Soon, scores of newspapers and magazines joined the Sound Dollar Committee in its nationwide mail-in campaign to fight inflation, balance the budget and protect the dollar.

It was an avalanche! Congressmen would walk into their offices on a Monday morning and be struck immediately with the clutter of mailbags. According to a *Chicago Tribune* survey on the Hill, the total response was *twelve million postcards, coupons, letters and telegrams.*

By mid-March, the public's attitude switched from apathy to intense interest. According to *Business Week*: "Just about anywhere you go these days, the talk will turn to inflation. The subject comes up with friends at cocktails, in the brokers' board rooms, and among businessmen who feel a responsibility to avoid price increases."

The most pronounced transformation was the one brought about in high levels of government. All of a sudden, Washington was a "city full of inflation fighters."

"For an explanation," continued the *Business Week* article, "there is no point in looking at the price indexes. They have been level for almost a year and there's no sign they are getting ready to start rising. What underlies the rising inflation fever is this: Leaders of both parties are convinced that making a record against price increases is the soundest political assurance for the presidential and congressional races next year. Leaders in Congress began the session talking like big spenders; now they are talking about cutting Eisenhower's budget."

Senator Proxmire, who had been steadfastly in favor of the spending programs, changed his mind and voted *for* the budget cuts. One Congressman after another shifted his vote to support the Eisenhower budget. The budget was balanced! Unfortunately, however, it was the last real balanced budget of the century!

In one sense, Weiss had been right in his discussion with Bernard Baruch: They did not have to wait to be effective. In another sense, however, *Baruch* was right: The country was led in precisely the opposite direction from the one desired.

14

The First Superboom

Kennedy won the 1960 presidential election precisely because unemployment remained high and the economy was below "full capacity."

According to the economic theorists of that era, the full capacity level of a nation is calculated in terms of factors stemming from within the economic system, such as unemployment. Only later did a more sophisticated definition of capacity emerge—the concept of "carrying capacity."

Carrying capacity represents the growth limits—determined by the environment and by the level of progress—which a society must not exceed if it is to maintain its balance. This does not imply that there are steadfast ceilings to growth. Rather, the limits should be there to prevent excessive *acceleration*. Acceleration requires a thrust, an aggressive, sometimes violent, push against the past in order to propel the system into the so-called "future" faster than the normal ticking of time. Acceleration requires a radical break, a sudden reversal.

Lyndon Johnson initiated such a thrust, and his successors followed suit. The results were favorable. However, their actions also brought negative reactions—backlashes, kickbacks, assassination, corruption, addiction and a series of other unexpected feedbacks—that in the end did great violence to the socioeconomic system, its people and its "enemies."

Johnson's El Dorado and Nixonomics

The economic system had just so much energy and money. There were definite limits as to how fast this energy could be transformed into goods and services, and how fast money could be pumped in. Lyndon B. Johnson, however, sought to simultaneously create the heavenly kingdom of the "Great Society" in America and support the hellish war in Vietnam. More than any other modern American President, he tried to create the best of all possible worlds. But the guns overheated and the butter melted. It was just too much for the domestic economy and the American people to tolerate.

Nevertheless, the nation raced forward—more money, more growth. The debt pyramid, still relatively small, continued to grow.

Later, in the first several months of the Nixon Administration, plans were made to tighten up the economy and deflate. But Nixon knew very little about the debt problem, let alone that as much as 35 percent of it was short-term. It was a time bomb, ready to explode.

Interest rates soared. Penn Central, Chrysler, Ling Temco Vought and other weak links were caught unprepared. The stock market broke to 627 on the Dow in May 1970.

Most frightening of all to those in power, the brokers were going broke. Later, DuPont, Glore Forgan, Walston, Dempsey-Tegeler, Hayden Stone and others would fall. The Special Trust Fund set up by the New York Stock Exchange would be depleted. And the Exchange would have to dip into its $25 million building fund—money it had set aside for building a new home for itself.

Nixon was terrified of fulfilling a prediction made by Eisenhower that he would battle inflation but be killed politically. He decided instead to fight recession, to fight it as no other President had ever done before.

Arthur Burns, the new Federal Reserve Chairman, cooperated fully. The companies that couldn't borrow money in the open market went to their banks. The banks went to the Fed, and the Fed furnished the money.

It was around this time that the domestic economy sprang a leak, and the world monetary crisis made its first major appearance. Nixon reacted with a series of economic bombshells. On August 15, 1971, he imposed a 90-day wage-and-price freeze. He declared a 10-percent surcharge on imports. He eliminated the requirement that the dollar be backed by gold held in Fort Knox. And he abrogated the international agreement—made at Bretton Woods in 1944—designed to maintain stable world currencies. In effect, he engineered the first attack on the U.S. dollar. At the time, it did not appear to be a very momentous event. But as you will see when we discuss the Crash of '87, it was *the* critical watershed for the dollar.

There are no clear-cut boundaries that separate the era of healthy postwar growth and the era of chronic international crisis. However, if someone wanted to select the one event that symbolizes this momentous transition in twentieth century history, it would be Nixon's dollar devaluation of August 15, 1971.

The growth in labor productivity, which had been increasing with only minor interruptions for nearly two hundred years, slowed down—a prelude to actual declines that would start by the end of the 1970s, later causing other nations such as Japan, Korea and Taiwan to leap ahead of the United States.

In the 1980s, this would be called "the most basic sickness of the American economy." But at the time, few made much of the change. The money-and-credit printing presses ran at a feverish pitch, propelling the economy on a collision course with the world's limited resources and the Arab oil embargo of 1973.

The inflation problem—long a sideshow in the play for economic and political power—now burst onto the main stage of American life. Interest rates soared again. Money markets were thrown into chaos. Franklin National and the West German Herstadt Bank went under. New York City teetered on the brink of collapse. Again the debt crisis appeared, larger and fiercer than ever before. Again the Federal Reserve came to the rescue.

It wasn't until this stage that inflation was finally recognized as "the most vexing and most intractable of all economic problems," "immovable," "hard to cure." Economists didn't recognize that too much debt stimulated too much growth. The demand for goods and services increased at a faster clip than improvements in the nation's ability to produce those goods and services. They didn't know that inflation was really the debt crisis in disguise.

Instead, laymen and professionals viewed inflation as a plague that spread from country to country, slowly destroying the society of each. Others saw it as a conspiracy by the rich to bleed the poor, by labor to bleed the rich, or by the politicians to collect votes from *both* the rich and the poor. Some economists went no further than saying inflation was "too much money chasing too few goods," which is only a description, not an explanation. Still others dwelled upon the different kinds of inflation: "creeping inflation," "rampant inflation," "runaway inflation," "galloping inflation," "hyperinflation," "cost-push inflation," "demand-pull inflation," "structural inflation," "inflation-fed inflation." Despite the plethora of terms, however, inflation was a problem that defied solution. And repeated plans by government economists to deal with its causes never got off the ground.

In early 1970, the President's Council of Economic Advisors (CEA) undertook a massive study to find inflation's "real causes." Herbert Stein, its Chairman, passed the responsibility to Ezra Solomon. Several months later he, in turn, passed the buck to an economist newly arrived at the CEA, Nicholas Perna. When Stein appeared before the Joint Economic Committee in October 1972, Senator William Proxmire asked about the status of the study. "We are not prepared to make the conclusions of that study public," Stein said. "We will have more to say about it in our report." But the report, when it finally appeared, made no mention of the study.

Perhaps the government economists knew all along that they were pumping too much money into the economy and feeding the fires of inflation. Their real concerns were preventing a recession and covering up the fact that inflation, along with the decline of the dollar, were the probable consequences of their policy.

Aside from a small number of farsighted observers, who could have known the consequences of Nixon's dollar devaluation? Who could have known that the dollar disease—with an incubation period of more than a decade—would not begin to do visible damage until the mid-1980s? Least of all, who could have foreseen that it would be the dollar's collapse which would finally topple the stock market on Black Monday, in October 1987?

Like a comet swinging back from distant space, Nixon's dollar devaluation of August 1971 would return—194 months later—to strike fear and panic into the heart of Wall Street.

15

The Debt Pyramid

After thirty years of unrestrained borrowing by consumers, corporations, banks and government, a great debt pyramid had developed. By the end of the 1980s, it would balloon to more than $11 trillion in bonds, mortgages and loans that threatened to sabotage nearly every government economic policy. A two-trillion-dollar debt emerged at the headquarters of our nation's corporations. A two-and-a-half trillion dollar debt burdened the Federal Government. And the greatest debt pyramid of all towered over nearly every home, office building and shopping center in America—over $3 trillion in mortgages!

A minority of Americans were able to escape its ravages by staying out of debt and keeping their money in absolutely safe havens. But for the majority, it was a horror story.

If you were a borrower in the 1980s, you were haunted by illiquidity. To the average consumer, illiquidity meant skimming at least one-quarter from each paycheck just to meet mortgage and installment payments, as opposed to only one dime back in 1929. To the average manufacturing corporation with $1 billion or more in assets, illiquidity meant they had only 17 cents in cash or equivalent for every dollar in debts coming due within 12 months. Back in 1930, even after the stock market crash of 1929, they had about 70 cents!

If you were a lender, you faced another aspect of the debt pyramid—the fear of inflation and big losses in your bond portfolios. During the 1970s and early 1980s, bonds (including U.S. Treasury bonds) suffered wave after wave of collapse, whittling the fortunes of small savers and decimating the holdings of great banks, S&Ls and insurance companies. In the mid-1980s, the bond markets did recover. But the danger of another collapse lingered.

Worst of all, the Chairman of the Federal Reserve faced the dilemma of fighting both aspects of the debt problem. He had to defend both the borrowers and the lenders *at the same time*—a nearly impossible task.

If he wanted to fight inflation—to counter the inflationary consequences of big budget deficits—he pursued a "tight-money policy," draining money from the banking system and temporarily taking it out of circulation. Suddenly, banks and corporations, already short of liquid funds, suffered an acute cash squeeze. A dangerous chain reaction of failures, panic and financial collapse loomed. Obviously, this line could not be pursued for long.

If he decided to attack on the opposite front of the debt crisis, he'd employ an "easy-money policy," printing more dollars to be put into circulation. The money supply would grow and the value of each dollar declined. To investors who owned bonds, this signalled inflation, and inflation meant their fixed-income bonds were worth less and less. What was their response? For a while, these investors might remain complacent. But sooner or later, they would refuse to buy any *more* bonds. Worse yet, they would decide to *sell back* bonds from their portfolios. Sure, the Federal Reserve Chairman might make some headway by helping everyone else with *their* debt troubles. Trouble is, now the government itself would have a hard time selling *its* bonds to finance *its* debts!

In sum, if he persisted in belt tightening, he squeezed the borrowers and the liquidity problem appeared. If he tried to stimulate the economy to resolve the liquidity problem, or to help collect votes for the next election, inflation fears would pop up and the lenders were hurt.

And if he decided to do nothing, then he confronted the most treacherous problem of all: *Time*. With every tick of the clock the debts were coming due: $1,127 per second, $406,000 every hour, a total of $3.5 trillion within 12 months.

The crux of the problem was this: *Either side of the debt pyramid—illiquidity or inflation fears—forced interest rates higher than they would have been otherwise.* No matter what the politicians did, and no matter which way the economy went, until the debts were reduced, those interest rates could not come down to normal levels. Nevertheless, most economists belittled its importance.

If the debts had grown at the same pace as the economy, they might have been right. But this was not the case. Between 1970 and 1988, new debts created every year grew over 6 times, but the economy grew by only 3 times. We had run into the law of diminishing returns: more debts, less results.

If the growth in stock equities had kept pace with the growth in debts, the problem would not have been so severe. But this too was clearly not the case. In 1968, the total market value of all common and preferred stocks in the United States was approximately equivalent to the total debt ($1.03 trillion versus $1.36 trillion). By the late 1980s, however, the value of debts outnumbered stock values by more than four to one.

If there were enough cash reserves to back up these debts, it would have been fine. But by the end of the decade, the cash available to cover each dollar of debt held by corporations, banks, consumers and governments was at the lowest point in the twentieth century.

If the average maturity of the debts had been stretched out to the distant future, the debtors might at least have had some time to raise cash. Instead, the debt had become a lighted fuse burning closer and closer to the crisis threshold.

The huge debt pile-up was so appalling that most economists pretended it didn't exist. Some tried to explain it away by saying that "for every liability on the balance sheet of one economic entity, there is an equivalent asset created on the balance sheet of another" and, therefore, "the system is in constant equilibrium." All they were really saying, however, is that "all balance sheets balance." They forgot that accounting was a man-made device *designed* to balance.

With that rationalization, the authorities managed to hide the debt disease from the public and from themselves. But its symptoms were everywhere: Higher-than-normal interest rates, periodic bond market collapses, surging business failures and more frequent bank closings. How did they fight the debt? How did they keep the economy going despite these burdens? That responsibility fell squarely on the shoulders of the Federal Reserve.

The Great Bond Pool

In theory, the Federal Reserve controlled the supply of money pumped into the economy. In practice, the Fed was really trying to control the *cost* of borrowing money—interest rates. This strategy caused two problems.

The first problem was the impact on inflation. To keep interest rates low, they pumped more money into the banking system which boosted the economy in the short term, but caused higher prices in the long term.

The second, more poorly understood problem was illiquidity—the great scarcity of cash and abundance of short-term debts. By 1975, U.S. corporations had built up $401 billion in debts which had to be repaid within twelve months, but they had only $75 billion in cash or equivalent, leaving a huge *cash deficit* of $326 billion. Banks, governments and consumers were in the same hole. In other words, if they tried to pay all their current bills, it would not only wipe out their checking accounts, it would drop their cash balances deep into the red.

This illiquidity, in turn, gave rise to a chronic shortage of money and a natural, often explosive tendency for interest rates to move up. *To compensate for this shortage, the Federal Reserve was forced to increase the money supply at a faster pace than was theoretically desirable.* The rapidly growing money supply then fueled more speculation, more demand for funds and, finally, even greater cash deficits.

Apparently, the Federal Reserve governors were not aware of the importance of these chronic cash shortages on the economy. But they were painfully familiar with the consequences: They discovered that, whenever they fought inflation by holding back money-supply growth, a credit crunch popped up out of nowhere. Thus it was—with a sense of moral obligation and patriotic duty—that they deliberately went about their business of pumping in still more money in an attempt to hold interest rates down artificially.

Crucial to your understanding of this chapter is a clear grasp of what a "bond" really is. Bonds, as well as bills, notes and other "paper," are nothing more than that—paper. Although often fancy and engraved, they are simply IOUs printed up by a government or a corporation. You loan them your money. They give you the piece of paper. So when you're "buying Treasury bonds," you're really just loaning your money to the U.S. Treasury Department. When you're buying General Motors "commercial paper," you're loaning your money to General Motors.

Sometimes you let them have your money just for a few days or a few months, and they give you their "bills" or "paper." Sometimes you're willing to trust them for a few years and you get their "notes." Or you may let them have it for 10-30 years, in which case they give you their "bonds."

No matter what the term, the idea is essentially the same. They promise to pay you interest (say 7%) every quarter or every six months and, of course, they promise to give you back all of your money on the due date. In other words, they guarantee that your note or bond will be worth 100% of its face value when it matures. Instead of saying 100%, however, they just say that "the price will be 100 at maturity."

It follows then that if you can buy these bonds for *less* than 100—say 90—you could earn more than just the interest they pay you. You could also make a little extra profit on the deal. You would earn a profit of $10 plus the 7% interest. So the cheaper the bond, the more you earn; the lower the price, the higher the yield.

This concept also works the other way around. Say you own a Treasury bond and decide you want your money immediately. If you go to the Treasury Department, they'll politely tell you to please call again on February 29, 2017 (or whatever the maturity date is). "If you can't wait," they say, "you can go to a dealer who specializes in secondary (second-hand) government securities."

You go to the dealer and you say: "Please take this bond off my hands."

"Sure. But there's one problem."

"What's that?" you respond, a bit uneasily.

"Your bond only pays 7%. The new bonds offered by the Treasury pay 8%."

"So?"

"So you're going to have to sell it to me for 95 instead of 100."

"You mean I have to take a loss?"

"Absolutely. Why should I buy your old 7% bond for 100 when I can buy the Treasury's new 8% bonds for that price? Would you buy a 1989 Buick for $18,000 if the 1990 improved model was going for the same price? Of course not. The same is true for bonds."

Thus, when the yield on new bonds goes up, the price of existing bonds goes down. This doesn't mean that you should never buy long-term bonds. If yields go *down*, the market value of your older, higher-yielding bonds will *improve*. The trick of course is to buy them when yields are near or at their peak.

What makes bond prices go up or down? It's all a matter of supply and demand. Buyers bid the price up and sellers bid the price down.

The very biggest buyer and seller of already-issued bonds is none other than the Federal Reserve Bank of New York. In fact, the Fed uses the government bond market as its primary tool for manipulating interest rates. Like private investors, they have a complete portfolio of Treasuries—bills, notes, bonds, etc. And, as you might imagine, their portfolio is huge.

Here's how it works: The Fed buys the government securities from New York bond dealers. The dealers deposit the money from the sale of the bonds into their commercial bank accounts. This puts extra cash into the banking system. So when banks need the money, to cover their cash requirements or for any other purpose, there is plenty available. End result: Interest rates go down.

The Bond Market Bailout

Very few know what the Fed is saying behind the scenes. However, in the August 1977 issue of my newsletter *Money & Markets*—two and a half years before the bond market collapse of 1979—I offered an informed guess. The balance of this chapter is based on that newsletter issue. (While the facts and figures are from actual Federal Reserve statistics, the dialogue is fictional.)

The time is April 14, 1975. The place is the Federal Reserve Building, Constitution Avenue, Washington, D.C. Eleven members of the Fed's Open Market Committee sit at a long conference table. Chairman Arthur Burns opens the meeting.

"Only eight months ago," he says, "debt markets were on the verge of a full-scale collapse. We managed to ease credit dramatically, and we breathed a sigh of relief ... but only for a moment. Three weeks from today, the Treasury Department will go to the bond market to raise money for financing the deficit. They need $3.8 billion to pay off maturing bonds plus another $2 billion in fresh cash—the most massive financing week on record. Unless we do something about it, they'll sop up all the available cash out there and interest rates will rise. Hubert Humphrey has been on my tail, trying to find out what we intend to do about it. Unfortunately, there is no way of estimating the impact. He is right about one thing, though. We may not be doing enough to soften its potential damage to the financial markets."

The man at the far side of the conference table is perplexed. "What else can we do? In the past thirty days, we've already bought $7 billion in Treasuries to hold down interest rates. That's twice our previous record. And what good did it do? We did manage to stop three-month Treasury bill rates from soaring past 6% last week, but the bond yields are still rising. I honestly think there is nothing more we can do."

A prolonged silence descends on the conference room. Each man searches for alternate solutions, realizing that there is only one way out. Finally, a fourth member puts it into words.

"Buy *more* bonds! Pump *more* money in! Hold down those interest rates!"

The Chairman makes no effort to hide his impatience. "How? Where? We're already out on a limb. We have to maintain some semblance of balance in the money supply, don't we?"

"Not if it means letting short-term rates hit 12%. Not if it means killing the incipient recovery! The automobile and housing industries were hurt badly by the last round of tight money, and their wounds have yet to heal." A man who normally sides with Burns suddenly turns against him. "You said yourself, it's the only tool left. If $3-$4 billion isn't enough, we must do it again and again until we're over the hump."

And so they did. The unprecedented $7.1 billion in U.S. Government securities purchased between March 12 and April 16, 1975, was followed by another $6.2 billion between April 16 and April 30. Within several weeks, the Federal Reserve had pumped $13.3 billion into the economy. With the Fed's April purchases totaling 250% more than the previous record, it is little wonder the Treasury was able to sell their bonds so easily. The Federal Reserve rolled out the money from its printing presses.

There arose a new wave of enthusiasm among bond dealers, and cheers resounded from the back offices of Wall Street to the Oval Office of the White House. They didn't realize that, even as the Fed was saving the day in the spring of 1975, it was creating a new and fiercer debt dilemma that would emerge several years later, first toppling the bond market and finally the stock market as well.

A Big Killing

Two weeks go by. The scene shifts to the phone-cluttered desk of John Hartman, a New York government securities dealer. His business is to buy Treasury bills, notes and bonds from the government wholesale, mark up the prices, and sell them to investors retail. Like an automobile dealer, he temporarily owns the merchandise (in this case, government securities) while they are in his inventory. If prices go up, he stands to make a profit. But if prices fall, he also risks big losses.

"John, do you know how much the Fed bought this week?" a junior associate asks one Friday afternoon.

"No, how much?" responds Hartman.

"Would you believe $5 billion?"

"You must be kidding!"

"No—looks like the Fed's jumped in all the way. They're scared the growing federal deficit will bring on another panic, and that's good, because it means they're going to just keep right on buying. Bills, notes, bonds—anything that needs support!"

The younger man, eager to make a quick profit, becomes enthusiastic. "Let's get in on the act," he exclaims. "I know our inventories are kind of big, but with the Fed practically guaranteeing they'll buy 'em back, we can't lose. Let's load up on anything we can lay our hands on."

The veteran trader isn't quite as enthusiastic. There's something in the tone of this brief exchange that echoes a conversation he overheard as a teenager nearly fifty years ago: "Hey! You know who's buying?" said the voice. "Raskob. That's who. He's going to run up the price till kingdom come—our chance to make a killing, a big killing."

That was 1929. The Dow Jones was going great guns, and the stock pools were hot. In those days, he was an errand boy at Ungerleider & Company. Now he is Senior Vice-President in the government securities division of a top investment banking house. He begins to wonder whether this flashback is a subconscious warning or merely a random association, when his junior associate breaks into his thoughts again, saying those familiar words: "This is our chance to make a killing, a big killing!"

The fact is there were striking similarities between the stock pools of the late twenties and what I call the Great Bond Pool of the late seventies. As in 1929, a handful of large buyers led the flock. In those days it was the Durants, the Raskobs, the Mitchells and the Wigginses. This time it was the Federal Reserve and a select group of Wall Street brokerage firms.

In both eras, investors felt they were secure beneath an umbrella of protection from huge trading volume. Then, the big volume was in stocks like Radio and GM. This time, the big volume was in the Treasury notes and bonds—securities that enjoyed large price swings but needed only a small cash investment for margin. Most important, like the 1929 stock pools, the majority didn't get in on the deal until *after* the lucky few had made most of the profits.

I discovered this alarming fact in 1977 when I analyzed Federal Reserve statistics on government securities. For over 25 years, the trading volume of government securities had increased at a steady rate of 26% per year. Then, with the Treasury issuing bonds like crazy and the Fed buying them up in huge amounts, the market went wild. The growth in trading soared by 221%. Within 28 months, average daily volume mushroomed from $2.5 billion to $15 billion. *The equivalent of five new bond markets were created virtually overnight.*

There is nothing wrong with big volume *per se*. The problem is that most of the buying came *after* bond prices approached their peaks. In other words, most investors were suckered in at high prices. They were lured by the aura of safety, assured by promises of government support and finally won over by aggressive promotion techniques.

Prudential-Bache used its relatively recent Halsey-Stuart acquisition to enlarge its government bond division. Other big houses, including Lehman Brothers and Paine Webber, alerted account executives to push all kinds of bonds. Smaller regional houses found that their consumers were natural buyers. Virtually the entire investment community joined the bond market bandwagon. The fever soon spread to government agency bonds, local revenue bonds and mortgage bonds. And still the same words echoed around the country: "You know who's behind this thing? The Fed, that's who!"

In 1929, stockholders were surprised to discover that there was little or no buying support in the marketplace, even at relatively low levels. The hundreds of thousands of buyers had committed the bulk of their resources and refused to buy more, complaining they already had too many paper losses. They were locked in at relatively high prices. When they belatedly heard that the pool leaders themselves had gotten out, they unleashed wave after wave of selling.

My conclusion: The same was about to happen in the bond markets and, eventually, in the stock market as well.

16

The Collapse Of '79

It happened in October 1979—precisely the fiftieth anniversary of the 1929 crash.

The leader of the Bond Pool, the Federal Reserve, had to withdraw its support for the bond market. Reason: The Dollar Decline. In 1971, President Nixon had cut the dollar loose from its moorings. The Fed's Chairman, Arthur Burns, with his record-shattering pump-priming operation, had pushed it into unchartered waters. Now, the new Federal Reserve Chairman, G. William Miller, confronted the impossible task of sailing with no compass and no rudder.

"What went wrong?" Miller asks his assistant. "We pumped the money into the bond markets, right?"

"Right."

"The bond dealers deposited it into the banks, right?"

"Right."

"The banks loaned the money to U.S. corporations; the U.S. corporations invested the money in plant and equipment; and the U.S. economy got all the benefit, right?"

Wrong! The majority of America's giant manufacturers were *multinational* corporations. They received one-third of their earnings from overseas and funnelled investments to those areas where production costs were low and worker productivity high—the nations with the lowest inflation.

With the U.S. Treasury running back-to-back budget deficits in 1976-77, totalling a then-mammoth $101 billion, and with the Federal Reserve pumping in more money and credit than ever before, it was only natural that the U.S. inflation rate was among the highest in the West.

At the same time, American corporations enjoyed greater access to credit than their counterparts in Europe and Japan. They established subsidiaries abroad, beat down the foreign competition and received higher investment returns than in the United States. IBM, for instance, noticing that domestic business was falling off in 1969, pushed sales at foreign subsidiaries. Coca-Cola, running into stiff competition from Pepsi, gave top priority to its overseas markets. DuPont, Kodak, ITT and the oil giants were also at the fore.

These multinationals took some of their dollars to London, Paris or Frankfurt. They opened bank accounts in branches of American banks located in those cities. And they deposited these dollars in dollar-denominated accounts. Like some Americans abroad who want to talk their own language and have their own social club, American companies abroad felt more comfortable if they had their own currency, in their own banks. These new overseas dollars became the first "Eurodollars." And it was this foreign enclave of U.S. currency which later became known as the "Eurodollar market." It functioned much like our own debt markets except for one difference: It was beyond the control of the Federal Reserve.

Following the Americans' lead, European and other companies found it convenient to do business in U.S. dollars. Later, when OPEC came into its own, the Eurodollar market emerged as the center of the world's oil money.

In 1960, the Eurodollar market had $500 million on deposit—a mere niche in the back offices of European banks. By 1970, it had grown to $50 billion. By 1980, it had ballooned to $820 billion! Later, prior to the big Crash of '87, it amounted to $1.75 *trillion*! The crux of the problem was this: Foreign holders of U.S. dollars were far more prone to sell those dollars and convert them into foreign currencies, sending the dollar's value downwards. In the 1950s and '60s, the dollar was the sun around which all other currencies revolved; now *it* was spinning wildly off-balance.

Analysts often wondered why these deposits grew so fast. One important reason was the Fed's money pumping in the United States. In fact, the pace at which new money was added every year to the domestic economy was closely correlated to the growth in Eurodollars abroad. Despite many crosscurrents, this is the picture that emerges: The Federal Reserve pumped the money, and the money escaped overseas.

As a result, Fed Chairman Miller was faced with a Catch-22 dilemma: If he held down U.S. interest rates despite accelerating inflation, international investors dumped their dollars in massive amounts, causing the value of the dollar to collapse. On the other hand, if he let interest rates rise, domestic trouble emerged, especially in the savings and loan industry. The thrifts suffered massive withdrawals and the housing industry threatened to collapse.

His choices, therefore, were clear: *Either fly outward or collapse inward with the risk of a depression and the certainty of defeat for the President in the 1980 election—either rampant inflation or rampant deflation; either burst or bust.*

He chose the former. Between early 1977 and late 1978—within less than twenty-four months—the dollar plunged from nearly 300 to 175 against the Japanese yen, from 2.4 to 1.8 against the West German mark, and from 2.5 to 1.5 against the Swiss franc. It was the sharpest drop in American currency since the collapse of the Continental currency precisely two hundred years earlier. But *it was merely a sneak preview of the dollar disaster which would later precipitate the stock market crash of October '87.*

Finally, by the fall of 1979, key OPEC countries were balking at accepting payment for their oil in dollars that were worth progressively less. Instead of dollars, they threatened to demand payment in a basket of currencies—a move money experts predicted would surely destroy the world's financial structure. With one of the turning points of economic history unfolding, I kept a detailed diary of the key events and of my thoughts. Here are some excerpts:

Belgrade, October 1, 1979. The newly appointed Chairman of the Federal Reserve, Paul Volcker, has flown to this East European city for the annual convention of the International Monetary Fund. He is under intense pressure from West European central banks to take swift action to protect the dollar. At the convention, some are predicting a new dollar collapse that will make the 1977-78 debacle look like a picnic.

Washington, October 6, 1979. After a sudden departure from Belgrade and round-the-clock meetings with Administration officials, Chairman Volcker has announced a "Draconian bombshell." He's raising the discount rate two full percentage points. He's imposing stiffer controls on Eurodollar borrowings by U.S. banks. And, most important, he has decided that the Fed will no longer try to manipulate interest rates directly. Instead, he is going back to the old principle of controlling the *amount* of money in the economy. The implication is that the Fed has literally given up trying to hold interest rates down and, from now on, will let rates rise to whatever level is necessary in order to balance the forces of supply and demand. His goals: To conquer inflation permanently and help the dollar regain its place as a world leader.

New York City, October 11, 1979. The new Fed Chairman's actions have revealed the dimensions of the debt crisis. Prices on 30-year government bonds have plunged four points in four days. A $1-billion IBM issue—hailed weeks ago as a brilliant piece of corporate finance—is now being described by Wall Street analysts as "the greatest underwriting fiasco of all time."

Teheran, November 4, 1979. Iranian students seized the U.S. Embassy. Fears of a new oil crunch are sweeping the globe.

Kabul, Christmas 1979. The Soviets have invaded Afghanistan.

New York, January 1980. Talk of "a new cold war economy," plus month-to-month consumer price inflation running at an annual rate of some 18 percent, are sending bond markets into a nosedive. Will it be as bad as the October collapse of last year?

New York, February 5, 1980. Yields on longest-term U.S. Government securities have just broken through the 11% level—the all-time peak reached during the Civil War. "Faced with a prolonged buyers' strike," one seasoned pro told the *Wall Street Journal,* "we decided to throw in the towel and get yields up to a level where some cash buyers might be shocked off the sidelines." But even at 11%, most Americans aren't interested.

Wall Street believes that the Afghanistan invasion and the resulting inflationary fears are the causes of the collapse. Why should investors buy bonds yielding 12% or even 13% if they expect inflation to be at 18% or 20%?

What most analysts don't understand is that the real, underlying cause of the bond market collapse is the debt—the fact that there has been a speculative boom in bonds similar to the 1920s speculative boom in stocks. And one reason the collapse in bonds is so severe is because the Bond Pool has been abandoned by the pool leader, the Federal Reserve. Buyers, lured in at much higher levels, are now looking for any excuse to get out. The threats of war and inflation are the most obvious ones.

New York, February 6, 1980. Some panicky bond holders are unloading at any price, but there are few takers. *According to the Wall Street Journal, the flood of sell orders prompted all except four or five of the largest, best capitalized bond houses to effectively abandon their "market-making role."*

The dealers are actually dropping out of the market! This is no longer merely a case of a *price* collapse. It's a *market* collapse in the literal sense of the word; the brokers themselves are going home!

New York, February 11, 1980. The pressures on the government to take outright deflationary measures are mounting by the minute. If Uncle Sam cannot find enough investors willing to buy his bonds, he will have to literally close up shop and start a new government. At the same time, by some estimates, investors have had losses totaling at least 25 percent of the market value of their bond holdings in recent months, or more than $400 billion.

The *Wall Street Journal* quotes a source at one sizable bank in the East who says that, if he had to liquidate his Treasury notes, the loss would amount to more than $225 million, wiping out the bank's capital. And look at this message off the Dow Jones wires:

> Unless those that brought us this disgusting inflation want to see a government, corporate and tax-exempt market worth $3.5 trillion, along with a mortgage market worth $2.5 trillion, wiped out, it is clear they are going to have to do something ... If that includes taking away the money that has made this sickening inflationary party possible, then we could have an awesome hangover.

Hangover? Sickening? Disgusting? These are not words one expects to see coming off an international teletype machine, normally replete with technical mumbojumbo and commentary couched in language of the highest professional caliber. Is it a warning of graver dangers still ahead?

New York, February 19, 1980. The collapse continues to gather momentum. According to the Dow Jones wire, the bond market is reeling through "an even blacker Tuesday as inflation and interest rate fears send prices lower." Treasury bonds lost over 5% of their face value in yesterday's trading, surpassing the 2.5% drop that had caused traders to refer to February 5 as "Black Tuesday." If the Dow fell by an equivalent amount, how many points would that amount to? Ironically, however, since the crash is occurring in the relatively obscure bond markets, virtually no one—including those who faithfully watch their network evening news—has the faintest idea of what's going on.

New York, February 24, 1980. Pessimism on Wall Street is reaching a peak. The bond market collapse is now about *three times worse* than the October 1979 collapse. Will our nation survive it? Strangely, there are still very few Americans who even know what a bond market is, and fewer still who understand its ultimate impact.

Washington, early April 1980. President Carter is huddling with top advisers and with Fed Chairman Volcker at Camp David. What will he do to end the bond market crisis? Respected Wall Street economists are predicting an end to our democratic system of government unless some immediate action is taken.

Washington, April 15, 1980. The White House has just announced credit controls. For the first time in history, a Democratic President, in an election year, has taken actions which will deliberately force the economy on a downward path. This demonstrates the power of the debt pyramid to overwhelm even the strongest of political yearnings—a President's desire to be reelected.

My diary ends here. Before we resume our trek through time, however, let's try to understand what really happened: First, the bond buyers disappeared. Then, most dealers abandoned the marketplace. Finally, the entire market nearly closed down, making it next to impossible for the politicians to borrow the funds they needed to run this country.

Could it happen again? If the government decided to pump up the money supply again, yes! On the day George Bush was elected President, millions of investors—both at home and abroad—owned over $11 trillion in U.S. Government bonds, corporate bonds, municipal bonds, mortgages and loans. This was *three and a half times* the value of all common and preferred stocks in America. These investors and creditors had frequently suffered huge losses in their portfolios, and they blamed this on inflation or on the dollar's decline. Whenever they expected a *revival* of inflation or another dollar disaster, they would sell their holdings and cause another bond market collapse. It was a disaster of unprecedented dimensions.

But it was not all bad. If these investors had not risen up in rebellion, literally boycotting the bond market, no one knows what the politicians might have done. They probably would have just flooded the country with worthless paper money and brought on triple-digit inflation like Germany experienced in the 1920s or Brazil and Argentina suffered in the 1980s.

Fortunately, the politicians needed us—the investors and savers—a lot more than we needed them. Unlike other countries in other eras, we had a bond market where we could express our vote of confidence or no confidence.

If you owned a Treasury bond, you didn't have to wait until the next election to make your mark. You didn't have to run down to Washington to bang your fist on the desk of some faceless bureaucrat. All you had to do was pick up the phone, call your broker and utter one four-letter word: *Sell*. Your message would go straight to Washington.

Yes, politicians made some horrendous mistakes in the twentieth century and probably will make many more in the years to come. But the bond owners have consistently prevented them from going too far. As a result, inflation never got off the ground and, eventually, it was deflation—lower prices—which took over. This was the sole benefit of the debt pyramid.

The debt pyramid was not a new phenomenon. As we have seen, its roots can be traced back to the 1960s and 1970s, when credit crunches flared up with the regularity of a nuclear clock: 1966, 1970, 1974. The 1980s, however, were far worse. What previously had been a regular—and almost expected— credit flare-up had now evolved into full-blown debt crises that struck without warning, at any time and in any place.

After the U.S. bond markets nearly shut down and President Carter tried to shut off the inflation, he lost to Ronald Reagan, whose policies merely compounded the debt problems. In 1982, Mexico suddenly reeled into a bottomless pit of unpayable debts and a downward spiral of the Mexican peso. In 1983, it was Brazil's turn. The pressure was building to a crescendo.

17

Nineteen Eighty-Four

1984 was the year which was to have been, according to George Orwell's novel by that name, one of total state control and utter enslavement of the individual.

For most Americans, it was anything but. However, it was also a far cry from the rosy scenario being painted by most economists—low inflation, low unemployment, steady growth and a strong financial system.

Rather, 1984 is remembered in our twenty-first century textbooks as the pivot point between stability and chaos. It was the year in which four decades of growth *should* have come to an end. They should have, but they didn't!

Entire volumes have been written about 1984—on how the business and political leaders of that time ignored the danger signals; how they patched together bits and pieces of data to generate an idyllic picture; and how they masterminded a long series of cover-ups to keep the truth from an unsuspecting public.

Some historians call it a conspiracy. But those who hold that view misunderstand the nature of human psychology and the dynamics of its changes over time. The business leaders and economists who built the smoke screen fooled no one but themselves. In fact, there is plenty of historic evidence that the public got what they wanted: More false prosperity.

By midyear 1984, the perception of our economic leaders was that the very earth was shaking beneath their feet. Continental Illinois Bank, the seventh largest in the United States, suffered a sudden wave of withdrawals by big institutional depositors, threatening to tear asunder public confidence in the entire banking system. The Comptroller of the Currency himself forecast that more banks would fail that year than in any year since the Great Depression. ESM, a Ft. Lauderdale bond brokerage operation, collapsed, setting off a chain reaction of events which led to the closing of all Ohio-chartered savings and loans. Maryland S&Ls were the next dominos to fall.

A short while later, just when everyone thought that the foreign loan crisis had faded, the Brazilian problem popped up again. A small minority of bankers, torn between the prodding by the IMF to lend Brazil more money and their own better judgment, seriously considered calling it quits. But they finally went along in order to keep Brazil—and the big city banks—afloat. Had they known that, two years later Brazil would wind up defaulting anyhow, they might have reacted differently. And had they known that, in the Money Panic, they would wind up losing as much as 90 cents on every dollar of foreign debt, they might have decided to take their losses right then and there.

But in those days, most city bankers cared little about the long-term protection of their depositors' money. Their main concern was the immediate impact on profits and stockholder PR. Time and energy which should have been spent on the task of shoring up their loan portfolios, i.e. shifting from weak to strong areas, were instead spent on figuring out how to hide the mess from depositors.

Later, when Brazil declared a moratorium on its debts, the major banks had no choice but to boost their loan-loss reserves substantially—despite the fact that it would cause huge losses on the books. It was a desperate attempt to put it all behind them, but it was to no avail. There were plenty more losses yet to emerge. Several weeks after the 1987 stock market crash, Brazil would unveil a special program to allow foreign creditor banks to swap debt for shares in Brazilian enterprises. And still later, Brazil's President Sarney would unveil another economic package, creating yet another Brazilian currency, the novo cruzado. But these were merely desperate gimmicks in ever more desperate times.

No matter what new gimmicks were invented, one fact remained immutable: Throughout most of the 1980s, rather than face reality, the bankers preferred to throw good money after bad, trying to postpone the inevitable. The banking and monetary authorities of the world still failed to grasp the most shattering truths about the debt situation.

First, they didn't realize that the far broader problems—to surface in 1985 and 1986—were not overseas but right within our own borders: Bad agriculture loans and bad energy loans, along with bad real estate and consumer loans! For every one dollar of foreign debts outstanding, there were seven dollars of domestic debts!

Second, they ignored, until much later, an issue which made all these problems look tame by comparison—the *principal*. It was only after the Money Panic began that they would begin to ask the *real* question of the day: *What is the true value of the banks' loans to Third World nations?*

Everyone agreed that it was certainly *not* the full 100% at which the loans were carried on the books. But for several years, no one dared to guess what the markdowns should be. To the unbiased observer, a 30% markdown was hardly enough. Yet, even at that time, before the truly severe economic declines, a 30% markdown of bad foreign loans would have wiped out *all* of the capital of both Manufacturers Hanover and Bank of America and roughly three-quarters of the capital of Chemical, Citicorp and First Chicago.

Jim Grant, the former credit-market columnist of *Barron's* and the editor of *Grant's Interest Rate Observer*, developed an index that measured the market value of Third World loans. It was not 30% or even 40% below par. It was 60%. In other words, *if the banks tried to pawn off their Third World loans, the most they could raise for the typical portfolio would be 40 cents on the dollar*. That was even *before* the Money Panic began!

If the full extent of their massive losses had been admitted, virtually every major bank in America would have required a larger bailout than Continental Illinois. No wonder the authorities stopped at nothing to bury those sour loans!

Not learning from previous mistakes, they again convinced themselves that the debt shocks were behind them. Nothing could be further from the truth. *The debt shocks of the early 1980s were merely a mild foreshadowing of the real debt explosion still to come.*

It is with this backdrop that the Great Money Cover-Up got under way on all levels of government and the financial community. And it was this concerted cover-up that paved the way for thousands of unwary investors to march blindly into the stock market trap of the mid-1980s.

18

The Great Money Cover-Up

Robert Sheppard, the President of Metrobank, is a troubled man. Outwardly he prefesses the bank's optimistic line, encourages his staff to look positively towards a bright future, and carries a demeanor of confidence which sets the tone for all those who know him. Tall, slim and white-haired, he has no difficulty in filling this role. Inwardly, however, he feels intense subconscious doubts which are bound to surface in the midst of a true crisis.

For now, however, it's business as usual. The time is late 1984. The place, downtown New York. Sheppard and executives of the bank gather for breakfast in an exclusive restaurant.

"We've got to reduce our exposure," says Sheppard.

"You mean our loan exposure?"

"Certainly not! That would be a disaster in itself. We'd be lucky to get 50 cents on the dollar for some of this garbage."

"Then you must be referring to our interest rate exposure—the big short-term borrowings we've loaned out at long-term fixed rates?"

"No, there's nothing we can do about that either, except sit tight and wait for rates to decline."

A few moments of silence ensue as each man tries to figure out what the boss is actually talking about.

"The reason I called this little powwow is to set specific strategies for reducing our *media* exposure! Look at this bombshell!" he exclaims, slapping on the table the *Wall Street Journal* of March 19, 1984.

"Look at these poor blokes: First Tennessee Bank, 516%; First Peoples Bank of New Jersey, 121%. Need I go on? You don't want to see our name in a column like this, do you? We'd probably be up to at least 400%!"

"516%? 400%? What in God's name are you talking about?"

"The bank's capital, man! The capital! That's how much of our capital would be wiped out if we took a total loss on our Third World loans!"

"So what do we do?"

"First, we tell the world how we've *generally avoided* foreign loans due to 'our ultraconservative philosophy.' Next, we *reduce* our provision for loan losses, giving earnings a lift. We tell 'em it's the 'just reward for our careful approach and the inevitable payoff of the brisk recovery.' Finally, and most importantly, we sell off some of our German marks and Swiss francs—the ones we have big profits in."

"But ..."

"Yes. I know the portfolio as a whole is still in the red. And I know it's not really going to make a difference in our balance sheet. But look at the PR value! We get some local business editor to do a story on Vance here—how he astutely invested in foreign currencies, how he's making a big killing!"

The men leave the room with a surge of confidence. At first, there is some initial success. But the plan soon backfires. The reduction in reserves calls the attention of federal regulators. This, in turn, raises the eyebrows of an out-of-town newspaper reporter who digs into the facts. Not only does he find agricultural and real estate loans in disarray, but he learns that the bank is on the government's list of problem banks.

At first, the reporter is pleased to see some regulators take an interest—only to realize a few days later that, rather than busting the cover-up wide open as he had expected, the government officials decide to take charge of the cover-up operation themselves! They call a press conference, tell the depositors all is well and the crisis passes.

How long would they be able to maintain this charade? And if the truth came out into the open, what would be the final outcome? Could the financial system—already severely weakened—survive the additional shock of a confidence crisis in the banks?

Federal Reserve Chairman Paul Volcker didn't wait for the answers. In fact, he didn't even wait for the questions. By late 1984, he was well on his way to the first massive money pumping operation of his career and, for that matter, the biggest one in the history of the American economy.

Oftentimes the Chairman was known to balk, to refuse to go any further lest it "wreck the system structurally," "destroy everything we've ever fought for," "do permanent damage no Fed Chairman could ever repair."

True. The Fed Chairman did refuse to do it—over and over again. But it was done anyway. In fact, it was his continued reluctance to accommodate the wishes of the Reagan Administration that gradually led to a major leadership shift at the Federal Reserve Board. Chairman Volcker, previously the champion inflation fighter, began to avoid the limelight, receding gradually into the background. Others, not committed to the fight against inflation, gained influence.

The stock market, still unaware of what was really going on, languished for a couple of months, dipped to new lows and then exploded into a buying frenzy. By all measures, it was more powerful than the wild stock market boom of the late 1920s.

The economy suddenly perked up and lurched into high gear. Within twelve short months, the optimists were describing a Panglossian transformation from a manufacturing economy to a high-tech, service economy. Even the pessimists talked about "mulling through from crisis to crisis," but "always avoiding a true panic or depression."

Like a painkilling drug, the extra money injected into the system duped the economic brain centers into believing there were no financial wounds to worry about. What did this portend? What new calamities and crashes would this lead to?

Sick Prosperity

The President of Metrobank, Robert Sheppard, sits quietly in the darkness of his sixtieth-floor office suite in lower Manhattan and mulls over recent events until the early morning.

Back in the 1960s and 1970s, he could cope with any crisis: At the peak of an inflationary boom, he dealt with a decline in the market value of his long-term bond portfolio. At the bottom of a recession, he turned his attention to bankruptcies and the danger of defaults.

Now he is confronted with *both* problems at the same time. On one side, he sees the rapid money-supply upsurge. Still unaware of the big oil-price collapse ahead, he is convinced it will lead to an inflationary revival some time in the not-so-distant future. On the other side, he sees the aftermath of the recession and the foreign debt crisis.

These fears are legitimate. Sitting on his desk are the latest figures showing the losses in the bank's assets as of the end of the fiscal year. They are staggering. In search of consolation, he picks up estimates for a couple of other banks in trouble. "Maybe we're in better ... or rather less bad ... shape than these other guys," he whispers to himself. It is a pleasant thought—until he discovers, to his utter dismay, that they are all in essentially the same boat.

"Damn it! Why did our bond traders have a knack of always buying these bonds and munis at the peak—just like everyone else? Why did we go wild with these foreign loans at the worst time—just like everyone else? Why is it that we dove headlong into these 'sure-fire no-risk' agricultural loans—just like the other guys? What a disaster!"

Adding to the urgency, his thoughts shift to the election in Argentina, bringing to power a President who will pick and choose how and when to repay their foreign debts, throwing into question nearly half of his bank's capital. The executive leans back in his chair and begins to plan for the worst. He starts writing a secret memo to the Board of Directors, outlining a new set of contingency plans:

(1) Begin joint efforts by top banks to petition regulatory bodies for redefinition of nonperforming international loans. It's currently three months. Ask for six months and settle for four or five! Compare it to Iran or the communist takeover of China in 1949.

(2) To the *authorities*, stress the *importance* and urgency of this problem in private communications. For the *public*, mount a campaign on the *unimportance* of foreign debts as a percent of liabilities.

(3) A similar redefinition of nonperforming *domestic* loans might alarm the investing public. Pursue such efforts with utmost secrecy. At the same time, repress complaints by country banks that seek equivalent leniency on *their* bad farm loans. If everyone wants it, no one will get it. The leniency must be limited to a privileged few money center banks.

(4) If all else fails, freeze deposits nationwide at the first sign of panic. Avoid the term "bank holiday." Call it instead "liabilitymanagement."

As the sun rises over New York, a flicker of reality penetrates his consciousness. Sheppard realizes that the real steps—a thorough housecleaning of loans—should have been taken long ago; that now there is really nothing that can be done to stem the tide.

He crumples the would-be memo into a ball and tosses it into the trash can.

19

Merger Mania

Only a few blocks away from Metrobank's headquarters, four men sit quietly in the executive conference room of the Consolidated Industries of America, awaiting the arrival of the Chairman. Harry Pinkerton, a stocky and slightly bald middle-aged executive, walks into the room, opens his briefcase and pulls out a yellow pad. There is an extra touch of arrogance in his voice as he begins to speak.

"Our expansion strategies were all right for the Sixties and Seventies, but this is a new era. We need a *new* strategy, a *new* plan, a *new* philosophy."

It is the spring of 1985, and business volume has picked up rapidly from the recession. Such strategy meetings are being held in one corporation after another throughout the country to plan for what will prove to be the greatest merger boom of all time. Some firms are still hesitant because of the close call with financial insolvency earlier in the decade. But Consolidated, although relatively small, is one of the first to have switched to the new "gung-ho" philosophy.

"But, Harry," queries an assistant, "the last plan we called 'Project Acceleration.' What shall we call the plan this time?"

"Project Explosion! Of course."

"Ah, yes. Of course."

The financial vice-president is somewhat perplexed. "But haven't we already borrowed heavily from the banks? Aren't we already expanding as fast as possible? What *more* can we do?"

"The trouble with us," answers the Chairman, "is that we give equity a positive value and liabilities a negative value. Most of us were brought up with the idea that savings are good and debt is bad. But now we must struggle to purge ourselves of the prejudices and fears of bygone generations. It is time to declare war on equity and embrace debt with all our energies."

Pinkerton lowers his voice as if speaking in confidence. "Go find yourselves a corporate giant that has been sitting on a hoard of cash—and *take it over!*"

In previous years, it was almost impossible for a small company to gobble up a large multibillion dollar corporation. But now, in the mid-'80s, anything goes! Corporate raiders of previous decades would be dumfounded and envious if they could witness how corporate dwarfs—such as Wickes, Pantry Pride, Mesa Petroleum and others—gobble up multibillion dollar giants many times their size.

"We have the staff," continued the Chairman. "We have the expertise. Best of all, we have the guts!"

"And the gall!"

"Sure. If you want to put it that way. Sure, why not?"

"How do you propose to pull this off?"

"First, the usual way. Behind the scenes, we quietly and steadily start buying up their stock. Do it through third parties. Pick up big blocks privately whenever you can."

"Then what?"

"Then we move into the Octopus Strategy—eight new ways to use leverage and attack the cash-rich giants. Number one," he continues, counting on his fingers, "we tap the banks, playing one against the other if necessary. Either the banks say 'yes' or they lose our business."

"Sheppard at Metrobank seems anxious."

"Great! But that's not enough. Tell him to double the ante or we're going elsewhere for our big deal!"

"Such as?"

"Such as part two of my strategy: We float big junk bond issues to the public—and when I say float, I really mean *drown*. Drown them in our junk bonds. I know they'll come along because they're desperate for high yields to make up for their losses in other areas."

Back in the 1970s, junk bonds—high risk, high yielding bonds issued with virtually no real assets to back them up—were virtually nonexistent. In the late 1980s, at the peak of the merger craze, they had enjoyed a virtual explosion of growth to an estimated $250 billion outstanding. Thus, the junk bond market was the epicenter of the merger boom—the central powerhouse that provided the needed cash fuel.

The Wall Street brokerage firm which specialized in this area, Drexel Burnham, became an overnight success by luring big investors—pension funds, insurance companies, mutual funds, and savings and loan associations—into the junk bond market.

Back in the old days, most brokerage houses were staid, reliable partnerships. Relations with long-term clients were important. The ethics of the profession were emphasized. And the partners stood behind their firm personally with their integrity and wealth. If the firm got into trouble, they were *personally* liable!

But by the time the 1980s superboom came around, all this had changed dramatically. Old-style partnerships were few and far between as brokerage firms hid behind the anonymity of larger and impersonal corporations. Moreover, they found they could make more money from "doing deals" than from ordinary commissions.

The most notorious example of these excesses was E. F. Hutton. Most people paid little attention to what was going on, and never would have dreamed that a scant five years later, despite the greatest boom of all time, it would suffer a meteoric decline. As long as the stock market continued healthy, none of this came to the surface. But in the Money Panic, the consequences of these ventures would erupt.

All were attracted by the lush double-digit yields. All thought that they had little or nothing to lose. None—let alone the chairman of the fictional Consolidated—were prepared to face the true consequences.

"Number three," Pinkereton continues, "we push our commercial paper. We give 'em the best rate we can. We show 'em we mean business." (Commercial paper represents IOUs sold by a corporation in the open market in order to raise money from other corporations or from individual investors.)

"What rate?" interrupts the financial vice-president again.

"Two percent above the market, maybe more!"

"Harry, you're insane," he half whispers impulsively. Then, catching himself, says: "Excuse my ignorance, but can we really afford it?"

"Of course! With the kind of return we're going to get on our investment, we can afford practically anything within reason. So what if the funds cost more? Inflation will soon be running nearly at that rate anyhow. The important thing is, the money is *there*. It's there for the taking.

"Number four: Don't hesitate to saturate the media with ads attacking the companies we want to take over. First, tear their management apart. Ridicule their performance. Remember the word 'takeover' is taboo. Don't let me catch anyone in this room or at the advertising agency ever using that word! This is a merger—a normal, healthy merger, and nothing more."

Harry Pinkerton pauses for a moment and then says: "Oh, yes, one more thing while we're on this topic. Tell the ad agency we want our campaign to stress how this *merger* will give rise to a more efficient and more competitive company."

"Is that it?"

"No, also tell them to use phrases that appeal to the stockholders' patriotism, that invoke the images of people like Lee Iacocca and Bruce Springsteen. Tell 'em that we represent the great new force which will bring you a leaner and meaner Corporate America—one better able to generate renewed economic vigor and better equipped to compete with our counterparts abroad."

"Do you really believe this?" the VP countered, challenging the Chairman's sincerity.

The Chairman is visibly angered. He resents the financial VP's insinuation that there might be the least bit of hypocrisy in his intentions. Sure, the media campaign is PR, he thinks, but what's wrong with that? He stares the VP down for a brief interlude and then, very deliberately, makes these comments: "After a takeover, we will lay off scores of middle management positions. We will sell or close unprofitable operations. We will reduce overhead and boost profit margins. In short, we will lay the groundwork for an earnings explosion. That's why I call this 'Project Explosion'!"

"I see," responds the VP, greatly humbled.

And so it was that Consolidated embarked on one of the most ambitious takeovers of all time: United Oil Company.

In theory, Pinkerton's concept of striving for greater efficiency was not a bad one. In practice, things didn't quite work out as planned. Fixed costs remained at peak levels. Staffs were too large. And confusion reigned. More importantly, no one at the meeting considered the risk of big debt in the merger game. As long as the stock market kept surging and the economy kept muddling along, these risks were camouflaged. But, later, as soon as the invisible threshold from boom to bust was crossed, *the great debts incurred before the crash would explode with devastating power.*

Back in the 1920s, a similar boom had prompted Congress to pass laws to prevent a recurrence. They had vowed to stop "unrestrained corporate mergers and the deleterious effects they can have on the economy." They had limited takeover activity and curbed the involvement of commercial banks. In short, they had done everything they possibly could to prevent another great disaster.

However, laws made by men were unable to stop the tides of nature. Like waves pounding on soft stone, with each business cycle, the antimerger legislation was eroded. New pathways were carved out, new gimmicks invented. Finally, after fifty years of this gradual but persistent change, the obstacles were circumvented. By the 1980s, an uninhibited, Roaring-Twenties-type boom was under way.

In fact, it was often the government itself that inadvertently *promoted* the boom. For example, it was no mere coincidence that the huge takeovers among the oil companies commenced in the early 1980s. That's when the Justice Department's Antitrust Division, the agency in charge of regulating mergers, was silenced by the Reagan Administration. And that's also when they leaned on the Fed to provide funds to the bond markets and the banks which, in turn, lent the money to merger-hungry raiders.

This opened the door to raiders in other energy sectors, the railroads, broadcasting, manufacturing, advertising and, later, even banking. It was "supply-side economics" at its worst!

There was nothing wrong with the *theory* of supply-side economics—the idea that the nation's chronic ills could be resolved by removing obstacles blocking greater productivity. It was the *practice* that was a disaster. Unfortunately, it was the umbrella of supply-side economics that made the merger boom possible. It effectively defused the Justice Department and the Securities and Exchange Commission (SEC) which, under previous Administrations, would have stopped the madness.

On Wall Street, the merger mania led to the phenomenon called "insider trading," whereby investors or brokers illegally profited from confidential information about upcoming takeovers.

In the 1970s, with the SEC's presence more widely felt, experienced traders had been more careful. And in the 1980s, these same traders were acutely aware of suspicious activity. Indeed, they knew about it as much as six years *before* the SEC brought its first cases to court.

They knew about it, but they had no power to stop it. In fact, as time wore on and as their junior associates passed them by in the mad race for quick profits, they finally yielded to temptation. Many were quite aware of the harmful side effect of excessive leverage, but that knowledge didn't stop them from taking the risks anyway.

These brokers, investment bankers and commercial banks provided the corporate raiders with the necessary financial muscle, transforming them from mere mortals into super-raiders, and allowing them to go for what they called "the big banana"—the corporate giants of America. All with no previous experience, with no understanding of the consequences of over-indebtedness, and with no restraint from a government that had been charged with the duty of protecting the public from such escapades.

When the SEC finally did fight back, it argued that the raiders were ripping off the public, that the public was getting shortchanged and not allowed to participate fairly in the stock market boom. Yes indeed! What they forgot to mention, however, was the fact that *the merger maniacs and those in and out of government who lent them support were destroying the financial system as a whole, themselves included.*

No-one cared. Their only concern was to somehow keep the party going. Wall Street earned hundreds of millions in commissions, advisory and finder's fees. The bankers earned premiums above the prime rate on the billions lent. And the public enjoyed the price appreciation in stocks which benefited from the takeover frenzy. *All* players were concerned only with their immediate gains. Few worried about the long-range damage to the economy.

Ironically, the greatest damage done by the merger boom was not from the permissive attitude of Uncle Sam. Nor was it from attacks by the raiders. Rather, it was the *defensive* strategies by corporations under attack which made the big hole in the balance sheets.

Running Scared

Since it was previously unheard of for small corporations and raiders to take over big companies, management under attack initially ignored their threats. But after some of the largest oil companies fell prey to raiders in the early 1980s, corporate boardrooms across the country were truly shaken. Management adopted a series of defensive tactics designed to keep their companies independent.

The scene now shifts to one such company, a competitor of United Oil. The President and his most trusted officers debate as follows.

"Did you see what has just happened to United? Consolidated pulled it off! I never believed they could do it. I was so sure they'd fall flat on their face. I was wrong! The really bad news is that I think we're next on their list."

The man on his left shakes his head. "I doubt it. They must have completely exhausted their cash in the United deal."

"You mean Metrobank's cash!"

"Whatever. Anyhow, it's going to take them at least six months to recharge their batteries for their next shot." The man seems to be leaning toward a mood of complacency ... until suddenly he says: "I've heard a rumor that it's ABC Industries that is aiming for us."

"Does it really matter *who* attacks us? No matter what, we're vulnerable. All I want to know is: What the hell can we do about it?"

"Not much right now. We'll have to wait."

"Not on your life. I want defensive strategies in place immediately! I've given too much of my life to this company to see it suddenly usurped by some junk-bond-carrying yuppies."

"What do you have in mind, sir?"

"Everything: Greenmail, the white knight tactic, scorched earth, super dividends, leveraged buy-outs."

Only a few years earlier, all this would have been gibberish to the average investor. But during the merger mania of the mid-1980s, everyone on Wall Street was familiar with the terms. It was the "newspeak" of corporate America which came into vogue circa 1984. However, virtually no one was willing to admit that these tactics were completely contrary to sound management.

With *greenmail*, target companies retaliated by buying back the raider's stock at above market prices. This did eliminate the immediate threat, but it severely depleted their cash.

In *white knight* deals, the target company sought another merger partner which would give existing directors and managers a better deal. This might have helped the existing directors and managers save their jobs, but it was of little long-term benefit to the company.

In the *scorched earth* strategy, management launched an even more direct attack on their own balance sheet. The target company actually went out of its way to make itself an *undesirable* candidate by reducing its cash liquidity, buying out another company, or sharply increasing its long-term debt. This is why twenty-first century historians call the 1980s the "era of financial masochism" or the "decade of corporate suicide."

The *super dividend* strategy was great for the stockholders at that moment. To pull it off, however, the corporation had to go deeply into debt, sometimes even exceeding their assets. End result: A capital deficit—a gaping hole in their balance sheet.

The ultimate speculation arrived with the *leveraged buy-out* (or LBO) when a company went deeply into debt to go private and take itself off the market. However, in the end, this destroyed one of the most important pillars of capitalism. Here's why: Traditionally, a company raised capital by selling shares to the public. The stockholders participated in the profits and shared the risk. Leveraged buy-outs changed all that. Instead of raising money by selling stock, the corporations did precisely the reverse. They borrowed money to buy back their own shares or the shares of other firms. Instead of earning profits for their stockholders, they now served the profit needs of their creditors. Instead of capitalism, they practiced what I call *"debtism."*

If this transformation had been subtle or behind-the-scenes, we could understand how most analysts might have missed it. However, it was anything but that. The Federal Reserve periodically published two graphs (Graphs 10 & 11) that illustrate—beyond any vestige of doubt—what was really going on.

The top graph shows the funds corporations raised from bonds (debt). The bottom graph shows how much they raised from equities (stocks). In the past, fund raising was balanced between the two. Then, in the mid-1980s, as the merger boom went into full swing, they actually began to buy back more shares than they issued. For the first time in history, they abandoned the most basic capitalist principles; they reduced their equity base while switching completely into debt.

In the bottom graph on page 175, this shows up in the form of the large black area, representing net sales of equities to the tune of $100 billion or more each year. The top graph shows the mirror image of this phenomenon in the form of a sudden surge in debts.

This was much more than just a passing footnote in the history of the merger boom. It was the prelude to the merger *bust* which hit during the Money Panic.

It resulted in the most dramatic erosion in the balance sheets of corporate America of all time. As documented in Table 9, cash resources were depleted in the late 1970s; and, as you can see in Graph 12, equity was eroded in the 1980s.

Graph 10 & 11. How Corporations Practiced "Debtism"

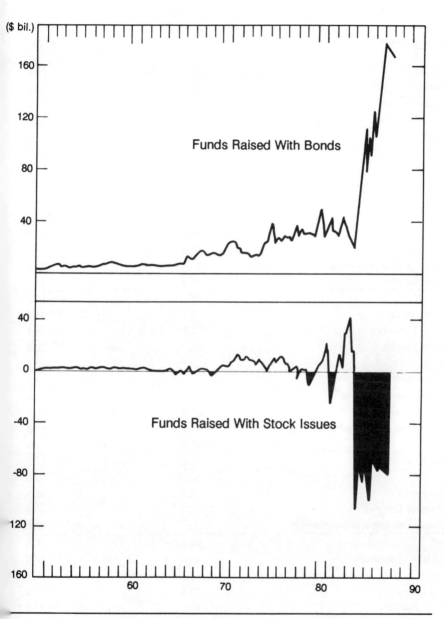

The way corporations raised money was totally transformed. Previously, ey sold shares and built capital. But in the 1980s, they sold debt (such as junk nds) and reduced their capital by actually buying back more shares than they sued. The increase in debt shows up in the top graph in the form of an surge. The decrease in their capital is depicted in the bottom graph in the rm of a sharp decline into negative territory. Data: Federal Reserve.

Table 9. The Liquidity Of The Industrial Giants

Company Name	1988 (%)	1976 (%)
Allied-Signal	7.7	15.1
American Tel. & Tel.	20.0	27.9
Amoco	27.1	34.1
Anheuser-Busch	5.3	81.3
Atlantic Richfield	93.5	43.7
Boeing	59.5	85.3
BP America	15.6	18.6
Caterpillar	2.8	107.3
Chevron	51.5	11.0
Chrysler Corp. *	43.2	15.6
ConAgra	10.3	35.2
Digital Equipment	86.6	46.4
Dow Chemical	13.6	7.8
Du Pont (E.I.) De Nemours	17.5	22.3
Eastman Kodak	24.8	64.9
Exxon	14.2	48.2
Ford Motor Co. *	6.2	21.2
General Dynamics	8.7	6.1
General Electric *	18.7	20.3
General Motors *	9.7	25.1
Georgia-Pacific	7.0	4.8
Goodyear Tire & Rubber	9.8	1.9
Hewlett-Packard	30.9	56.1
Int'l Business Machines *	45.7	150.8
ITT	28.3	7.9
Johnson & Johnson	36.2	92.1
Kraft	50.6	7.2
Lockheed	2.5	16.5
McDonnell Douglas	1.3	5.6
Minnesota Mining & Manufacturing	33.6	48.9
Mobil	20.3	18.7
Occidental Petroleum	21.2	26.0
Pepsico	45.7	52.7
Philip Morris	13.8	8.0
Phillips Petroleum	42.9	64.9

Liquidity is defined as the amount of cash and equivalent on hand to cover each dollar of debts coming due within the next 12 months. In good times, low liquidity is usually not regarded as a problem. But during a recession, those firms with insufficient cash and/or too much short-term debt will face severe financial difficulties. Data: Corporate reports.

Table 9 Continued

Company Name	1988 (%)	1976 (%)
Proctor & Gamble	25.2	84.4
RJR Nabisco	30.9	10.1
Rockwell International	31.0	18.4
Sara Lee	9.9	31.5
Shell Oil	15.3	42.9
Sun	55.9	30.2
Tenneco	13.0	7.7
Texaco	41.8	15.6
Unisys	1.7	7.0
United Technologies	5.4	38.7
Unocal	12.4	24.4
USX	42.1	34.2
Westinghouse Electric	22.1	24.1
Xerox	9.5	62.2

* Includes captive finance subsidiaries.

Graph 12. The Great Plunge In Corporate Health

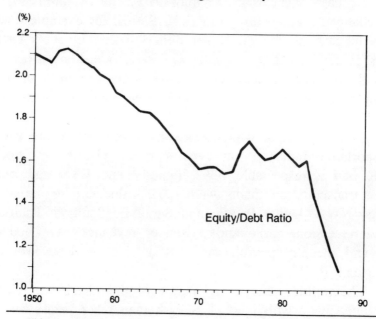

This graph answers the question: "How much do all nonfinancial corporations have in equity for every dollar of debt?" As you can see, it fell steadily throughout the 1950s and '60s, and then plunged in the mid-1980s from $1.60 to $1.10. This left corporate America extremely vulnerable to recession. (Conventionally, this ratio is expressed in reverse – as the amount of debt per dollar of equity.) Data: Federal Reserve.

Among the 50 largest industrial firms in America, only 15 escaped the 1980s borrowing binge. Only 15 could be considered relatively liquid—flush with cash and devoid of large short-term debts. At the top of the list were Atlantic Richfield, Digital Equipment, Boeing, Sun Oil and Chevron. Most of the others were skating on very thin ice. McDonnell Douglas had barely one cent in cash per dollar of short-term debts. Unysis was only slightly better off with 1.7 cents in cash and equivalent per dollar of debts coming due.

Most striking was the overwhelming trend of deterioration over time, especially between the mid-'70s and the late '80s. A decade and a half earlier, one could scan the corporate landscape and find numerous cash-rich companies such as IBM, Caterpillar, Anheuser Bush, Proctor & Gamble, Johnson & Johnson and Xerox—just to mention a few. But by the late 1980s, most of these had greatly reduced their cash holdings.

The retail firms were taking even bigger risks. With only a couple of exceptions (such as May Department Stores), all had very big cash balances in the mid-1970s. But by the 1980s, this had changed dramatically. American Stores, for example, had 48 cents in cash or equivalent per dollar of current debts back in 1976. *In 1988, it had less than one cent.* Wal-Mart Stores had virtually no cash whatsoever in 1988—only one third of a cent to cover each dollar of debts coming due within the next twelve months!

The only sector which was somewhat more secure was the transportation industry, but even here the picture was uneven. AMR had a respectable 53% liquidity and CSX had 46.5%. Three transportation giants were quite vulnerable to the Money Panic—NWA, Union Pacific and Santa Fe Southern Pacific. In a real recession, cargo and passenger revenues were bound to fall, and meeting payrolls as well as current debts would be touch and go.

The utilities, due to the nature of their business, felt they could get away with much less cash than other firms. But they abused this privilege and reduced their liquidity far below the minimum standards they set for themselves. This was especially apparent among some of the electric power companies such as Public Service Enterprise Group (1.3%), Southern California

Table 10. The Liquidity Of The Largest Retail Companies

Company Name	1988	1976
American Stores	0.9	48.0
Dayton Hudson	6.9	4.7
JC. Penney	9.1	43.0
Kroger	6.2	25.7
K Mart	15.7	36.3
May Department Stores	62.3	5.8
Sears, Roebuck*	6.0	4.4
Wal-Mart Stores	0.3	7.3

*merchandise group only

Table 11. The Liquidity Of The Largest Utilities

Company Name	1988	1976
American Electric Power	20.2	33.6
American Information Tech.+	11.3	21.1
Bell Atlantic+	13.1	10.6
BellSouth+	18.7	N.A.
Interior Energy	60.1	12.5
Commonwealth Edison	7.6	3.0
Detroit Edison	0.4	1.0
FPL Group	4.9	3.1
GTE	4.2	1.0
Middle South Utilities	30.8	29.0
Nynex+	5.1	16.9
Pacific Gas & Electric	6.2	4.2
Pacific Telesis Group+	0.3	N.A.
Philadelphia Electric	6.5	11.5
Public Service Enterprise Group	1.3	4.7
Southern Company	25.1	28.4
Southern California Edison	1.1	2.3
Southwestern Bell+	8.4	21.8
Texas Utilities	19.1	12.7
U. West+	16.1	21.1

+1984 data used in lieu of 1976 data.

Normally, utility companies didn't need as much cash on hand as industrial firms. Therefore, it was normal to see ratios which were lower. However, many utilities in the U.S. had abused this privilege and were now in much worse shape financially than at any time in previous history. The deterioration in their liquidity was especially evident when comparing 1988 to 1976. Data: Moody's.

Table 12. The Liquidity Of The Transportation Companies

Company Name	1988	1976
AMR	53.2	61.3
Burlington Northern	15.1	11.2
CSX	46.5	42.4
Delta Air Lines	36.7	16.2
NWA	1.7	16.6
Santa Fe Southern Pacific	8.7	69.8
Texas Air	29.5	33.5
Union Pacific	9.9	11.1

Edison (1.1%) and Detroit Edison (0.4%). They said they didn't need the cash on hand, that if they wanted it, they could always borrow more. In normal times, yes. In the Money Panic, no!

In previous eras, America had at least maintained its stature as a world economic power. Now, however, in order to prolong the boom, our leaders would force the dollar down. This, plus other risky escapades, set the stage for an even greater threat—one which made the merger boom seem tame by comparison.

20

The Dollar:
The Ultimate Sacrifice

Prior to 1984, recessions in the U.S. economy were considered a natural, even desirable, event—temporary interludes during which the economy rested, recuperated from the stress of rapid growth and regenerated itself for the next cycle. In the mid-1980s, however, our economic leaders, perceiving that our financial system was vulnerable, sought to prevent a recession at *all* costs. But in the end, they sacrificed the one pillar of the U.S. economy—which remained the dollar.

To see how this happened, we look to the nation's capital around March 1985. Three of the most powerful officials in government sit at a long table covered with computer printouts and charts. They shake their heads in amazement.

"In all my life," comments the eldest of the three, "I've never seen anything like this. Sure, banks have been in trouble before. But this many closings in one year? And look at these business failures! They're literally off the chart! You realize, of course, what this means?"

"Yes, I do," responds the second man. "But give me your interpretation anyhow."

"OK. Here's the bottom line: This is the most precarious financial situation we've had in this country since the Great Depression. What is most shocking is that these disasters are occurring at a time when the economy as a whole, according to all our traditional measures, is actually performing quite well. We've had quarter after quarter of nonstop recovery, and that recovery has been one of the fastest of the postwar years. It's downright frightening and uncanny."

"Because?"

"Because just as soon as the economy stops growing or, worse yet, turns on a downward path, all hell will break loose. Another recession will be the spark that ignites the fire. We cannot—*must not*—permit the occurrence of another decline! *This country will simply not survive another recession!*"

Soon a new figure took center stage, a man who in a few short months would help destroy all that Fed Chairman Volcker had so painstakingly achieved during the previous five years. His name: James Baker. And in order to achieve his goal of prolonging the recovery, he made the ultimate national sacrifice—the near-destruction of our currency. All in the name of saving the economy from the dreaded nightmare of a recession which, in previous decades, would have been considered normal or even desirable.

Mr. Baker thought that, by cheapening the dollar, goods made in America would become cheaper to foreigners. The foreigners were then supposed to buy more U.S. goods and America's trade deficit would disappear. Unfortunately, it didn't quite work out that way. Instead, other nations which were not directly affected by the currency fluctuations—the so-called Newly Industrialized Countries or "NICs"—jumped into the picture. The NICs included Taiwan, South Korea, Singapore, Hong Kong and, to some degree, nations such as Brazil and Indonesia. As Japan and West Germany had done earlier, these countries continued to undersell U.S. manufacturers. And the U.S. trade deficit remained stubbornly large.

The dollar, meanwhile, continued to plunge with Mr. Baker's blessings. At the outset of this dangerous escapade, in early 1985, the U.S. dollar had reached a peak against the world's major currencies. One dollar could buy 3.45 West German marks, 2.94 Swiss francs or 263 Japanese yen. But within twenty-four short months, all that had changed. Now, the dollar was worth only 1.56 marks in West Germany and only 116 yen in Japan. In Switzerland, it was down to 1.25 francs!

This was far worse than the great dollar collapse of the late 1970s. In fact, *against the Japanese yen, the dollar's fall of the mid-1980s was more than twice as bad as the earlier disaster.*

What did that really mean? Let's say you travelled to West Germany, Switzerland or Japan in early 1985 when the dollar was at a peak, spending $100 on meals, taxis, and such. Then, let's say you went back to one of those countries two years later. Your $100 would now be worth less than $44!

At the time, most people in Washington didn't care. They didn't recognize that the dollar was more than just a symbol of American might. They didn't understand how it was directly related to inflation, monetary policy, interest rates and the overall stability of the entire nation.

It had taken Fed Chairman Volcker over six years to restore the dollar's value. It took Treasury Secretary Baker one-third that time to destroy it again, throwing America into a deeper hole than the one Mr. Volcker had encountered on his first day at the Fed.

Never before—even during our darkest moments as a nation—had our currency been battered so far so fast. And never before was the American public so oblivious to a calamity with such widespread future repercussions on their daily life.

The U.S. Government knocked the dollar down by running the dollar printing presses at a breakneck speed and pumping the money into the economy. Naturally, the more excess dollars there were around—both in the U.S. and abroad—the less they were worth. For a better understanding of how this took place, consider a strange conversation which took place during that period.

The Money Explosion

A West German central bank official visits an intimate friend at the Fed in Washington, D.C., with whom he can speak openly. "My God! What have you done here? I just saw your latest chart of the money supply growth rate and, I must admit, I am shocked!"

"But what about the deregulation? What about the—"

"I don't care if you transformed the American banking system into a Danish chocolate factory!" the German says. "There isn't any way to justify this growth in money supply. Besides, it's not just the money supply anymore. It's bank reserves. It's credit. It's any measure you pick out of the hat. And

Graph 13. The Surge In Money Supply

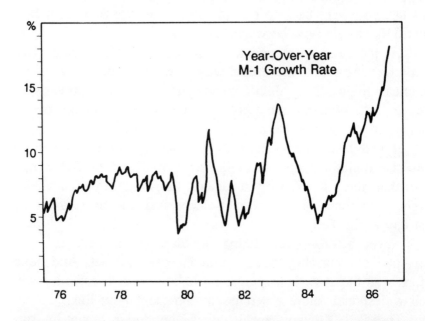

This shows, in effect, how the money printing presses nearly ran amuck during the mid-1980s. The surge in the money-supply growth rate helps to explain how the stock market boom of the mid-1980s was possible despite relatively weak corporate profits. Later in the decade, economists tried to discredit the validity of this particular barometer (M-1). However, the same basic trend can be seen in other measures such as nonborrowed bank reserves and total credit creation. Data: Federal Reserve.

you want us to do the same thing in Europe? You're absolutely, unforgivably, out of your minds!"

"Well, I must admit we did give ourselves some leeway."

"Leeway? Are you serious? No, you must be joking of course. You're not? Is it possible that you haven't seen this chart? It is? I find that hard to believe. We watch it every week at the Bundesbank. Look at these year-over-year growth rates! Back in January of 1984 it was 4% or 5%, which was very reasonable, maybe even a bit too conservative. But then it shot straight up. 10%. 15%. 20%! Did you hear me? 20%!! I have only one question for you."

"Which is what?"

"You know where all this money is *coming from*. It's being manufactured right here at the Fed. But do you know where this money is *going*?"

"Well, no, not exactly."

"It's going into speculation—gambling, the roulette wheel. It's running overseas. It's everywhere. What on earth has motivated you to take such drastic steps? Do you think that the dollar collapse will be the magic wand that saves you from depression or financial calamities?"

"What speculation?" asks the Fed official.

Obviously he didn't see what is now apparent to most economic historians. In the mid-1980s, while the farm sector was being devastated, while manufacturing and mining were floundering, the greatest gambling binge of the twentieth century occurred. (Later, turn-of-the-millennium novelists would call it "the last hurrah of the American miracle" and "the eleventh-hour Mad Hatter's tea party." But at the time, most of those involved believed it would never end.)

Washington and Wall Street rejoiced. Like magic, the money pumping transformed what could have been a great disaster into an even greater recovery! Sure, the budget deficit failed to improve. Yes, the trade deficit was worsening. But who cared? As long as the voters were content and the yuppies made money, what difference did it make?

In sum, we can now look back at that critical mid-1980s period and see the true sequence of events: (1) The fear in high levels of government that a recession would trigger a financial collapse, (2) an all-out effort to pump in more money, (3) a disastrous decline in the dollar and (4) a stock market surge.

Did they defy history? Not really. It wasn't the first time that powerful negative forces spurred desperate men to create temporarily positive events. But the good news of the mid-1980s planted the seeds for the bad news of the latter part of the decade. By the late 1980s, the U.S. and world economies faced financial dangers that were far more severe than those of 1984!

In 1984, we had surging business failures and a rash of bank closings. In early 1987, we *still* had the failures and the bank closings, both at record postwar highs. On top of that, we now also had the money supply surging out of control, rampant speculation in stocks and a collapse in the dollar!

Nothing had been gained. Everything had been lost. We had made the ultimate sacrifice as a nation—the destruction of our currency and the disintegration of our financial health. And after all that, the money and credit being pumped in was not even producing real growth. It went into speculation in the stock market or escaped overseas. Very soon, it would all wind up in the Great Crash of '87.

Again, as in early 1980, that crash began in the bond markets.

21

The Crash Of '87

John Hartman is far less gullible than he was during the fatal bond market collapse of October 1979. He is more alert to the possible traps and more skeptical of the consensus view of the market. But he is still not prepared for what will happen next. Rather than dealing in U.S. Treasury securities, he now trades only "mortgage-backed bonds."

Most people don't know what those are, yet nearly everyone who has a mortgage is indirectly involved in this market. When you take out a mortgage on your home, the mortgage contract you sign with the bank doesn't necessarily stay locked away in a file cabinet at the local branch. It can be sold to third parties.

Frequently, your mortgage will be shipped out to a mortgage broker who throws it into a "basket" with a pile of other mortgage contracts. Since the basket is too big to sell to any one investor, the broker prints up a number of certificates which, in effect, represent equal shares of whatever's in the basket. These certificates are the "mortgage-backed bonds" sold to investors around the country.

Therefore, when you send your monthly mortgage check to your local bank, the money probably doesn't stop there. Most likely, it goes to the broker who then parcels it out to the investors who bought the mortgage-backed bonds.

Now suppose many homeowners miss their payments. Some investors, somewhere, are going to be very upset. This is where various government (or government-sponsored) agencies step in to guarantee the principal and interest payments to the investors.

The largest of these agencies is the General National Mortgage Association (GNMA) which guarantees its "Ginnie Mae" bonds. But like Treasury bonds, although GNMA guarantees the regular payment on the bonds, they *don't* guarantee their market price, which can fluctuate depending on the supply and demand.

These fluctuations are now of grave concern to John Hartman. He nervously watches the computer screen, waiting for changes in the prices for the Ginnie Maes.

The time is 8:00 AM, Tuesday, April 14, 1987. The place is the back office of a major New York broker-dealer specializing in these bonds.

"I'm a bit queasy about this opening," Hartman remarks to a colleague.

"Why?"

"Just a gut feeling. I'm afraid the Ginnie Maes could be off as much as two points. We're holding $50 million, so that would be a $1 million loss!"

The traders turn their attention back to their monitors. The day's opening offer appears on the screen, blinking to signal that it's a new quote.

A shiver goes down Hartman's spine. Never before in his lifetime has he seen these securities, held by hundreds of thousands of unwary savers throughout the United States, fall so far so fast:

The opening prices for Ginnie Mae bonds are down ten points—over 15% of their value. It means that the interest rate on these and other mortgages is up by over two percentage points!

Anyone who owned these and other long-term bonds was taking a beating and probably didn't even know it. Anyone who wanted to buy a home suddenly faced a jump in mortgage rates. Even worse, those who had a variable-rate mortgage would be hit with higher monthly payments.

As recently as 1970, there had been no mortgage-backed bond market worth mentioning. Then it went wild with growth—mortgage-backed bonds surged from less than $30 billion in 1970 to over $800 billion by the end of the 1980s.

When I first saw these numbers, I was dumfounded. If this superboom had been proportional to the overall growth in

Graph 14. The Boom In Mortgage-Backed Securities

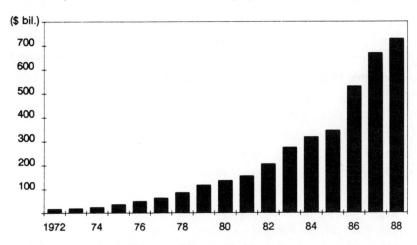

These securities are issued by government or government-sponsored agencies which hold the actual mortgages. The growth was phenomenal during the 1970s and '80s. But there was insufficient attention paid to the potential risks in the event of widespread mortgage delinquencies. Data: Federal Reserve.

mortgage lending, it wouldn't have been alarming. But this was not the case. Until 1981, these pools produced an average of 15.5 cents of each dollar of new mortgages. By 1988, they provided 71 cents of every new mortgage dollar—a phenomenon never before witnessed.

If Ginnie Maes and other mortgage-backed securities had been backed by solid values, a rise in interest rates might not be so threatening. But the fact is that, by the late 1980s, the homeowners of America, the people who had to make the mortgage payments, were in their worst financial condition since the 1930s.

If the owners of those securities had been well-capitalized institutions, it also might not have been so bad. But in fact the single largest group owning the mortgages happened to be the weakest link in the economy—the savings and loan institutions.

The end result was a combination of fundamentally suspect assets and financially weak holders of those assets! When the savings and loans needed cash, they started dumping.

Other institutions followed suit, selling not only their Ginnie Maes but also their municipal bonds, corporate bonds and Treasury securities. The result was the most severe bond market decline since 1980.

But the bond market collapse of 1987 was merely the trigger of a much more severe financial panic to occur throughout the Western World. My diary shows the extraordinary sequence of events which ensued:

Tokyo, June 1987. Japanese Government Bonds are plummeting. The bellwether 5.1% bond of 1996, which reached a historic high of 125 two months ago, has just plunged to 100. Meanwhile, the yield which dropped to a historic low of 2.6% has jumped to 4.6%, an amazing 77% increase. Despite a slight time lag, the spring panic in the United States has precipitated a summer debacle in Tokyo.

Chicago, September 11. The Commodities Futures and Exchange Commission (CFTC) has just released its "Commitment of Traders Report," which reveals *who* owns *what* in the futures markets. (In the futures markets, investors buy and sell stocks, bonds and commodities at today's prices for future delivery.) Of special interest are two of the categories used by the CFTC:

- *The commercials* or the *strong* hands. They are the big players and, for the most part, they are in the markets for protection—not speculation. Their primary goal is to use the futures markets to offset any losses in their actual holdings.
- *The small speculators* or the *weak* hands. They're the little guys and they're in the game for the quick buck, reacting to the emotions of greed and fear.

If there's going to be a big downward break in the markets, it's bound to begin when the commercials start selling, catching the small speculators by surprise.

Our messengers in New York and Chicago have just picked up the latest statistics and have called them in to our office. I am especially interested in the stock index futures because that's where I think a stock market crash is bound to begin.

In the previous month, the data showed that the commercials (the strong hands in the market) were big buyers. Meanwhile, the small speculators were big sellers. The burning question now is, have the commercials dumped their holdings? If so, it could be the signal we've been waiting for. We have entered the new statistics in our computer. The resulting chart is reproduced in Graph 15.

Graph 15.   Who Owns What In The S&P Futures Index

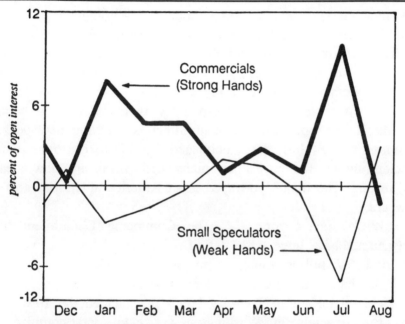

In the 1970s and '80s, the futures markets, originally designed strictly for commodities, were adapted and transformed to allow the trading of Treasury bonds and bills, foreign currencies, bank CDs and stock indexes such as the Standard & Poor Index. A speculator could buy the S&P Index in the futures market — representing a portfolio of 500 stocks — with very little margin, unusually large profit potential and equally big risks. By the late 1980s, these futures markets had emerged as a dominant force, often having a greater impact on price movements than the actual trading on the floor of the New York Stock Exchange. Therefore, this analysis — showing who was buying (or selling) — was very helpful in determining the timing of major market moves. In this graph, the thick line represents the commercials — the institutions who are the strong hands in the market. The thin line shows the activities of the small speculators — the weak hands.

A decline in the line means they are selling; a rise indicates buying. Look especially at the changes which took place from July to August. This is when the commercials suddenly dumped their holdings and even went short. At the same time, the small speculators bought heavily, thinking that the market was headed for the 3,600 level. But it was a trap for the small investor and a solid signal of a top in the market.

In September, the commercials dumped all their holdings! They're completely out of the market. That thin line popping up represents the small speculators. They're buying like crazy. I think this could be *the* top!

September 21. We have never seen such a wide divergence between falling bond markets and a still-surging stock market. Don't investers see the handwriting on the wall? Merrill Lynch, the largest brokerage firm in the nation, is still running ads saying that they're "bullish on America," meaning they believe the stock market—and the entire country—is going up.

We are among the very few surviving *bears.* We're not bearish on America as a whole but, for the reasons I will be writing about in my book, we think the stock market—and the entire economy—are in for a big setback.

First week in October. Despite the twin collapses in bonds and the dollar, optimism on Wall Street is reaching new peaks. *Business Week* has just published its October 5th issue, proclaiming on the cover that many U.S. firms are now "lean and mean." The image portrayed is an America at the dawn of a new era.

Wednesday, October 14. The Commerce Department has just announced a huge trade deficit for August: America has imported $15.7 billion more in autos, VCRs, clothes and other products than it has exported. The Dow is down 95 points and the yield on long-term Treasury bonds has pierced the 10% barrier. But officials in Washington are calm and complacent. They're going out of their way to say there are "no signs of resurging inflation." Of course not! Who ever said inflation was the main problem? They still don't understand that the real problem is too much debt—not too much inflation!

Throughout the world's financial centers, brokerage firms are retrenching—bailing out of the stock market. Salomon Brothers has dropped out of the municipal bond business, given up trading in commercial paper, and laid off 12% of its work force. Shearson is cutting back its municipal bond operations and getting out of British securities. Chemical, Citicorp and Merrill are cutting staff or selling real estate.

The *Wall Street Journal* puts it this way: "The Wall Street game of the 1980s always seemed too easy. Mathematicians, musicians-turned-stock-analysts and newly minted M.B.A.s are reaping vast riches. Thirty-year-olds with condos, BMWs and more money than they know what to do with ... Suddenly reality is setting in. Wall Street has laid off nearly 1,100 people in the past month—many of them with six-figure salaries."

Do they see the crash we see? Impossible. Otherwise they'd have to be crazy to hang on to the huge positions in stocks showing up on their balance sheets.

Thursday, October 15. The Dow Jones Industrial Average has just plummeted by 58 points, piercing its 200-day moving average for the first time since the bull market began. While I don't think the 200-day moving average is important, a lot of people do, especially the mutual-fund switching operations that follow it like gospel. Tomorrow morning they will walk out of their strategy meetings with big sell orders.

"Time to tell our subscribers to go short," I announce to my staff. "It's the best way to profit from a crash."

This is the transaction we recommend to our subscribers before the crash.

Friday, October 16. My father, Irving, who is now a senior consultant to my firm, is more bearish about the stock market than ever before. In fact, I have just returned from a big discussion with him in his office, which is strange inasmuch as I walked in there extremely bearish myself. It started when I asked rhetorically if we should take our profit on yesterday's trade. "After all," I said, "the Dow was down another 138 points today which means we have a windfall profit. Shouldn't we take our profit now?" I asked.

In response, he had me look at his big chart of the Dow. Then he started on a long explanation about Bernard Baruch and Black Tuesday of 1929. Except this time he thinks it's going to be Black Monday instead of Black Tuesday. And he's not talking about next month or next year anymore. He's talking 72 hours from now, next Monday, October 19th. I agree. I tell subscribers to *hold on no matter what*.

"When you go home," advises an official of a Wall Street firm, "walk close to the buildings." He's referring, however, strictly to the market's decline through Friday afternoon—which is just a warmup for the big crash we believe will hit Monday morning.

I wonder if others on the Street are finally turning bearish. Not likely. *Wall Street Journal* reporters Tim Metz and Beatrice Garcia put it this way: "By 8 AM, at Harry's Bar, the Wall Street watering hole, hordes of yuppie brokers and traders clearly were preoccupied with getting dates for the evening rather than with the market collapse." Obviously they have never seen a really sick market before. Most of them blindly assume it will shoot back up 100 points on Monday! They add parenthetically: "Of course, no one is forecasting a crash like that of 1929." Of course.

Monday, October 19, 7:00 AM. This is going to be the big day but you'd never know it if you're reading the latest news magazines. "The quarter looks golden," says *Business Week.* Little do they realize that today will go down in history as the greatest crash of all time.

Fed Chairman Greenspan, who has a reputation for hard-nosed skepticism, is one of the most optimistic of all. Like nearly everyone else in Washington, he has no inkling of the impending disaster.

10:00 AM. This is it! This is the great crash we expected. Back in October 1979, the *bond* market collapse finally broke the back of the wild inflationary spiral in tangible assets— homes, land, commodities, precious metals and consumer goods.

Now, in October of 1987—a full eight years later—the *stock* market collapse is breaking the back of the *financial* assets—stocks, junk bonds, options and futures.

Eight years may seem like a long interlude to those of us living through it. But some day, historians will look back at this period and call it the "deflation decade" or the "panic decade." They'll see the eight years between the twin collapses as a short synase linking the two.

1:00 PM. I just spoke by phone with our brokers, Lee Finberg and John Emery at Pru-Bache, Orlando, who handle many of our managed accounts. They called to congratulate us on our short positions but, at the same time, to pass along the latest from their technical analyst, who thinks this is the bottom. John hastened to add that any timing indicators had become worth-less, because the New York Stock Exchange's new, high-speed computer has fallen behind by a record 85 minutes.

So the stock prices reported on the brokers' screens are next to meaningless. Trading volume is plowing right past its previous record of some 340 million shares *and there are three hours of trading left!* My guess is that, with the main stock fu-tures index down by a full 50 points, the Dow, which is about ten times higher, might crash 500 points before it's over. I decide to hold firm with our shorts.

3:30 PM. The final rally attempt has collapsed. The market is cascading in a climactic panic, led by heavily indebted traders threatened with total financial ruin.

No one knows where the market is or what price they will get for their shares. Investors who punch in stock symbols on their quote machines are being given prices that are three hours old! That's how far behind the computers have fallen. But they're selling anyhow!

5:00 PM. The closing bell rang almost an hour ago, but the cascade of selling continues around the globe. The Dow Jones Industrials are down 508 points, or 22.6%. (On Black Tuesday, October 28, 1929, the loss was "only" 12.8%!) Over 600 million shares have changed hands—*double* the previous record!

Long ago we warned our subscribers that we had crossed an invisible threshold in which historic precedent had lost all meaning. Now we have the proof! The five-year, $2 trillion bull market is mortally wounded.

According to the *Wall Street Journal*: "The reaction around Wall Street, from traders, money managers and securities analysts, was mostly of stunned disbelief ... As stock prices col-lapsed, the U.S. Government stood by powerless ... Officials met at the White House, the Federal Reserve and the Securities and Exchange Commission. But as the market continued falling, they concluded that there was little they could do other than to stay calm in the face of Wall Street's panic ... Optimistic state-ments rang hollow as sell orders poured in on Wall Street ..."

5:25 PM. It's time to record today's Daily Hotline for our subscribers: "This is Martin Weiss with the Daily Hotline for October 19, 1987. For some time we have thought that we would soon see a crash that would be equivalent in magnitude to the Crash of 1929. We were wrong. *Today's decline was twice as bad as Black Tuesday of 58 years ago*, even in percentage terms.

"Therefore, there can be no doubt whatsoever that *today is the first day of the Money Panic*. For now, however, the time to take our profits has arrived. Tomorrow, Tuesday morning, October 20, hold your shorts in the December NYFE until 10 AM Eastern Standard Time. Then, at exactly 10 AM, pick up the phone, call your broker, and tell him to cover the shorts at the market. If the market keeps falling, so be it. Do not be tempted to jump back in again. Let's take the money and run! This concludes the Daily Hotline. Next update, tomorrow, Tuesday, before 5:30 PM."

Why 10:00 AM? There's bound to be a follow-through to the downside in the first half hour of trading and then the market should bounce back. But it's just a guess.

Tuesday, October 20, 9:00 AM. Wall Street is looking to Washington to end the agony and prevent a market Chernobyl. In the coming days and weeks, they're bound to try something—anything—to bring about a rally. But it will be too little too late. The damage has already been done—not just to investor psychology, but also to the infrastructure of the world economy!

5:00 PM. As it turns out, the bottom in the stock futures came at around 11:00 AM. Today is bound to go down in history as "the day the stock market died," only to be raised from the dead two hours later:

- Trading in many major stocks—such as IBM, Merck, plus scores of lesser issues—was frozen.
- Stock options and futures all but stopped trading for several hours.
- The "specialists" on the floor of the stock exchange, who are supposed to buy or sell specific stocks in order to help maintain an orderly market, are themselves devastated. Two-thirds of their capital is lost.
- Banks, frightened by the collapse, refused to extend credit that dealers desperately needed. Others have called in previous loans.

• Some big houses are rumored to have *begged* the New York Stock Exchange to close down, to artificially put a halt to the endless panic.

What most people don't realize is that this is a mere foreshadowing of the true market gridlock still to come when the entire nation is gripped by depression, and banks are on the verge of closing down.

Wednesday, October 21. Many small investors who have been devastated in the crash blame themselves for their losses. Not only has it hurt their pocketbooks, but it has also punctured their egos—their confidence in their own ability to make sound investment decisions. They chasten themselves for being amateurish, just "little guys" who "should never have competed shoulder-to-shoulder with the large speculators." On this last score, however, they are wrong.

The only difference between the two is that small investors know when to quit; the big speculators keep on losing money hand over fist. Media magnate Rupert Murdoch and his family have taken losses of over $1.5 billion, but he clings to his empire in the hope that it will survive the crash's aftershocks. Li Ka-Shing, who controls 15% of the value of the Hong Kong stock market, has lost $5 billion. The big corporate raiders, the survivors of the insider trading scandals, and the twentieth-century counterparts of the old "robber barons" have lost even larger sums. In the near term, their policy—to hold on no matter what—may prove correct. But later a second crash will again devastate their fortunes.

Thursday, October 22. Investors in mutual funds are in a state of shock. Between October 15 and today, the net asset value of equity mutual funds has plummeted 16.6%, hand-in-hand with the overall market. In fact, for the 20 million Americans who put their money into these funds, it turned out to be a lot harder to get out of the market than to get in. The toll-free lines at the mutual funds were overloaded and their main switchboards were jammed. By the time the investors got through, most of the initial crash was over; and by the time their sell orders were finally executed, the value of their shares had

Table 13. How The Mutual Funds Were Hurt By The Crash

Mutual funds	8/87 High	10/87 Low	Decline (%)
Affiliated Fund	13.90	10.01	28.0
Dreyfus Fund	14.92	11.64	22.0
Fidelity Equity Income	31.27	24.25	22.4
Fidelity Magellan Fund	60.75	41.95	30.9
Fidelity Puritan Fund	15.16	11.41	24.7
Investment Co. Of America	17.38	12.34	29.0
Mutual Shares	75.58	60.05	20.5
Pioneer II	24.62	15.65	36.4
Templeton World	19.29	14.51	24.8
Twentieth Century Select	44.60	30.35	32.0
Washington Mutual Inv.	15.12	11.44	24.3
Windsor Fund	18.21	13.62	25.2

Most mutual funds were severely hurt by the crash in two ways: First, the market value of their portfolio declined causing a parallel drop in the value of the mutual fund shares as shown here. Second, they suffered large redemptions. The net result was the first major decline in overall mutual fund assets in many years. Data: *Wall Street Journal.*

fallen still further. Here are the hits taken by the top 12 stock mutual funds:

Table 13 is evidence that size did not provide protection against loss! Nor did the funds change their ways after the crash. After all, stock mutual funds had one single purpose—to invest in stocks. One could not expect them to suddenly switch completely into safer investments.

Many of the funds actually took a beating that was worse than that suffered by the Dow Jones. Since the market's peak on August 27, the 44 Wall Street Equity Fund has fallen by 63.7%, *leaving investors with only about one-third of their money.* The Fidelity Select Industrial Material Fund is down by 48% and New England Growth is off by nearly 42%.

Even funds owning convertible bonds, supposedly the best of all possible worlds, have been hit hard in the crash, despite a big rally in most other bond markets. Dean Witter's Convertible Fund is down 25%. Putnam Convertible is down 21% and Value Line's Convertible is off 19%.

Friday, October 23. Finally, some people are beginning to recognize the grave dangers ahead. For example:

- FDIC and FSLIC officials are privately admitting that the stock market plunge could deal another costly blow to the government's deposit insurance funds, already reeling from record numbers of bank and S&L failures. Until now, the stock market boom helped cover up the banking crisis. Private investors poured money into failed banks in the belief that, in a strong stock market, they could sell their shares at a profit. No more! The FSLIC, which is itself insolvent, has more than 50 failed S&Ls on the block for sale, plus many potential candidates in line behind those. But in the new postcrash environment, selling *any* assets—no matter which kind—is going to be tough.

- Congress is responding to the crash by revamping its agenda for the securities industry. Our elected representatives are again saying that "program trading"—the never-ending stream of sell orders automatically fed into the New York Stock Exchange's computer—was responsible for the crash. They're talking about ways to curb it, along with a number of other "crash-prevention" laws. Next time, they should act *before* the savings of Americans are swept away!

- Some brokerage firms, already in trouble before the crash, are now on the brink of failure. One of the first casualties is E. F. Hutton. The firm has suffered from a terminal personality conflict between two men at the top. And it already ran into big trouble in 1985 when it had to plead guilty to 2,000 counts of mail and wire fraud. In addition, the firm had extended itself in other areas, paying the highest commission in the industry to salespeople, sponsoring lavish company trips to exotic locales, leasing swank offices. To say that Hutton is typical of Wall Street would be unfair; most firms have not gotten involved in speculative excesses to that degree. But to say that Hutton is the *only* firm to make grave mistakes would also be a gross misstatement. Still more trouble looms beyond the horizon.

The government was having enough difficulties dealing with the deficit before the crash. Now, huge capital losses have erased what would have been big capital gains taxes.

Monday, October 26. Dazed government and stock exchange officials are still trying to pick up the pieces. "This is 'The Week After,'" remarks one stock exchange official. He was referring to the TV docudrama, "The Day After," about the aftermath of a nuclear holocaust. "Never again should we be at the mercy of market forces such as those that struck the world last week."

The goal of stability is unanimous, but the way to achieve it is not. Some believe that the best solution is to shore up the inadequate capital of brokers. Others want more coordination among the stock exchanges worldwide to prevent the rippling of shock waves—from New York to Tokyo to Hong Kong to Sydney to London and back to New York. Still others say the main problem resides in the high-risk options and futures markets.

Each makes an important point, but no one recognizes that all of these weaknesses are tightly interwoven in the fabric of debt. Simply patching up certain flaws in the fabric will not prevent its unravelling over all!

November 16, 1987. After many years of cheerleading the boom, the editors of *Business Week* have temporarily joined those of us who are trying to shake Americans out of their dangerous lethargy:

"WAKE UP AMERICA" is their front cover headline this week. "The stock market may recover somewhat," they say, "but the message underlying the crash remains largely unheeded. We have spent too much, borrowed too much and imported too much. We have lived beyond our means, relying on foreigners to finance our massive budget and trade deficits. The bill is now coming due. America's standard of living is bound to suffer."

The numbers are clear to anyone who dares to look at them. In a few short years, America has squandered 75 years of capital accumulation abroad, swinging from the world's largest creditor nation to its biggest debtor! In 1983, our investments overseas exceeded foreign holdings in the United States by some $100 billion. Two years later, in a frightening turnabout, our tenants had become our landlords as foreign assets exceeded our holdings abroad by $112 billion. By the time the next president moves into the White House, this foreign capital deficit could exceed $500 billion. And by the time the panic finally reverses the trend, it could reach a whopping $1 trillion!

The Postcrash Interlude

Late December of 1987. The shock of the crash has been wearing off. *Business Week*, for example, is already back in the camp of the optimists with a new headline: "THE LONG-TERM CASE FOR STOCKS REMAINS STRONG." Meanwhile, the architects of the speculative boom, especially the raiders and speculators, have not learned their lesson. Yes, some were utterly crushed on Black Monday. But most are aiming their takeover guns at new targets. Rather than receding to the sidelines, big buyers like Carl Icahn, Asher Edelman and Paul Bilzerian are plunging into new areas.

Similarly, after the crash, you'd assume there would be a rapid demise of Wall Street's yuppie culture. Not yet! According to the *Wall Street Journal*, "far from demoralizing Wall Street's youth—or denting their bank accounts—the volatile stock market seems to have rekindled their enthusiasm. Many say they are exhilarated by the market's wild swings and claim that the current risks will only make them richer."

Early 1988. The bulls are rallying around high-spending consumers who, after the initial shock of the crash, started buying as if nothing had changed. They are finding allies among manufacturers who are revving up their expansion plans, aiming for a 9% increase in capital spending for the year. Everywhere, we see signs of optimism, yet everywhere there is evidence of trouble, ignorance and complacency, alongside the same blind euphoria that led to the crash.

It's shocking how few people are ready to accept the reality. It seems as if everyone prefers excuses and scapegoats. If we were psychoanalysts, we might say this behavior is typical, but as economic analysts, we strive to warn as many people as possible that, by deluding themselves about the gravity of the situation, they are merely making it worse, heading for an even more severe crisis.

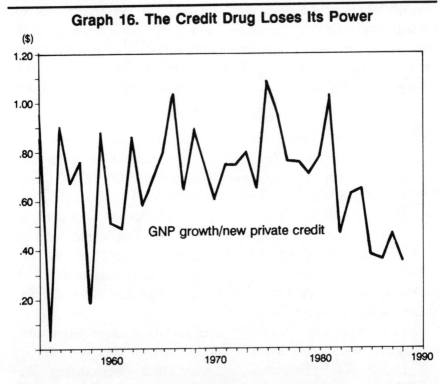

Graph 16. The Credit Drug Loses Its Power

GNP growth/new private credit

Banks and other lenders made loans and created credit. This was then supposed to generate more business activity and production. The question was: How much? This graph illustrates that, throughout the 1960s and most of the 1970s, each new dollar of private credit generated roughly one dollar of growth in goods and services (GNP). But in the 1980s, the power of credit fell sharply as a larger proportion went into speculation and other nonproductive areas. Data: Federal Reserve, Dept. of Commerce.

November 1988. Eight years ago, Ronald Reagan began his presidency when things looked their worst. So he got credit for the longest economic recovery in postwar history. His timing couldn't have been better. George Bush, however, will move into the White House at the very end of the Reagan boom. He will preside over what could be one of the longest economic declines in American history.

Throughout the boom, the authorities have been pumping in huge amounts of money which, in turn, prompted banks and other lenders to distribute even greater amounts of credit. Like a drug addict, the economy has come to need larger and larger injections of credit merely to sustain the previous pace of growth. But now they are cutting back the dosages. As a result, the economy is bound to suffer severe symptoms of withdrawal.

Graph 17. Surging Bankruptcies Despite "Good Times"

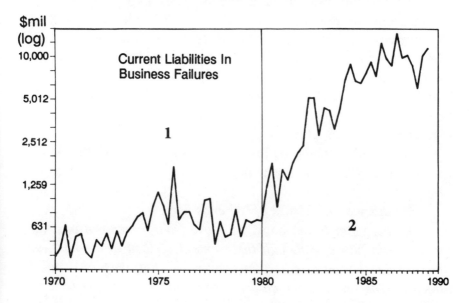

This shows the total amount of current liabilities involved in business failures each quarter, in millions of dollars. Throughout the 1970s, it rarely exceeded $1.5 billion. But in the mid-1980s it surged past $15 billion, or over ten times as much. Even if this had occurred during a recession, it would have been surprising. The fact that it took place during a long economic recovery was literally shocking. Data: Dun & Bradstreet.

Already, the new credit is losing its power to stimulate growth in the economy. Only a few years ago we saw a dollar in growth for every dollar of private credit. Now it's down to about 40 cents (see graph 16).

Another way of looking at it is this: During the 1960s and '70s, it took only one dollar and change to get one dollar of growth in the economy. Now it takes $2.25! Obviously, we're not getting our money's worth! Rather, we're getting the law of diminishing returns *par excellence*. Why? Where is all the credit going?

A big chunk of it is still going to nonproductive use—the takeover mania, the leveraged buyout craze, and the surge in stock buybacks—not to mention the speculative real estate deals which are now beginning to collapse in the Southwest and even the Northeast. This is not just a waste of money—it completely undermines the American economy!

Another big portion of the credit goes into companies that go bankrupt. In the previous business cycle (period 1 in graph 17), business failures rose when the economy was weak and fell when the economy recovered. But in the current cycle (period 2), they have gone up during the bad times and *they have continued to go up during the good times*. Now, as we enter another bad economic period, they are bound to surge once again. For several months—or even longer—the economy may hold up and the stock market could enjoy further strength. But the longer the day of reckoning is postponed, the more severe it will be.

My diary on the Crash of '87 ends here.

At this point in the book, we move from the known past into the unknown future. Although the events described in the next section are in the past tense, the reality is that they are strictly forecasts. The statistics which are associated with specific dates are factual. But those which appear with unspecific expressions (such as "during the panic") merely represent guesstimates.

As you read the chapters which follow, you will no doubt find some events which match closely with those you see happening around you in the months ahead, and some that do not. No one can predict the future with accuracy; the best we can do is to prepare ourselves and achieve safety.

Book III

THE FUTURE

22

The Worst Panic In History

The Money Panic was unlike any panic or crash in American history.

The panic of 1901 revolved around an attempted takeover of the Northern Pacific Railroad, and culminated in a battle between the Morgan-Hill and Harriman-Kuhn-Loeb groups for its control. The 1907 collapse, which later became known as the "rich man's panic," followed a speculative spurt in copper stocks and a boom in corporate mergers. The crash of 1920-21 resulted from the postwar accumulation of inventories. The great crash of 1929 collapsed the huge stock pyramid built by brokers, banks, utility tycoons and individual investors.

On the surface, the Money Panic was all of these wrapped up in one. In reality, however, it was *none* of these.

As in 1901, the Money Panic was provoked by powerful corporate groups who used massive debt to gain control over corporate giants through mergers and acquisitions.

Like the 1907 collapse, the Money Panic involved speculation in commodities. That time, it was primarily in copper and coffee. This time, it was in stocks, junk bonds, mortgages and a series of other financial instruments which had been transformed into "commodities" by the new futures markets.

As in 1921, the Money Panic caught business loaded with inventories and productive capacity. Back then, auto and tire makers, sugar producers and cotton farmers suffered most. This time, it surprised virtually every manufacturer and distributor in the industrialized world, plus farmers and cattle ranchers.

Most previous panics and crashes had been relatively isolated, limited to one geographic area, to one privileged class, to
a few powerful cliques, to the weakest sectors of the economy.
Previous panics were cushioned by relatively liquid or flexible
groups, who reduced the steepness, the speed and the depth of
the declines. The Morgan group limited the 1907 panic to New
York City. The DuPonts and powerful banking houses supported General Motors, Goodyear and others during the 1920-
21 crash. The giant manufacturers and the Federal Government
relied on the cash and gold reserves accumulated during the
roaring twenties to fight the Depression, win the Second World
War and build the military-industrial complex.

During the Money Panic, however, no single source of
support would emerge. Giant corporations and other powerful
economic groups periodically convinced the Administration to
bail out favored corporations and banks, but these schemes
tended to backfire and were ultimately abandoned. Once under
way, the Money Panic was both pervasive and relentless, always
returning with greater and greater power despite several
postponements, interludes of apparent calm and sharp stock
market rallies.

The debt crisis set into motion a unique vicious circle, a
chain of events no one could control. In simple terms, when the
economy fell, it caused a sudden and acute shortage of money ...
and this shortage caused the economy to fall that much more.

In previous panics, the stock market was the centerpiece
of the crash. In the Money Panic, the stock market merely sym-
bolized a broader, pervasive crash which occurred in three main
arenas: The U.S. bond markets, where the panic first began; the
foreign currency markets, which helped transmit the panic to
the four corners of the globe; and the real estate market, where
much of the wealth of Americans was tied up. In short, *the worst
aspects of past crises converged into one time and place.*

That's where most of the similarities ended. Because the
underlying problems were so much worse, the government and
the people tried that much harder to stop it from happening.
And because they intervened so frequently, the crisis, coming in
fits and starts, dragged on longer than it would have otherwise.
Meanwhile, during the long intervals of apparent "prosperity,"

Americans chose to enjoy life to its utmost, giving the impression that the crisis was less severe than that of the 1930s. However, those who endured the years since the panic know that, in the long run, it was actually far more severe, wearing down our energy, depleting our recovery powers.

Back then, it was believed that, since we had already endured one depression in the 1930s, we had more devices to combat the Money Panic. True; but what people didn't realize was that, in the final analysis, combating the crisis may not have been as desirable as it appeared. It merely deepened and prolonged the suffering.

Unlike previous panics, there were also less tangible, but no less powerful positive factors—modern communications, sophisticated nonviolent conflict resolution and international cooperation. To the surprise of some pessimists, most Americans had the fortitude to withstand the psychological pressures. After being bombarded by many shocking episodes for decades, they had been "future shocked" to a higher level of tolerance for rapid change. Unfortunately, there were also many exceptions.

23

Real Interest Rates

The money panic was caused by a collision between two of the most powerful economic forces of all time: *debt and deflation.*

For the average American, this meant lower earnings and higher mortgage and car payments.

For the Federal Government, meanwhile, this collision produced the balooning budget deficit which, despite a rapid succession of new budget laws and tax reforms, surged past the $300 billion mark.

The collision was the primary cause of the depression in smokestack America which continued despite a temporary export-led recovery in 1988.

It lay behind the collapse in commodity prices, the dollar, the bond market and, finally, the stock market and the economy.

Most important of all, the collision between debt and deflation was the key to understanding why the power of the government was so limited.

There is no mystery about the sequence of events which led to the panic. Inflation began to heat up temporarily due to an increase in the cost of imported goods and a rally in world oil prices. The Federal Reserve responded by tightening money and reducing the amount of credit available. Interest rates rose.

This, in turn, dried up the money which was feeding the merger boom, toppled the stock market and put a squeeze on business.

Finally, after years of all-out effort to avoid an economic decline, the inevitable recession got under way. But unlike any recession since the end of World War II, America was too over-burdened with debt to tolerate it. When corporate profits declined and unemployment rose, debts went unpaid, setting off a chain reaction of delinquencies, defaults and bankruptcies.

Did Uncle Sam try everything possible to cover up, postpone or offset the Money Panic? Yes. But the answer to the more critical question—did Uncle Sam *succeed* in those efforts?—is "No."

In fact, as you will soon see in the chapters which follow, it can be argued that the government unwittingly contributed to the *acceleration*—not the prevention—of the crisis which enveloped the nation. Their biggest mistake? Interest rates!

One of the most widely accepted textbook theories of the time held that interest rates move *up* during inflation and *down* during deflation. Government and private economists, business planners, banking executives—even those pesimists who anticipated some sort of economic crisis—generally accepted this theory. In the past, this theory *did* hold true. Inflation and high interest rates had been synonymous. In the 1950s, '60s and '70s, whenever inflation went up, interest rates followed along and vice versa.

However, starting in 1979—nearly a decade before the crash—something different began to take place. First, interest rates surged well above inflation. Then the inflation rate tumbled *but interest rates stayed high.* In other words, contrary to the theory, the difference between interest rates and inflation grew wider and wider. We call this difference the *real* interest rate because it represents the *true* cost of money.

If you were a saver in the 1980s, high real interest rates were good news. The net yield on your money, after subtracting inflation, stayed high even though there were temporary declines. However, to guarantee the value of your principal, and to make sure your funds were available, it was essential that you stashed it away in the safest possible place.

If you were a borrower, however, high real interest rates were bad news. It meant that the cost of money would be chronically high no matter what the government tried to do.

When business executives complained that the two were supposed to be linked together, the majority of economists explained it as a temporary abnormality. They promised that either interest rates would soon come down or inflation would go back up—one way or another, they would come back into synch.

They didn't! Instead, the real interest rates—the difference between interest rates and the inflation rate—emerged as the most critical force operating in the world economy.

The real interest rate is very easily calculated. Take for example, the 20-year T-bond rate (let's say it's 10%) and subtract the inflation rate (for example, 4%). The real interest rate is 10 minus 4, or 6%. If you repeat that calculation for each year and plot it over time, the result will be similar to that shown in Graphs 19 and 22.

Note how the real rate stayed nearly flat around 3% or 4% for the first 20 years of the postwar period. Economists considered this "the normal level," so when it shot upwards in 1979 and 1980, it was only natural for them to say it was "abnormal." Some blamed the Federal Reserve for easing money too aggressively. Others blamed them for tightening money too persistently. Still others said the trouble was that they *shifted back and forth* too frequently from easy money to tight money. All agreed it was an anomaly which would soon correct itself. Instead, real interest rates stayed high.

As we look back at the last two decades of the twentieth century, however, it is not hard to find the real causes: The surge in business failures and the huge federal deficits.

On page 215, the top graph correlates real interest rates with the business failure rate. Notice how the two were relatively steady until the early 1980s. Then see how they shot up in parallel from that time onward; as failures proliferated, all lenders had to charge more to cover their growing risks.

The bottom graph on page 215 shows a similar correlation between real interest rates and the budget deficit. The more Uncle Sam borrowed, the more he crowded out other borrowers; and the more competition for scarce funds, the more everyone had to pay for them—*over and above the inflation rate.*

Graphs 18 & 19. Real Interest Rates Surge

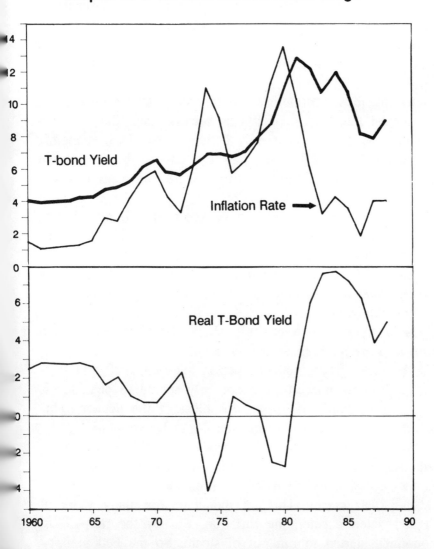

During the 1960s and '70s, interest rates tended to fluctuate around the ation rate, with only minor discrepancies between the two. But in the 1980s, ough the inflation rate fell sharply, interest rates remained relatively high. a result, there emerged a big gap between the two.

The real T-bond yield represents the difference between the two lines in top graph. It is the yield on Treasury bonds minus the average inflation rate each year. For example, at the peak in this graph (in 1984) the yield on asury bonds was close to 11% and the inflation rate was about 3%. The erence between the two—approximately 8%—was the real T-bond yield. s was dramatically higher than the previous decades. Data: Federal Reserve.

Thus, *real interest rates were high for real reasons*: Overspending and overborrowing by government, by corporations and by individuals, combined with a gross failure to save money that included every sector of the economy. In short, they were the direct result of the debt pyramid and the problem of illiquidity.

Why did most economists fail to recognize the importance of real interest rates? Perhaps it was because their time horizon was too narrow. They unabashedly believed that "U.S. economic history began in 1950." They had no interest in the period before World War II. If they had, they would have seen an entirely different picture. (See page 216.)

In this broader time perspective shown in Graph 22, you can see how real interest rates were high in the 1980s. But they were nowhere near as high as in the 1920s!

Thus, *there was no historical evidence to justify the idea that real interest rates had to come down. In fact, history indicated they could go much higher!*

What's more important, this chart shows that *high real interest rates were the prelude to depression!*

In the same graph, note the period between 1920 and 1929 (labeled "A"). Real interest rates not only soared to peak levels but they *stayed* near those peaks for most of the decade. That led to the stock market crash and the Great Depression!

Next, examine the postwar period (B). Real interest rates plunged below zero. In other words, the interest charged by lenders was actually less than the inflation rate.

Money was cheap! This set the stage for many years of growth and, later, accelerating inflation. But by the mid-1970s, the economicy started to run out of steam. So the Fed pumped in massive amounts of new money, forcing real interest rates below zero for the first time since the early 1950s (C). By the late 1970s, double-digit inflation resulted.

Then, in the 1980s, *real interest rates soared to the highest level since the '20s and they stayed at those peaks for several years (D).* The impact was devastating!

Graph 20 & 21. Why Real Interest Rates Were So High

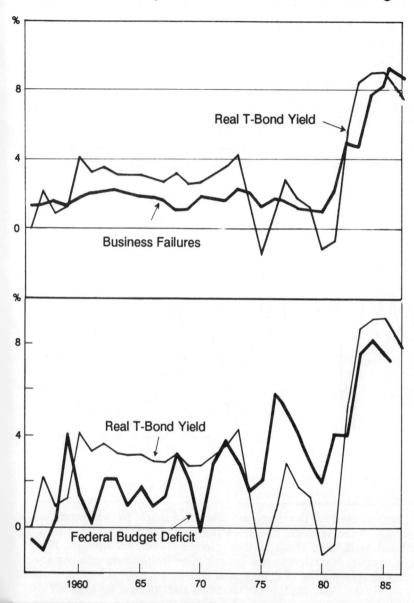

The majority of economists felt that real interest rates were abnormally high; and that they had to come down sooner or later. However, these graphs demonstrate that real interest rates were high for *real* reasons. The first correlates the real T-bond yield to business failures (as a % of GNP). The second shows the correlation between the real T-bond yield with the federal deficit (also as a % of GNP). The real T-bond yield is the nominal T-bond yield minus the inflation rate. Data: Federal Reserve, Dun & Bradstreet.

At times, the Fed forced real interest rates down temporarily and the immediate crisis was avoided. But to do so required such a Herculean effort that it revived the fear of inflation. This frightened investors in bonds and in the dollar to such an extent that interest rates bounced right back up in response. Money was chronically expensive! Debt crises erupted periodically. American families were constantly pinched, needing two incomes to make ends meet.

Graph 22. The Real T-Bond Yield Since 1900

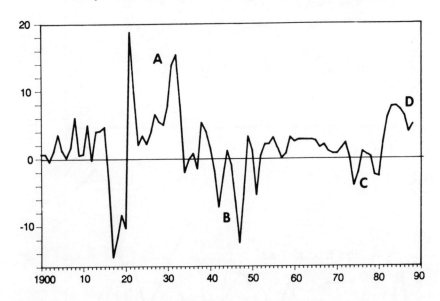

The numbers used for this graph are calculated simply by subtracting the yearly average of the inflation rate from the yearly average of the 20-year Treasury-bond yield. The result is then plotted from 1900 through 1988, providing a complete overview of real interest rates for the twentieth century. The most striking revelation of the graph is this: Although real interest rates were very high in the 1980s, the levels of the 1920s and '30s were far higher. This implies that, strictly in terms of historic precedent, there was no reason why a further upsurge could not occur during the 1990s. Data: Federal Reserve.

Thus high real interest rates *kept* the world on a consistent downward course, despite long interludes of prosperity. But soon, the roller-coaster ride—from crisis to euphoria and back to crisis again—would end in one final crash.

24

The Merger Bust

On a cold rainy morning, the second stock market crash began. The main cause was the unraveling of the 1980s merger boom.

It is in the nature of speculative orgies that every sector is swooped up into madness, as individuals and institutions also rushed in to lend support or to grab their share of the purported benefits. The big banks, the brokerage firms, insurance companies and the Federal Government itself all participated in the Great Merger Boom of the 1980s.

Likewise, when the merger boom fell apart, it followed that these participants were dragged down with it.

The second stock market crash was not quite as sudden or as steep as the first. But it was larger in scope and depth. Before it was over, the decline in the Dow would be greater than that of October 1987, impacting twice as many investors and inflicting much greater damage on the economy.

Large companies were now undergoing severe financial difficulties. Why were they in such sorry shape? Because of the merger boom and corporate America's heavy debt load, even the slightest economic downtick mushroomed into a convulsive contraction. The merger boom of the mid-1980s fed the longest economic recovery of the postwar era. Likewise, the *merger bust* during the Money Panic became one of the paramount causes of the sharpest economic decline since the Great Depression!

Isn't stepped-up merger activity a normal element in the business cycle? Yes, but the 1980s merger and takeover craze was unique in the history of corporate finance. It overshadowed all prior periods, both in the relative dollar amounts and the leverage used. In previous eras, it was unheard of for small firms to take over the giants. During the 1980s, it was a common occurrence. Previously, junk bonds were virtually nonexistent. Now they were everywhere.

After the Crash of 1987, corporations stepped in to buy their own shares, thereby giving the market some much-needed support. But when the market tumbled for a second time, a major source of buying power that had previously boosted stocks disappeared.

Rumors of major corporate bankruptcies swept the news wires. Selling pressure, which had been very mild throughout the postcrash rally, cascaded into an avalanche as investors stampeded the exits. Most frightening of all, unlike Black Monday, 1987, when bond prices rallied sharply, both bonds and stocks descended in leapfrog fashion.

The First Domino

The rumors were true. One of the greatest success stories of the mid-1980s merger boom was on the verge of default and one of its major financial backers on the brink of bankruptcy. Our fictional Consolidated Industries and Metrobank became the first victims of the merger bust. It didn't take a genius to figure out why: Like many illiquid companies in America, Consolidated had too many debts coming due. When the sales of its various subsidiaries declined, it could no longer afford to pay them.

Even before the second crash began, corporate raiders were beginning to discover that the legislative and regulatory environment for mergers was turning cold. Before 1988, states passed laws effectively blocking hostile takeovers. Dart Group's bid for Dayton Hudson, for instance, was derailed by a quickly passed antitakeover law.

The U.S. Congress actively considered several bills to abolish greenmail and make hostile takeovers difficult. And with a more active Securities and Exchange Commission, damaging information about raiders was becoming public. In 1987, Maxus Energy (formerly Diamond Shamrock) sued Kidder Peabody, Ivan Boesky and Martin Siegel for $300 million because of stock manipulation. Others filed similar actions.

Consolidated didn't realize that the party was over, that mergers and leveraged buyouts *needed* the stock market bubble to keep them going. Indeed, the rationale for many LBOs was to sell "undervalued assets" at higher market prices. This was the only way they could ever expect to repay the debt and build net worth in order to avoid bankruptcy. In a weak market and a poor economy, that door closed quickly.

And yet, even after the crash, Consolidated didn't want to give up. Most important, they failed to reconcile themselves to the reality that the junk bond market had been decimated. When the stock market crashed again, bids for many bond issues vanished. The overnight success story was now an overnight disaster, saddled with huge supplies of unsold bonds.

The S&Ls and mutual funds wanted out but were locked in. Not only were fewer investors willing to accept the higher risk, but many previous buyers became sellers. For example, in 1977, Southland's inability to get $1.5 billion from junk bonds left two major Wall Street firms and five commercial banks stuck with an unwanted bridge loan for $2.7 billion. Now, many other examples abounded.

The decision makers at Consolidated, however, were slow to act—always fighting the last war. As they plunged ahead with irrational optimism, their junk bond holders suffered severe losses. Metrobank, as well as several brokerage houses that provided the bridge financing, took big hits. Suppliers who gave them trade credit were being drawn into the melee. Everyone was demanding their money.

Financial newspapers throughout the country reported the failure of Consolidated's "Octopus Strategy," which was designed to raise cash from a range of financial media, but wound up concentrated in dangerous short-term instruments. They reported the fiasco of the "Project Explosion," in which earnings gains from efficiencies of scale were eradicated by huge interest costs. The press, however, did not mention another factor: The Trust Departments of Consolidated's banks were dumping their long-term bonds to raise cash.

One day, two New York bank officers, comparing notes over lunch, made an interesting discovery.

"We finally scratched up some money to participate in the rescue of Consolidated Industries. I don't think they'll get as much as they want, but at least it'll tide them over until this great fog overhanging the junk bond market clears up."

"Consolidated, did you say?"

"Sure, what's wrong with them? They've got a pretty good rating."

"I don't believe this. You just made a loan to Consolidated so that they can take more time with their new bond issue?"

"Sure! Why not? Do you have something on this company?"

"No, that's not it. Only that this morning I did some liquidating of my own and cleaned out 25 percent of our portfolio including, believe it or not, $20 million in long-term bonds and $30 million in ninety-day commercial paper issued by Consolidated."

The Money Panic was accelerating.

Near the end of the merger boom, four big firms—Unysis, Zenith Electronics, Burlington Northern and Conagra—were among the least liquid of the large corporations in the nation. If cash inflows suddenly faded, their resources would be wiped out in a matter of days.

In the 1970 money squeeze, it was Chrysler that had gone through this kind of a crisis—a surprise to most analysts because they had forgotten to consider the debts of the affiliate company, Chrysler Financial. This time the analysts made the same mistake. They paid little attention to the *de facto* collapse of large manufacturers—and even less attention to the plight of the captive finance companies.

Returning to the fictional Consolidated, in the first phase of the panic, it was already on the brink of bankruptcy. The finance subsidiary had over $3 billion in commercial paper (short-term corporate IOUs) and bank loans. To stay afloat, it ran on a treadmill, paying its creditors $50 million a day—over $2 million per hour! Meanwhile, the parent corporation struggled under the dual burdens of a slow junk bond market and growing rumors of default.

The bankruptcy tripwire tightened, awaiting only the slightest tremor. Commercial paper owners—mostly cash-starved corporations themselves—decided not to renew. The standby credit at the banks, which was supposed to back up this commercial paper, could not be implemented. Attempts to borrow money from employees' pension funds were blocked by the unions. Layoffs were ordered, but there were no immediate savings because of the severance-pay provisions in the new labor contracts. When Consolidated's financial vice-president raced across the Atlantic on the Concorde to raise money in the Eurodollar market, the rumors arrived before him and he returned empty-handed. An emergency meeting called between a group of bankers and Congresspeople, which was expected to result in a Chrysler-type rescue proposal, resulted instead in a cul-de-sac.

Consolidated had no choice. The lawyers were called in and the books were spread out on the boardroom table. A brief discussion followed, after which the lawyers simply snapped their briefcases shut and took a last limousine ride—to the bankruptcy courts.

Harry Pinkerton, the stocky, balding Chairman of the firm, disappeared from Wall Street and has not been heard from since. But his counterpart at Metrobank, Robert Sheppard, suddenly turned over a new leaf. After years of cover-ups and pretense, and after a personal life crisis, he resolved to clean house. He moved swiftly to increase the bank's provisions for loan losses. He sold off a large chunk of the bank's riskier securities. He closed branches and laid off employees.

But it was too little too late. His staff who had known only his other side for so many years could not accept the sudden change in personality. Stockholders rose up in rebellion. He had no choice but to resign from the bank. Later, Sheppard would join a small group of country bankers and emerge as one of the nation's leading advocates of sound banking practices.

Meanwhile, the commercial paper market died. "If Consolidated could go under," reasoned the commercial paper buyers, "what about GMAC? Sears Acceptance? Citicorp? Ford Motor Credit?" Nearly all issuers, whether solvent or insolvent, came under suspicion.

The stock market, which had managed to stage a sharp rally, suddenly dropped another three hundred points within four days of trading. All stocks were hit with big selling pressure—the high-tech, the energy stocks, the bluechips, the gold stocks—whether interest sensitive or noninterest sensitive. There were no exceptions.

This is also when the brokerage firms suffered their most acute crisis of that era. One of the primary sources of their difficulties, in addition to the junk bond fiasco, was mortgage-backed securities.

Investment bankers and brokers had packaged hundreds of billions of dollars worth, selling much of them back to the S&Ls where they got the mortgages in the first place. *I estimate the total outstanding was approaching $800 billion.*

As the crisis deepened, and as the FSLIC and Congress were hard pressed to bail the S&Ls out, *these securities were dumped back on the market—and into the laps of the brokers.* This would have been no great trauma if their positions in these securities had been minor. The problem was that they owned over $210 billion of them! For the brokerage firms, it brought big losses. And investors who owned mortgage-backed securities found the exit doors slamming shut.

On the network news, one analyst put it this way: "High interest rates and high inflation we could stand. And, in retrospect, the market did quite well considering that the prime rate was so high. Then deflation was also tolerable because of the good news on the interest rate front. In fact, by looking cross-eyed at the deflation, we could actually see it in a very positive light and got a great bull market going. But when high interest rates, deflation and recession hit all at roughly the same time, it was just too much to handle. We suddenly woke up to the fact that we had been looking at a mirage."

Stockholders were dumping their shares of the bankrupt retailers and oil companies. The retailers, in turn, were dumping their stocks of clothing, appliances and assorted consumer articles. This prompted manufacturers to unload inventories of steel, chemicals, textiles and other raw materials, while the oil companies dumped crude oil. As a result, grain and metal prices tumbled on the commodity exchanges, dragging down the price of most industrial and agricultural commodities. Soon nearly all corporations joined the selling rush to gain liquidity and to seek protection against further money-market shock waves.

In the earlier stages, most economists and businesspeople anticipated an "L"-shaped recession, a leveling off in the economy following the initial steep decline. The main reason for their relatively optimistic outlook was the assumption that this kind of inventory panic could not occur.

"We learned our lesson the last time around," they declared. "Since we've been anticipating the business decline, we've kept our inventories trimmed to the bone."

Superficially, they were right. But it soon became obvious that businesspeople and economists were making four cardinal mistakes.

First, they underestimated the extent to which sales had been artificially boosted by credit card and installment buying— and the speed at which they would sink when credit became scarce. The auto industry was a frightening example. For months, Detroit executives had proceeded as if everything was under control. But when the shortage of credit hit the auto business, they ran to Washington to ask for easy money and protection against foreign imports.

Second, economists and managers made the mistake of using the inventory levels of the 1970s—an era of accelerating inflation—as the norm. The trouble is that what might have been considered normal during the years when prices were rising was dangerously high when prices were soft.

Third, they underestimated the fragility of the financial underpinnings that supported the inventories and receivables of America. In 1988, U.S. manufacturers had $1.19 in current debt for every dollar of inventories and receivables as opposed to 54 cents in 1960. Among giant manufacturers (with $1 billion or more in assets), the situation was even worse. As soon as it became too expensive to finance their inventories, the pressures mounted to reduce them. And as soon as major corporations began to feel the effects of the Money Panic, the sole choice left them was to resort to mass dumping at cut-rate prices.

Fourth, businesspeople and economists—almost without exception—ignored what later came to be known as "regurgitated inventories." Marketing experts of that era tended to assume that if a consumer item was taken into the sanctuary of the household, it was absorbed and, in essence, gone forever. They forgot that consumers, in a financial pinch, could readily become net sellers of durables; that these new sellers could find a ready marketplace for their wares; and that this market was one of the most elaborate networks of secondhand dealerships, flea markets and garage sales in the world.

It was at this stage that one of the most unusual economic events of the century occurred. There was an upsurge in inventories. Simultaneously, there was a decline in revenues sharply *below* the outflows needed for meeting debts coming due. The result was a sudden *cash* shortage—what some economists called *illiquid demand for money*. What made this demand for money so unique was that it took place while the economy was contracting—not while it was expanding.

When this demand could not be met, the alternative solution was bankruptcy or, as many prayed, a government bailout. Reports surfaced that Zenith Electronics was in grave financial difficulty. General Dynamics, Kraft, General Mills and Wendy's were said to be "on the brink." Xerox, Avon and Goodyear Tire were rumored to "have only a few weeks left." Zayre, May Department Stores, Whirlpool and McDonalds joined the reports as "one step away." The casualty list grew daily.

Why were these particular firms hit the hardest? Because they were among the most cash poor and the most debt-ridden of all the large firms in America.

Nevertheless, most investment bankers, executives and economists still hung onto the belief that, when presented with the magnitude of the crisis, the White House, Congress and the Federal Reserve would come up with a bailout plan. They believed that the government "had the power," that "where there was a will, there was a way." They also felt that it was their moral responsibility and patriotic duty to send a delegation of influential leaders to meet with the President and convince him to do something—anything! If the government did *not* take immediate action, they believed the economy would be plunged into a morass from which it might never emerge.

25

The Big Bailout

The financial and business leaders urgently meet with the President and his economic advisers. A previously scheduled meeting with the Secretary of the Treasury and the Chairman of the Federal Reserve is expanded to include the heads of several major corporations, top farm and labor leaders, plus an expert on the bond markets—John Hartman.

Treasury Secretary: Gentlemen, we have come to a crossroads. We're in a business slump, maybe more than a slump, and many of you are feeling the pinch. I want you all to understand that the Administration is well aware of that. You want the recession ended. We understand that also. But there is one question we must answer first: Can we afford to give up the battle against inflation?

[The Treasury Secretary glances at Hartman but he receives a blank stare in return. So he continues.]

I am convinced that this is not the right time, that it would be premature and rash. We have made substantial progress against inflation. But much of that progress could be threatened by a collapsing dollar. I am convinced that if we let the dollar collapse one more time, imported goods will soar in cost and, sooner or later, inflation will spiral out of control. If the reason you are here today is to ask for more money—which, by the way, would really mean more inflation—well, I'm sorry to say, we simply can't take that chance.

[The labor leaders murmur protests and shake their heads. More money is precisely what they have come to ask for. Some feel like leaving right then and there.]

Labor: I'm confused. In the past, I've always associated inflation with a growing economy and recession with a falling economy. Now you're telling me that we have the threat of both at the same time? How can that be? How can we have both? Besides, with oil prices tumbling again, why are you scared of inflation?

Fed Chairman: I'll tell you why. Each dollar decline has been worse than the previous one. First the late 1970s; then the mid-1980s. The next one—if we give in to your desires—*simply won't be survivable!* It will destroy the bond markets!

[Although Labor remains adamant, the business leaders are conciliatory.]

AT&T: We don't want a big boom. All we want is to prevent a big bust.

Ford: Exactly! We don't expect you to dish out money to anyone and everyone; we don't need a shotgun approach. What we need here is a sharpshooter strategy that brings relief to key areas and industries.

Metrobank: I suppose you're talking about automobiles.

Ford: Of course, I'm talking about automobiles.

Metrobank: And you're talking against foreign imports, I presume.

Ford: Absolutely! But that's not all. Our big competition isn't only from abroad anymore. It's also right here at home— the used car market! Let me give you some background. First, our primary objective was to shift production from the large, low-mileage autos to the fuel-efficient small cars. Then, when energy costs came down again, we shifted back to larger cars, vans and sports cars. But today, looking back, we see that all the shifting didn't really help prepare us for the current situation. It's a whole new ball game, the most uncanny combination of circumstances I've every seen—rising unemployment plus scarce credit at the same time! In fact, the two problems seem to be actually feeding on each other.

Fed Chairman: I don't quite understand what you mean. Our latest figures show there will be a recovery shortly and, in the worst scenario, a W-shaped pattern.

Adviser: I think it will be L-shaped.

AT&T: More likely V-shaped!

Ford: No matter what the shape, our business has been dropping fast. The last thirty days seem like thirty months, so your latest figures are way behind. Consumers have again suddenly vanished from the scene as though in some kind of silent rebellion. I'm telling you, this isn't your run-of-the-mill, inflation-recession crossroads.

Treasury Secretary: What is it then?

Ford: It's a tunnel straight to hell, that's what it is. We don't have the luxury of time. Either Congress and the Fed go out there tomorrow and initiate strong action—immediate action—or we're headed for a first-class depression.

Treasury Secretary: What do you gentlemen have in mind? More government spending? More money pumping by the Fed? More protection against foreign competition?

Labor: Yes! The answer is three times yes! You think Detroit is the only one? We have come here today to submit a four-prong proposal for the financial reconstruction of this country. But first, I would humbly suggest that each man here review the facts further so that we can have a broader grasp of the full dimensions of the problem we're up against.

[Each of the men nods].

Metrobank: You must do something immediately to stop the withdrawals from the banks. The thrifts are already losing savings hand over fist. The insurance companies are losing savings hand over fist. We ourselves are having difficulty renewing our CDs and commercial paper. If you don't restore confidence—and quickly—it won't be just housing and autos; every industry in the country will be trapped.

Fed Chairman: We've tried to pump in money before, but that merely prompted investors to dump their bonds because they feared inflation. We can't create confidence with more money. You're worried about money flowing out of the banks. We're worried about money leaving the country altogether, causing the dollar to collapse.

[The farm representatives who have, until this time, let the labor leaders take up the cause, now decide to speak for themselves.]

Farm Lobby: Throughout this discussion—and for many years—we have kept our peace. We have heard all the theoretical and academic arguments about inflation versus deflation, about high interest rates versus high unemployment. But nothing has been said about the real-life calamity now facing the farmers. You mention the dollar—protecting the dollar—as if it were some sort of an abstraction. You say it will collapse. But what about us? We have *already* collapsed! Every time we're told we've hit bottom, that the turn is around the corner, we're dealt a heavier blow. First it was the stranglehold of interest rates. Then came the fall in commodity prices, the repossessions and the fire-sales by the farm credit banks. As if that weren't enough, we got hit with the drought that destroyed our crops and forced us to slaughter our livestock, but didn't boost prices as much as we had hoped. And throughout all this, you have carried out the most insipid campaign of all—to destroy us via cutbacks in farm support programs. Now, here we are once again, and all we get is the same old light-at-the-end-of-the-tunnel routine.

We have talked to the most prestigious think tanks in the country—Morgan, Chase, Data Resources—whatever. You know what they told us? They told us that farm prices were going back up, that commodities were undervalued, that they couldn't get any lower. The analysts brought out all their charts on the business cycle, on the dollar and from their massive computer models. They were so convincing, we always wound up shaking their hands in gratitude, going home and waiting in vain for the turnaround which never came. Sure, there were a few big rallies, but those didn't last.

Today, many of us are looking back on those incidents and beginning to wonder whether there was a conspiracy to revive the economy on the backs of the American farmers!

Gentlemen, please excuse my bluntness, but your fears of a dollar collapse are just so much barnyard manure to farmers. All along you've told us that a cheaper dollar is precisely what *we* need to get us back into the world grain markets, to give farm prices a lift, to prevent a depression. Now we have the cheaper dollar. But what good has it done? Farm prices are still falling!

Treasury Secretary: Wait! You know full well why we're afraid of another dollar collapse. Because without the strong dollar, without all this money pouring in from overseas, you'd never have enough money to finance the deficit.

Farm Lobby: So what? Now you're getting the panic anyhow! All you did was postpone the inevitable!

Sears: The government is concerned with its cash flow—from abroad to finance the deficit. Farmers are concerned with their cash flow. Ford talks about cash flow. Well, what about the cash flow of the retailers? Ford Financial or GMAC can repossess cars if a consumer defaults on his auto loan. But what do we do when our customers can't pay their Sears charge accounts? Can we take back Sears jeans, Sears screwdrivers, or Sears gourmet foods? Obviously not!

[The Treasury Secretary has anticipated that cash shortages might turn out to be one of the focal points of the discussion. For this reason he has invited representatives of IBM and Exxon to the meeting. He has not yet worked out in his own mind the exact mechanics of his plan, but he feels confident that, with the help of cash-rich companies, he may be able to put together some sort of package. When he asks these firms about their "cash hoard," however, he is visibly shaken.]

IBM: What cash hoard? You must be thinking about the mid-Seventies. In 1976 we had over $200 million in bank deposits and almost $6 billion in marketable securities. For every dollar of short-term debts, we had $1.51 of cash and equivalent. But not today!

Treasury Secretary: No, I was referring to your latest balance sheet which shows 45 cents in cash per dollar of current debts.

IBM: A lot has happened since then. We're down to 30 cents!

Treasury Secretary: I don't understand.

IBM: We had to expand into new products. We were afraid we were going to miss the boat in the microcomputer field. We almost did too, until we began pouring solid cash into it. Then came the big worldwide shift from outright purchases of machines to the rental of machines, requiring over $4 billion in cash in 1979 alone. Most recently, our earnings have been hit by the latest war in computer standards—the fiercest competition ever from Hewlett Packard, Compaq, Japan, Taiwan and Korea.

Treasury Secretary: Certainly the oil companies are liquid!

Exxon: The oil companies are liquid all right—liquid in oil. We've got 360 days of oil stockpiled. Almost a full year's supply!

Treasury Secretary: Three hundred and sixty days? Are you serious?

Exxon: You bet your life I'm serious. We knew the big oil glut was not going away. But we figured that demand for petroleum products in the United States would continue to grow no matter what. We were wrong. Demand for gasoline has nosedived. We've gone through various stages in this thing. At first we hoped that OPEC, in coordination with non-OPEC producers, such as Britain, Norway and Mexico, could hold the line. But what we're discovering is that the impetus for price changes is not coming only from the Mideast. It's coming from the declining demand of consumers worldwide.

We've got only ten cents in cash for every dollar of short-term debts. This is less than half of what we had towards the end of 1987 and one-quarter of our cash position ten years ago! Where is all the cash? Probably at the banks!

Metrobank: Not on your life! At this late date, if nothing is done to stop the panic withdrawals, *we will run out of cash in less than a week*. Today's Tuesday. By next Monday we'll have to get an emergency infusion or else ...

[There is a long fifteen seconds of silence.]

Fed Chairman: Gentlemen, I'm not convinced. Don't you see what we're doing? We're falling into the same old pattern. Your predecessors pleaded to government in 1966, and President Johnson gave in. They were here in 1970, and Nixon did the same. They came in 1975, and it was the Ford Administration that bailed them out. Then, of course, came the so-called "Great Chrysler Rescue," the Reagan years and the big binges of the mid-1980s.

Each visit was always a little gloomier than before and always a bit more convincing. Each time we believed it, and we pumped more and more. More government spending. More easy credit. In the past five years alone we've helped create nearly $5 trillion in new credit—twice as much as the total amount of all common and preferred stocks in America just a few years ago. Then, lo and behold, came the dollar collapse, followed by the stock market crash, and you all said we had to do something to stop it. Now you're saying you want still more. How many times do you want us to ride this same seesaw?

You're saying that if we don't make emergency money available, you'll go bankrupt. But how much more credit do you think the country needs *this time*? Six trillion? Ten trillion? You thought the last round of runaway inflation was painful, ate away your profits, eroded the economy. Well, what do you think will happen if we create hyperinflation? What do you think might happen to American society? To world trade?

Metrobank: We all know the answer to that. Hyperinflation would destroy the entire banking system, wipe out the value of all our assets—corporate loans, home mortgages, investments, the works. But let's forget the "what-could-happen-if" arguments and examine the current situation. If nothing is done to remedy this crisis immediately, we won't have to wait around for some hypothetical inflation down the road. The banks will be wiped out right here and now. If you don't flood the banking system with emergency money today, you'll see a banking collapse the likes of which you've never seen!

President: Can't we steer a middle course?

Fed Chairman: Mr. President, we *have* been steering a middle course. These gentlemen see some temporary dislocations in the money flows, some prices falling, and they therefore believe that the Fed has been following a tight-money policy. The fact is we've been letting the money supply grow at a steady pace. We've been sticking to our targets.

Ford: Then why are real interest rates so damn high? Why is money so damn scarce?

Metrobank: It's the big utilities and the auto manufacturers. They're still trying to use the money markets to make up for lost revenues.

AT&T: I think it's the Treasury Department. They're the ones who have been grabbing all the available money from the bond market, and crowding us out.

Exxon: I can't figure out why the banks aren't dropping the prime rate.

Metrobank: Drop the prime rate? Are you nuts? We're running out of reserves. How can we drop the prime rate?

Exxon: Because prices are falling.

Metrobank: What the hell does that have to do with it?

Exxon: Everything!

Metrobank: In some college textbook, maybe. But in real life, money is in short supply. So the price of money—interest rates—should go up, not down.

Fed Chairman: Please, gentlemen, let me finish. The latest figures haven't been released yet, but I can assure you that our Open Market Committee has been more active in buying government bonds than in any week since I have been on the board.

Ford: So that's why the money supply jumped last week.

Metrobank: Come on now. Who cares about the money supply any more?

President: What do we do about the banks?

Fed Chairman: Actually, as I see it, the problem isn't only a matter of providing liquidity. We've been doing that already and it's still not enough. What they really need is an infusion of capital! I can visualize extending the Chrysler Rescue Act of 1980 to include the entire banking industry. I see problems, big problems. But I'm beginning to—

[John Hartman, the Wall Street bond expert, who has brooded silently with increasing unease, breaks into the conversation.]

Hartman: Gentlemen! You're forgetting the problems that first brought you here today, the problems that crush every argument raised so far: The bond markets!

We have two choices. Number one: We save the banks but destroy the bond markets. Number two: We save the bond markets but destroy the banks.

President: Why's that?

Hartman: Let's start with the first choice: We forget about the bond markets for a moment and we do our utmost to help the banks by pumping in unlimited amounts of new money to shore up their liquidity, even their capital. What happens? Confidence in the banking system is temporarily restored but the fear of inflation, maybe even hyperinflation, is revived. Bond investors recoil and the bond market mechanism—already severely weakened—disintegrates. This then forces interest rates to skyrocket and eventually shuts down the economy.

Now let's say we opt for choice number two. We let the banks fend for themselves and try to restore confidence in the financial markets. Unlike previous years, we can't support the market by simply buying bonds for the Fed's account. To convince bond owners that we're fighting inflation, we have to help push the economy into a recession. Needless to say, deepening the recession dooms the banks.

President: Why can't we do both? Why can't we save the banks *and* restore the bond markets at the same time?

Fed Chairman: Impossible, sir. To revive the banks, we'd need to pour money *into* the system. To revive bond markets, we'd need to pull money *out* of the system. Obviously, we can't put money in and take it out at the same time!

Metrobank: No wonder you've been seesawing back and forth between easy money and tight money!

President: I've had enough of this damned-if-we-do-damned-if-we-don't talk. What do you suggest we do?

Hartman: Nothing.

President: You mean you don't know?

Hartman: No sir, I know exactly what we should do in this situation: Nothing! Stand pat! Look at the experience of past Administrations. Every aggressive action produced an unexpected market reaction. And every action-reaction cycle has come with shorter and shorter intervals: Nixon's wage-and-price freeze led to runaway inflation and the Arab oil embargo. President Ford's budget deficits and easy-money policy were a prelude to the first dollar collapse. Carter's bond market rescue package of 1980 resulted in a near depression. The 1984-86 money-pumping binge produced still another dollar collapse and the stock market crash.

Now, regardless of the consequences, you have only one choice, and that is to keep your hands off—not because of some invisible force that will magically fix everything, but because, at this particular juncture, *the no-action choice is the most logical one a real leader can make.*

President: Do you want a do-nothing President?

Hartman: No. Temporarily at least, what we need is a neutral government. Let the market make the decisions. We have no other choice.

President: You're proposing that we allow the markets to take the bull by the horns and determine not only what the Fed and the White House do, but also what we think and what we say! I can't allow that to happen.

Hartman: But you already have! We've *already* lost control over the markets. The more we say and do, the worse it gets.

President: You mean they're telling us to shut up?

Hartman: Well, sir ... if you want to put it in those terms ... I'd say yes. Every time the White House chastises the Fed, the markets interpret that to mean you're planning to ride herd on the printing press operators and feed the fires of inflation, which in turn alarms the bond markets. Every time you've come out with this or that comment *in support* of the Fed, it's interpreted to mean you're going to get tough and the markets take still *another* nosedive.

Labor: We need action *now.* Millions of people's jobs hang in the balance. How can you just sit back and watch the show?

Hartman: Don't you see? This is not your typical inflation-deflation dilemma. Let me sum up the choices: Take the tight-money approach, and there won't be enough cash to keep companies going. Take the easy-money approach, and you'll kill the dollar, sabotaging the bond market.

AT&T: Sure, and if you follow a do-nothing policy, you know what happens? The debts still come due. With every tick of the clock, more debts come due. What do you propose to do next Monday when it's Metrobank's turn to bite the dust? Nothing?

Hartman: I seriously believe, gentlemen, that we have to let the marketplace make those decisions.

Sears: But there's no cash out there.

White House Adviser: What about the institutions?

Sears: I'm talking about the corporations, the banks, the cities and the states. That's what counts. Most important, the Federal Government. How is the Treasury going to raise the cash to rescue everyone else if it can't even get enough for itself?

Treasury Secretary: The government has to save itself first.

Metrobank: We have a plan.

President: Yes? Tell me about it!

Metrobank: In March 1980, the solution to the bond market collapse was to put into effect the credit-controls provision from the amended Federal Reserve Act of 1969. That failed but we can learn from our mistakes. Now I suggest we use the remonetization provision of the Deregulatory Banking Act of 1980.

President: Please explain.

Metrobank: The Federal Reserve has the authority to take over the debts of companies in trouble, of banks in trouble, even the debts of farms and foreign nations. The government has the power to *create cash*. The time has now come to use that power. Here's our plan:

First, erect selective trade barriers to stop any further damage from abroad.

Second, put into effect a wage-and-price freeze.

Third, as a temporary emergency measure, the Federal Reserve eliminates bank reserve requirements, freeing up large sums of liquid funds to revive the banking system.

Fourth, following the model of the rescue of Continental Illinois Bank in 1984, the Fed steps in to prop up the finances of Metrobank. The Federal Reserve goes into the open market and buys our debentures, our bonds. You can do the same for Ford or Exxon or any other company that's vital to the economy, to national security.

Hartman: You can't do that. For every dollar you loan to Metrobank, you have to borrow another dollar from the public. It just won't work. The bond markets won't stand for it!

Labor: Mr. President, do you save millions of jobs, thousands of businesses, hundreds of banks and the economy? Or do you protect the bond markets? The choice is yours.

The President knew it was a risky venture. The Federal Reserve Chairman and the Treasury Secretary harbored even greater fears. But in the minds of these leaders, it was even more risky to sit back and watch the American economy fail. Furthermore, a new law passed in 1987, mandated that they do everything necessary to guarantee America's bank deposits. They debated the pros and cons. The Wall Street economist insisted that the main reason for the current predicament was because no anti-inflation policy was ever followed to its conclusion, because every plan to solve the debt dilemma was abandoned prematurely. But they managed to override his objections. And they decided it was now time to pursue a rescue operation.

During the week that followed, although they rejected most of the proposal, intense pressures were brought upon the Treasury Department to funnel cash into the FDIC and FSLIC—the federal insurance agencies which guaranteed the deposits of banks and thrifts. Meanwhile, the Fed was pressured to make a symbolic gesture to reassure the failing private debt markets. Finally, it was rumored that a modest amount of Metrobank debentures would be bought directly by the Fed. In exchange, Metrobank was expected to lower its prime rate. The first reaction came from the bond market.

26

Why The Rescue Plan Failed

The cut in the prime rate was a joke. What good was it if the banks reduced their rate but had no money to lend? The idea of a wage-and-price freeze was also out of touch with reality. What people wanted was a wage-and-price *floor* to stop markets from falling.

Nevertheless, rumors that the Federal Reserve was planning to buy Metrobank paper and talk on the street that it would follow up with purchases of bonds of other firms—even junk bonds—triggered one of the sharpest rallies in the history of corporate bonds which, in turn, spilled over into the stock market.

One junk bond issue selling at 72 leaped in only a few hours to 79. Another jumped twelve points and settled down to a net increase of ten points. Utility bonds, municipal bonds and even foreign bonds leapfrogged each other.

Within hours, however, trading came to a standstill. If you called your broker, he gave you an "indication" of the market price, way up in the stratosphere. But it was a fiction—there were no buyers. This was the first sign of trouble. The next sign of trouble came in the government bond market. Prices went up, but not half as much as previously. Here's what came out on the news wires at the end of the week:

> THE DEEPLY DISCOUNTED MEDIUM-GRADE CORPORATES AND LOW-GRADE CORPORATES HAVE RALLIED SHARPLY THIS WEEK, BUT DEALERS AND TRADERS ARE WATCHING QUALITY

SPREADS CAREFULLY FOR SOME INDICATION OF THE REAL IM-
PACT OF THE RECENT FEDERAL RESERVE PLAN TO PURCHASE
CORPORATE SECURITIES IN THE HOPE OF BRINGING SOME
MUCH NEEDED SUPPORT TO THE HIGH-YIELD MARKETS WHICH,
IN RECENT WEEKS, HAD FLOUNDERED TO NEAR COLLAPSE AS A
RESULT OF THE RAPID LOSS OF CONFIDENCE IN THOSE COM-
PANIES IN THE PROCESS OF GOING OUT OF BUSINESS.

Bond traders who read this run-on sentence said it left them blank. Most, tired of the constant flow of "gibberish," did not bother to read it. Three days later the Federal Reserve Chairman called the President on the phone. "It's no good. The benefit of our plan to the corporate bond market is a drop in the ocean. On the other hand, to the government bond market, it's a potential hydrogen bomb. The quality spreads are narrowing—and in the wrong direction."

The President was not familiar with the meaning of quality spreads. "What are the causes and what are the consequences of changes in quality spreads?" he asked.

"I am referring to the difference in yield between a Treasury bond and a corporate bond. A big corporation always has to pay more than the U.S. Treasury to borrow money. Usually the difference is about 75 to 100 basis points (100 basis points = 1%). Then, several weeks ago, when the threat of bankruptcy was first apparent, the yield on corporate bonds went up by 2 1/4%, but the yield on the governments went up only 1/4%. In other words, the spread increased by 2%, or 200 basis points. Confidence in all corporations—no matter how creditworthy—declined sharply. But that was *before* our rescue package was announced."

"And now?"

"Now the opposite is happening. Top-grade corporate bond yields are back down sharply, but government bond yields are actually up. The spread between them has narrowed to practically nothing—a very bad sign." The Federal Reserve Chairman felt satisfied that he had put forth a very clear and straightforward explanation.

"Well, isn't that what we had said we wanted—to bring corporate bonds back up toward the level of government bonds?"

The Chairman tried to hold his voice steady so that his frustration with the President's lack of knowledge of debt markets would not carry over the phone. In the past he had tried several times to explain to the President how yields and prices moving in opposite directions always meant the same thing, but that spreads, although moving in the same direction, could mean a variety of different things. How does one make such things simple for a President to understand without sounding condescending? The Federal Reserve Chairman certainly didn't know how. He spent the next half hour going over the events in the marketplace until finally, after considerable effort, the President developed in his own mind an image of bond prices that resembled that of Graph 23.

"I see," the President said. "We wanted to bring the corporate bonds up to the level of the government bonds. What's happening is precisely the opposite. The 'governments,' as you call them, are falling down to the level of the 'corporates.' In short, we are not lifting them up; they are dragging us down. The question is: Why? Don't they believe our promise, our pledge? Why haven't we restored confidence? At the meeting it was said that we can create cash, that the law gives us the authority to funnel this cash wherever we please."

"The answer is we can create cash. But we cannot create credit."

"What's the difference?" the President queried.

"There's a very big difference. To create more cash, all we have to do is speed up the printing presses at the mint. And when we distribute it, no one is going to turn us down. But to create credit, we have to convince investors and bankers to make loans to each other—and in this environment of falling confidence, I can assure you that isn't easy."

The President was getting impatient. "So what's the point?"

"The point is that you can create cash; you can't create confidence."

"It would seem to me that the more money we give out the more confidence they'd have."

"No, no! It's exactly the opposite. The more paper money we create, the *less* confidence they have and the more they fear

Graph 23. Why The Fed Couldn't Buy Corporate Bonds

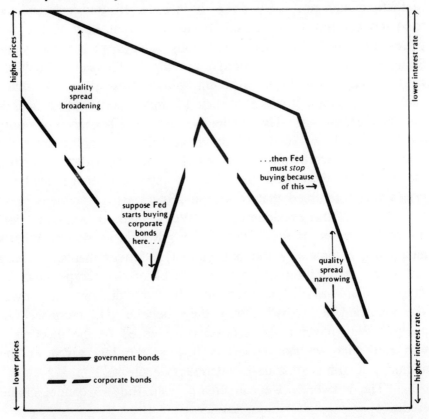

Most twentieth-century observers felt that a panic scenario such as the one described here could never occur because the government would step in and bail out all major corporations in trouble. However, as illustrated here, whenever they took any steps to support a corporation's bonds, it merely caused the government's own bonds to fall. The same would occur in any direct bailouts of banks or thrifts.

their money will be worthless. Look what happened the other day. The money supply went up by $10 billion. This scared bond investors and caused the market to fall by two points, implying $100 billion in losses. In effect, for every dollar that was created in new cash, we lost ten dollars in the market value of credit outstanding (bonds)."

"Oh. But why can't we just buy *more* bonds?"

"When we attempt to support bond prices through direct purchases of U.S. Government securities, the money is deposited in the banks, which means the money supply jumps. This scares bond buyers all over the world and causes investors to sell more—not only U.S. Government bonds, but also corporate, municipal and foreign bonds.

"If we go ahead and try to make direct purchases of corporate, municipal and foreign bonds—a radical break with tradition—it will create a tidal wave of selling not only in bond markets, but also in the markets for mortgage, financial futures and bank loans. Nearly all of the $11 trillion in debts outstanding are ultimately marketable in one way or another.

"Next, even assuming the remote possibility that we could somehow eat a big chunk of the $11 trillion in debt, it could not prevent the resulting dollar collapse. Finally, assuming we reverted to the sheer folly of permitting a rapid disintegration of the dollar, we would then confront the ultimate wall of resistance. We would not be able to purchase the oil from OPEC countries which, by this time, would be demanding payment in foreign currencies. We would not be able to provide 250 million Americans with food and shelter which, by this time, would require immediate payment in cash or even precious metals."

"But what about the law?"

"The law gives us the on-paper authority to buy public, private and foreign bonds. It does not give us the actual power to create real economic wealth."

"Why didn't we recognize this when we began the Metrobank rescue plan?"

"We did. But we hoped that the marketplace might swallow it. We underestimated the sophistication of investors."

Still the President sounded perplexed. "You're saying the market is sensitive. I see that now. But—"

The Federal Reserve Chairman's irritability was becoming more apparent. "Let's say I'm an investor and I own Treasury bonds. This implies that I trust the government; that I loaned you my money for the purpose of running the government. Now, you take my money and pass it on to a third party, the private bank. And I say to you: 'Now what did you go and do that for? If I wanted to loan the money to the bank, I would have done so myself—directly—in the first place. But I didn't. I didn't do it because I don't trust the bank. I trusted you. But no more. Now

I can't trust you anymore either. Now you're just like them.' So the investor sells his Treasury bonds and then we are in trouble. Then we, the government, default."

The President hesitated for a few tense seconds before responding, but it seemed like hours as the tension built.

"Then what?"

The Chairman couldn't believe his ears. The President of the United States had treated the government's default with levity, utter levity. He could no longer control his boiling frustration—and fear. "Do you want to be the last President of the United States? Do you want to risk a new government with a new constitution? Do you want to destroy, with one sweep—"

The Chairman's voice broke with emotion. Silence ensued.

"Mister Chairman, I appreciate the sincerity of your emotions, but you misunderstood me. What I said, in fact, was 'then *what*,' indicating to you my surprise and disbelief that this great country of ours could ever reach the point you described so dramatically moments ago.

"I request you take the following actions. Dispose of all Metrobank paper purchased thus far; make a pledge that the Federal Reserve, despite its current legal authority to the contrary, will not purchase, under any circumstances, securities of the private sector; and promise to discriminate always between corporates and governments. For my part, I shall proceed to take those actions I deem necessary to correct this extremely dangerous situation."

"But Mr. President, we haven't bought any Metrobank securities yet. The markets were shaken merely by rumors of our plans to do so."

27

How The Banking
Time Bomb Exploded

We go back a few months. Economist Richard Dexter, fully recovered from his two-year coma, is appointed to a senior position at the Federal Deposit Insurance Company (FDIC).

At first, he is thrilled by the responsibility of his new job. But he soon comes face to face with an impossible dilemma. He is responsible for guaranteeing the $1.7 trillion in bank deposits held by millions of Americans, but he has less than *one cent* in cash to cover each dollar deposited.

It is partially through his office that the decision to inflate or deflate will be implemented. If he pours money into every failing bank and provides unlimited bail-out funds, it will be inflationary. If his resources remain scarce and he only offers partial rescues, the impact will be *de*flationary.

The first day on the job, he thought he would have almost absolute power over the rescue operations. Within a week, however, he realizes that he is wrong. This very issue comes up in an animated phone conversation with a prominent Congressman, intent on rescuing every bank or S&L with any hint of trouble.

"Don't you see?" Dexter argues. "I don't control other governmental agencies. Just the other day, I was putting the final touches on a rescue package for a major city bank when the Treasury Department attacked the plan vehemently. I don't mind if they give us hell in private, but leaking it to the press rubs me the wrong way."

The Congressman shouts over the phone, "Just who's in charge here?"

"In charge? Are you kidding? *No one's* in charge of anything. But *everyone* has got their hands into every aspect of this problem. The Fed. The Comptroller of the Currency. Two Congressional committees. The SEC. The President. And we're in there too. To add insult to injury, no one controls the media. In fact, the more we try to persuade them not to write about something, the more we stimulate their curiosity. "But that's not the real crux of our problem. We don't control the funds available to our own agency—let alone the government funding to *everyone else* involved in this five-ring circus! The fact that, theoretically, the Fed can create money is meaningless. In practice, the money just isn't there."

"Be patient. I'm working on the Fed."

"What good is on-again off-again credit pumping? We need a reliable flow, an *accelerating* flow. We're losing control over the marketplace. It's too massive, too complex, with too many crosscurrents. We may manipulate it in the short term but that inevitably backfires, leaving the markets in worse shape than if we left them alone."

"For example?"

"The bond market. Since most people believe the Fed has the power to create hyperinflation by running up the money supply, even the slightest move in that direction scares the daylights out of anyone who owns bonds, triggering a price collapse and forcing the Fed to remain tough after all."

"So what *can* you do?" asks the Congressman with growing impatience.

"Sorry, all I can tell you is what we *can't* do: Although it's possible to put out the brushfires, we can't seem to stop the insidious trend of 'creeping withdrawals,' a steady loss of bank deposits everywhere around the country."

"So what's the bottom line?"

"It's simple. If the bank failures continue to accelerate, there isn't going to be any bottom line! We'll be scraping the bottom of the barrel in terms of our resources before we're halfway through."

Dexter pauses but the Congressman is silent, conveying a seething anger to which Dexter responds: "The real bottom line is that our agency and any other federal agency can only postpone the day of reckoning. If you think all this money buys *solutions*, you're deluded. All it does is buy *time*—less and less time for each new dollar spent."

Dexter was right. For years before the Crash of '87, the FDIC and FSLIC rescued one failing institution after another reducing their cash reserves to ever lower levels. But it was an endless cycle. For every bank rescued, two more took its place.

"So what?" exclaimed the perennial optimists. "Congress will simply throw in another few billion."

"Or," said others, "the FSLIC will merge with the FDIC."

"Maybe they can charge bigger insurance premiums and let the S&L industry resolve its own problems," suggested some.

"No matter what," everyone agreed, "Congress will solve the problem somehow!"

Most felt that the first option, more money from Congress, was best. But the Congressional debate dragged on for so long that, by the time funds were finally granted, an even larger cash drain had occurred, giving rise to more demands on Congress. In the end, the amounts needed were so immense that even the most liberal members of Congress recognized the futility of throwing good money after bad. Not only was this path too expensive, but the damage to the federal budget deficit, the bond markets and the dollar was incalculable.

The second option, merging the two insurance funds, was also blocked. As soon as the thrifts suggested this, the commercial bankers raised a wall of opposition that was impenetrable. "That's *our* money we've paid into the FDIC," the bankers complained. "What right do the S&Ls have to drain *our* insurance fund? Why should *we* pay for their errors? We have enough troubles of our own and we refuse to carry the deadweight of the thrifts."

The final option, raising insurance premiums that the S&Ls have to pay to the FSLIC, was another joke—but the S&Ls were not amused. "Insurance premiums are not just penny-ante contributions," the S&Ls protested. "Already, these payments drain our earnings. Any increase would merely add insult to injury."

Some "armchair analysts" of that period even went so far as to propose that thrifts in the worst financial shape pay the biggest premiums. "Make them pay for their mistakes!," was their philosophy. In theory, it wasn't such a bad idea. In practice, however, it would have been the last nail in the coffin. *There was little that the authorities could legally do to stop the confidence crisis from spreading.*

Perhaps this is why they resorted to methods which, by all definitions, must be considered illegal. In the early 1980s, regulators helped the S&Ls create bogus goodwill accounts to beef up their assets and keep them "solvent." They changed their definition of key elements in the balance sheet. For example, instead of "stockholders' equity," they invented the term "regulatory equity" which included outright debts—unacceptable under standard accounting practices.

In fact, it was common knowledge in the industry that two separate and unequal accounting systems had emerged—one for the public, where the terminology was camouflaged to hide the bad news; the other for the regulatory agencies, where the numbers were doctored to keep the S&Ls afloat.

The S&Ls repossessed assets of those who couldn't meet their payments. Then the government took over those S&Ls. Thus, despite all the "creative accounting," the government found itself the owner of a hodgepodge of assets—amusement parks, beer parlors, executive jets and retirement homes. If they could only sell off the assets and raise some money, they thought, this would help finance the cash-poor FSLIC. Thus, the Federal Asset Disposition Association (FADA) was created.

After 18 months, however, FADA had raised only $600 million from its garage sales despite offering $4 billion in assets. Worse still, this new agency actually lost $10 million in 1987. Later, when S&L failures accelerated, FADA would be so overwhelmed with unsalable assets, it would have to shut down just to stop its own cash hemorrhaging.

In fact, even while FSLIC officials said they were "seeking a solution," they were actually planning the own career changes which they would make after the FSLIC's demise.

First, private and state-run insurance funds were called into question during the run on the Ohio and Maryland S&Ls in 1985. Second, confidence in the FSLIC began to crumble. As early as 1985 and 1986, the professional journals and occasionally the financial press addressed this issue. It was only a matter of time before the mass media picked it up. Finally, the FDIC itself fell into disrepute.

People were temporarily reassured by the new law that Congress would guarantee all deposits covered by the FDIC or FSLIC. Before long, though, it became apparent that Congress talked loudly but carried a small stick. It was impossible for the government to back up its guarantees with consistent, concrete and aggressive action.

Fortunately, however, there were some who did manage to escape the carnage. They got out of all their CDs, whether with an S&L or a bank; used any temporary strength in the market to liquidate mortgage-backed bonds; placed the proceeds into 3-month T-bills; and later shifted into Treasury notes and Treasury bonds.

Those who failed to follow these steps were caught. Furthermore, those who were directly involved in the housing and construction industry, or whose business indirectly depended upon them, were washed away by the flood of S&L closings.

It wasn't long before a similar crisis spread to the commercial banks. Throughout the first few decades of the postwar boom, banks were failing at an average rate of roughly 10 per year. Then, in a lagged reaction to the back-to-back recessions of 1980 and 1981-82, failures quadrupled from 10 in 1981 to 42 in 1982. By 1987, the failure rate had jumped to 202—more than 20 times the "normal level."

The question I asked at the time was: "If we have still another recession, will bank failures surge again by a factor of 10 to 1?" If so, another banking holiday would be inevitable.

Eventually, the cascade became cataclysm that swept away all of the technical gimmicks and all of the government guarantees. We faced a shutdown of the thrift industry, a freeze on depositors' funds, and the evaporation of mortgage money that financed the housing and construction industries.

Indeed, it was primarily the decline of the banking system—and the sudden shortages of cash which followed—that precipitated the next phase of the crisis.

28

The Real Estate Debacle

With mortgage money becoming more and more scarce, the prevailing mood shifted rapidly from unbridled optimism to extreme caution. Those who had taken the precaution early in the game to reduce their debts or unload their properties were doing very well. But among the majority, those who had sat with their holdings, a major transformation was under way in family decision making—not only regarding when to buy a new home or a car, but also when to marry, when to move and when to have children.

Young adults lived with their families longer. New families were less anxious to start new homes and the growth rate in new households dropped.

Homes were offered for sale at deep discounts and the already large apartment glut became an avalanche. Ever so, until the money ran out, thousands of new units were completed each day. Rentals plummeted, but mortgage costs stayed high. Consequently, the gap between the cost of renting and the cost of owning widened, depressing real estate values even more.

The greatest shock, however, came from a different direction.

The Surge In Mortgage Delinquencies

Imagine a high-income neighborhood where homes are built along steep cliffs and scenic mountain tops. Then imagine its fate in an earthquake with the highest Richter-scale readings. This was an accurate picture of what happened to real estate—not only in certain highly indebted communities, but in the United States as a whole. The homes were built on the stilts of debt. The financial earthquake, along with its economic after-shocks, caused frequent and ever-larger defaults. Like a landslide, homes, apartment units and condominiums were dumped on the market.

Even during the 1983-1987 housing *boom*, the mortgage delinquency rate and the foreclosure rate kept rising. This fact, in itself, was most abnormal and ominous. The fact that we were then entering another economic downturn was downright frightening! Delinquencies and foreclosures soared to levels which far exceeded those of the Great Depression!

Also frightening was the bust in Adjustable Rate Mortgages, the so-called "ARMs," used to prolong the housing boom, allowing homeowners who otherwise might not have qualified to join the buying bandwagon. Out of every ten dollars in new mortgages written in the years before the crash, three to four dollars went into ARMs.

Since most ARMs were chosen by marginally qualified buyers, it didn't take much of an income decline to trigger still further delinquencies. Unfortunately, the problem S&Ls were already burdened with billions of dollars in unproductive real estate loans. So they had no choice but to unload their inven-tory of houses in a weak market.

For those who had sold their homes before the panic, this was the time to buy a new one. The proceeds from a modest home in a fair location could now buy a much larger property in a very desirable location.

However, those who thought this was a good time to rein-vest in commercial real estate for a speculative gain were great-ly disappointed. It would be several years before that market would bottom out and truly begin to recover.

The Crash In Commercial Real Estate

In the intermediate period after the Crash of '87, but before the economy turned sour, the construction of office buildings, shop-ping centers, hotels and motels began to slow. The glut in office space worsened and the prospect for commercial real estate darkened.

Despite the bad news—plus the stock market crash—the "experts" remained oblivious to the possibility of a commercial real estate crash. Their typical argument went something like this: "The big lenders and developers think long-term. They aren't concerned about a cyclical decline because they know they will always come out ahead by holding on. They have the vision to look beyond the valley."

With this rationale, they persuaded small and medium-sized investors to hold on to properties that had *not* been yielding positive returns. With newly completed office buildings and shopping centers going half empty for years, with promoters cutting leases to fill up space, and with individual investors continually getting shafted, they had obviously made a huge miscalculation.

Where had they gone wrong? Basically, they had expected another surge in inflation to boost property values and rent. When that inflation failed to materialize, they sought other justifications for their optimism. But the basic fact was that *supply had far outstripped demand.*

In 1985, the boom should have ended, but it didn't. Over $95 billion worth of office buildings, shopping centers, hotels and motels were built, compared with just $33 billion in 1977. Despite the office and retail space glut, developers just kept on building in near record volume.

What ever possessed developers, builders, investors and lenders to continue this huge expansion even after it became obvious that vacancy rates were soaring? Didn't they recognize times had changed? Clearly not!

They didn't realize that the persistent oversupply problem was not just a passing phase. It was a long-term fundamental trend, rooted in the chronic stagnation which would dominate the last decades of the century. According to Coldwell Banker, a major real estate firm, office vacancies in 1988 were 16% in downtown areas and 23% in suburban areas nationwide.

They didn't realize that service corporations—one of the largest users of commercial space—were about to cut back sharply. Already, Merrill Lynch, Shearson, Paine Webber and others in the brokerage business were laying off employees left and right. This was the industry that, for years, had been expanding its office space at double-digit rates. Now these firms were cancelling expansion plans.

They didn't realize that the negative cash flow to investors would be so persistent. To fill space, promoters were forced to slash prices and offer concessions, locking in their losses with unprofitable leases. The pension fund industry's returns from real estate turned negative in 1987. As a result, they severely restricted investments in new office buildings. Soon they would be cutting back in shopping centers, hotels, motels and other areas as well.

In 1987, commercial banks were hit with a 5 1/4% delinquency rate on all real estate loans, throwing nearly $30 billion into delinquent status. Meanwhile, the savings and loan industry was carrying some $23 billion in repossessed properties. According to government figures, the overhang of repossessed and delinquent real estate held by commercial banks, S&Ls and the FSLIC soared to $96 billion in 1987 from $76 billion in 1986.

And that was just the tip of the iceberg! Most of these real estate problems stemmed from a building bust in Texas and other energy producing states. What would happen when similar problems spread to the rest of the country? What would happen when highly margined investors and builders, no longer willing to absorb the severe losses, finally decided to bail out? The Money Panic quickly engulfed virtually every form of real estate in every region of the nation.

If neither paper investments like stocks and bonds, nor tangible investments like real estate were the answer, what was? Where could one turn for true safety? Many investors turned to the so-called "defensive" or "recession-proof" stocks such as utilities, gold and consumer-oriented companies.

Ultimately, they would be right. But in the interim, they were in for some big surprises.

29

From The Frying Pan Into The Fire

One of the least expected disasters of the Money Panic struck the utility industry. After the Crash of '87, many advisors naturally shifted their sights to the utilities as a conservative alternative. With the exception of a few unusual situations, that was a mistake. "I know you are upset with your stocks," brokers would say to their clients in 1988. "That's why I think utilities are a natural for you, especially the bonds." They argued that, in a bear market, it was *the* safest investment. This sounded logical and rational. Unfortunately, the half-truths trapped thousands of unwary Americans into some of the worst investments of that era. Few remembered that, in the 1930s, corporate bond yields surged to new all-time highs. In other words, the bonds' market value collapsed. Investors fooled by the earlier strength either lived to regret it, or left near-worthless assets to their heirs.

Analysts understood only the more recent past, when the utility industry had consistently benefited from a drop in interest rates, declines in oil prices and a steady growth in the use of electric power.

Only later, after the panic, did the real truth about the 1980s growth come out: Industrial use, the traditional mainstay of the utilities, had been flat for nine years. The only ones who had really been using more power were the commercial businesses which had been enjoying the boom in services. No one bothered to ask what might happen when credit ceased, when the service-industry boom turned into a service-industry bust. The growth in power consumption was bound to fall.

"The utilities are recession-proof," the brokers insisted. Not so! Electricity sales roughly paralleled changes in the economy. During the 1981 recession, for example, residential demand fell 0.4%, commercial demand fell 1.4%, and industrial demand shrunk by a whopping 6%. But that was just a recession! In the Money Panic, the declines would reach double-digit rates, especially in the highly vulnerable service sector.

"The utilities have a big cash flow," said others. This turned out to be another false assumption. For a full ten years prior to the panic, most of that cash was thrown into massive construction spending, committing the utilities to huge debts. In the years during and after the panic, any new cash would be needed to help meet the payments. In a declining economy and with scarce long-term capital, the debt crisis created and nurtured by the utility industry consumed their earnings and cash.

Before the panic, analysts were pleased to see that construction spending declining. They interpreted this to mean that most utilities no longer needed to issue new debt or common stocks. Again, this was only a half truth. The cutbacks in construction were not voluntary or planned. They were forced on the industry by a long series of blunders and political disasters. Since when was it good news to abandon nuclear power plants costing $10 billion?

The only way to escape this danger was to use any intermediate strength in the utility stocks or bonds to clear out. Unfortunately, utility stocks weren't the only unexpected disasters of the Money Panic.

Fannie Mae

Another big shock was the default by the largest private corporation in the world: Fannie Mae. No one expected it or even imagined it was possible. In fact, few even realized it was the world's largest corporation.

Created in 1938 by the government to help American families finance their homes, Fannie Mae later became a private corporation that was only partially owned by Uncle Sam.

The trouble was, in 1988, Fannie Mae owned $100 billion in mortgages, most of which were the riskier fixed-rate type.

When mortgage rates rose, it would immediately experience huge losses.

Fannie Mae *had* improved its income substantially by collecting guaranty fees on $170 billion in mortgage-backed bonds. But when the economy faltered and homeowners couldn't meet their mortgages, Fannie Mae had to pay the price. Its dilemma was the same as that of the commercial banks and the utilities: When the economy declined, delinquencies soared, Fannie Mae suffered severe cash flow problems and was forced to sell off assets.

Even during the economic boom of the mid-1980s, Fannie Mae was hit hard by delinquencies. According to their annual report, their provision for foreclosure losses surged from $2 million in 1982 to $360 million in 1987. During the Money Panic, it went from bad to worse—Fannie Mae was devastated.

As before, management sought to blame their failings on factors beyond their control. They complained that inflation no longer bailed out homeowners. In the past, they said, families would have sacrificed almost anything to stay in their homes because of rising property values. Now they were abandoning their homes because of falling values, leaving Fannie Mae holding the bag. They also complained about the long delay between the time they repossessed a property and the time they could finally dispose of it.

Even before the crash, Fannie Mae held huge inventories of unsold homes. As long as prices were going up and carrying costs were low, they didn't make a big issue of this; they merely reported their profits and kept quiet. When home prices declined while interest rates stayed relatively high, they complained repeatedly about "the Fed's lack of support for the real estate markets."

To this day most people don't realize that these problems first appeared during supposedly good times. "Just imagine," I asked, "what will happen when we move suddenly into truly *bad* times?"

The "Full-Faith-And-Credit" Charade

Many of those who searched for a safe haven in those turbulent decades fell prey to strategies that offered various types of "guarantees." On closer examination, it was later discovered that these guarantees often hid underlying weaknesses. The obvious but rarely-asked question was: "If this investment is *truly* safe, why can't it stand on its own? Why does it need a guarantee?"

Ginnie Maes were the most popular of these "guaranteed securities." "You can't go wrong," the brokers used to say, "because these bonds are backed by the *full faith and credit* of the United States Government. The yields are always higher than Treasuries and they repay both your interest and principal as you go."

Very few stopped to ask *why* the yields were always higher than Treasuries. Fewer still bothered to consider precisely what their money was invested in. They only wanted to know how high the yield would be.

The reason Ginnie Maes provided a higher yield was critical: The *quality* of these bonds was lower. The income of the General National Mortgage Association (GNMA) was far from certain. It relied on mortgage payments by homeowners and other borrowers. In the Money Panic, when mortgage delinquencies rose sharply, this income plummeted.

Only a handful of individuals in the late 1980s had the slightest inkling of the disasters in store for these supposedly "government-guaranteed" bonds. Investors liked the idea that they received part of their principal back each month, and they liked the relatively good yields.

The brokers, meanwhile, enjoyed the steep commissions. They didn't realize that, in many ways, the growth in Ginnie Maes paralleled the boom and bust of the speculative Real Estate Investment Trusts (REITs) of the mid-1970s.

Like the REITs, the growth was phenomenal. And like the REITs, they appealed to investors who sought "guaranteed" safety with high yield.

Unlike the old trusts, however, brokers selling Ginnie Mae in the 1980s invoked the name of Uncle Sam. They cashed in on the misleading "full-faith-and-credit" routine to lure new savers into an old trap. They did not tell you that, unlike a Treasury bond, the market for mortgage-backed bonds was thin. In the final stages of the Money Panic, as soon as supply greatly exceeded demand, buyers would disappear and brokers would renege on their implicit promise to buy them back from their customers.

There always existed a big difference between what was paid for the bond when bought and what was received for it when sold. In the technical lingo of the brokerage industry, "the spread between bid and ask was large." In a rapidly moving market, since brokers wanted protection from losses, it was even larger. Suddenly, investors found that it was almost impossible to get out. With the first whisper that the government might not guarantee the bonds after all, too many holders would try to sell. Prices would plunge, causing incalculable losses.

They were shocked to discover that Ginnie Maes were not backed by the full faith and credit, but only by a *partial* faith and credit. When push came to shove, owners of these securities would find themselves standing in a long line with the other savers and investors demanding their money back in the final days of the panic.

As the budget deficit grew, the government decided it could not back the Ginnie Mae bonds after all. The Treasury Secretary announced that "any payouts would be postponed" until they could be sure that they had enough money to run the essential functions of government. But there were still greater shocks to come.

30

The Leaky Lifeboat

Today, in the twenty-first century, investors and savers ask a multitude of hard-nosed questions before entrusting their money to anyone, no matter how large or well-established the institution might be. No one does anything on sheer faith alone. But during the late twentieth century, a combination of powerful media advertising and many decades of prosperity lulled the American public into unprecedented complacency.

Life insurance was a case in point. Most considered it among the safest of long-term investments. Some didn't even view it as an investment at all, bypassing the item on their regular portfolio checkups.

This was precisely the intention of the insurance companies. Their publicity campaigns traditionally sought to foster the image of solidity, stability and longevity. Brokerage firms contributed to the campaign by offering insurance annuity savings plans. Financial planners were trained to include insurance no matter what.

There was never any doubt that long-term planning and savings were beneficial. The problem resulted from the indiscriminate way in which insurance was bought—based exclusively upon the cost and the benefits, with virtually no regard to the relative safety of the investment itself. What the investors and savers of that era didn't realize was that, in the Money Panic, they would find themselves in a leaky lifeboat.

At the time it seemed preposterous. But now it is obvious: *Life insurance companies were increasingly taking on the appearance of mutual funds.* In fact, the bulk of their revenues no longer came from life insurance premiums but, instead, was derived from annuities and investment income!

In the late twentieth century, most people who bought life insurance policies were really buying two things at the same time—protection *and* an investment plan. This hadn't always been the case. In fact, from a long-term historical perspective, it is safe to say that the idea of using insurance as an investment vehicle was a relatively new one. Throughout the first half of the twentieth century, the industry's revenues came mostly from the sale of life insurance policies, especially *term insurance*. Investors paid strictly for the amount of life insurance desired for a predefined period. In other words, they were simply buying

Graph 24. Where Insurance Companies Invested Your Money

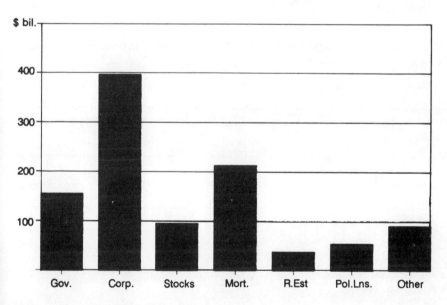

This shows, in billions of dollars, how much the life insurance companies invested in key sectors at the time of the Crash of '87. As you can see from the second bar in the graph, the greatest amount went into corporate bonds ($397 billion). They also invested heavily in mortgages ($212 billion), stocks ($94.3 billion) and policy loans. Although this would be a reasonably balanced and stable portfolio in normal times, during the Money Panic, it was subject to severe losses. Data: *Best's Insurance Reports.*

insurance protection and nothing more—much in the same way as they did with health, fire, theft or auto insurance.

The trouble was that the insurance industry felt they couldn't make enough money by simply selling insurance. Their premiums closely matched expenses. So there were no big profits and little chance for growth. Worst of all, since term insurance typically expired after one year, it was expensive for the company to get policyholders to renew every twelve months.

Their solution was to offer longer term insurance policies, get the insured to pay higher premiums up front, and boost the insurance agent's commissions. This was the concept behind the so-called "whole-life" policies. Regardless of the exact terminology, the truth is this: If you're buying insurance, the more you pay up front, the bigger *your* risk and the better it is for the company.

Some in the industry began to act like bankers, taking in "deposits" from customers. Others behaved like mutual funds. However, one fact remains crystal clear: Life insurance companies took your money. What they did with your money was

Table 14. The Largest Life Insurance Companies

Life Insurance Company	Gov't Bonds (%)	Corp. Bonds (%)	Stocks (%)
Aetna Life	16.6	22.0	2.2
Cigna Corp.	11.0	21.8	1.7
Equitable Life	6.0	23.9	1.0
First Executive Corp.	5.9	77.2	3.5
John Hancock Mutual Life	4.1	30.2	2.2
Metropolitan Life	20.5	32.9	3.9
New York Life	2.1	52.8	5.2
North Western Mutual Life	10.5	26.6	5.3
Principal Financial Group	2.3	24.3	3.7
Prudential Of America	8.1	31.6	2.3
Teachers Insurance & Annuity	0.5	45.8	0.3
Travelers Insurance	12.1	32.3	0.6

Although nearly all life insurance companies invested in roughly the same areas, there were significant discrepancies in the relative proportions which they invested. This table shows the percentage of their overall assets which they placed into each category. In the Money Panic, those that had the heaviest just as vital an issue as what any other company did with your money. It behooved investors to find out.

It wasn't long before the insurance companies began to earn more from the extra money paid in by whole-life policyholders than they earned from their regular term insurance. Their success with whole-life policies was so great that, by the end of the 1980s, these amounted to over $2 trillion—more than half of the individual policies written. Term insurance accounted for only one-third of such plans.

Once they became money managers, the next step was to make major inroads into endowments and pension fund annuities.

The basic difference between a life insurance policy and an annuity was that life insurance provided a one-time windfall payment to the beneficiary. Annuities provided a specified income flow *during* the policyholder's remaining life. This business grew from $960 million in 1970 to $26.1 billion in 1986. The growth in group annuities for pension funds was even more dramatic, catapulting from $2.7 billion in 1970 to $57.6 billion in 1986. As a result, life insurance companies had indeed become much like mutual funds.

Table 14 Continued

Mortgages (%)	Real Estate (%)	Policy Loans (%)	Other (%)	Cash (%)
27.3	0.8	0.6	27.4	3.0
17.1	0.6	0.9	42.6	4.3
26.9	18.6	5.9	12.0	5.7
0.2	0.1	1.2	1.7	10.2
31.8	5.4	8.3	14.1	3.9
16.8	11.1	2.8	9.3	2.7
20.4	1.3	15.9	1.1	1.2
17.1	3.6	21.2	14.3	1.5
48.2	1.0	3.4	16.3	0.7
13.9	1.9	3.8	35.4	3.0
45.4	5.7	0.1	2.1	0.1
28.0	1.6	0.9	20.3	4.2

concentration in government securities fared the best. Those that stressed corporate bonds in lieu of governments were more severely hurt by the merger bust. All were hurt to varying degrees when the Money Panic hit in full force.

Back in 1970, insurance premiums had been the dominant source of revenues. But by 1987, they represented only *one-third* of the total. Both annuity revenues and investment income had surpassed the industry's original mainstay. The bottom line was this: Between annuity reserves and life insurance reserves, insurance companies were now managing over $1 trillion in investor funds.

Big is not bad, but it's not necessarily good either. If the money had been kept in a safe place, there might have been no problem. Or if investors had at least been made aware of the potential risks associated with these investments, it might have been acceptable. Neither was the case.

The typical customer was attracted by the notion that his money was safeguarded for life in a solid institution when, in fact, nothing could be further from the truth. When the Money Panic hit and when the average American was in greatest need of insurance payouts, he was shocked to discover that some insurance companies were not able to meet their contractual obligations as they came due. They did not earn sufficient income to pay the promised returns on their annuities.

In order to meet the promised higher yields, the insurance companies found that they had to place an increasing proportion of funds into investments with higher risks. Today this is common knowledge. But before the panic, investors were generally unaware of what insurance companies did with their money. Graph 24 shows the industry's investment mix at that time.

Savers didn't know, for example, that life insurance companies had invested excessively in corporate bonds. The industry liked to advertise its "highly conservative investment philosophy." And to back this up, they put over half of investors' money into long-term bonds. But was this truly based upon conservative strategies? Not necessarily. They put the money in bonds because that's what it took to match future obligations with future income returns.

The problem was that only a small portion—15%—of the total portfolio was in the safer government securities. A whopping 38% was in corporate bonds mostly purchased during the years when their prices had been very high. In fact, between

1985 and 1987, life insurance companies bought $133 billion worth of corporate bonds, about a quarter of all corporate bonds issued during that period.

It just so happens that the 1985-87 period was when the merger boom took place (see Chapter 19). Not coincidentally, a large portion of the bonds bought by insurance companies was to help finance that boom. Very few—in or out of the industry—paid much attention to the fact that corporate America was, at that point in history, in the most illiquid position since the Great Depression. Very few bothered to ask why business failures in the United States, even before the onset of a recession, made new all-time highs. No one even *thought* it possible that, as a result of all this, the life insurance industry could be directly hurt by skyrocketing corporate defaults during the Money Panic.

Among the top 12 life insurance companies of those days, not one had steered an independent course—not one could claim it had bucked the trend. (See Table 14.)

There were some significant differences in the makeup of their portfolios. For example, Metropolitan Life kept over 20% of its assets in government securities, whereas New York Life kept only 2% in governments. Equitable had over 18% in real estate, much more than most insurance companies. Some were a bit more aggressive in buying corporate bonds and some were more conservative. Some took slightly bigger risks with their mortgage investments and some got more deeply caught in the South Texas fiascos of that period. But as a whole, these differences were only a matter of degree.

As the Money Panic unfolded, the truth emerged. Unfortunately, it was too late. Insurance companies experienced a 20-30% default rate in their corporate bond portfolios; these defaults translated into outright losses of $80-100 billion; and, worst of all, the policyholder had no recourse. Unlike bank or thrift accounts which were guaranteed by federal insurance (or at least nominally so), annuities carried no such guarantees.

Savers also ignored the variable nature of many annuities. Not wanting to be left out of the great bull market of the mid-1980s, life insurance companies had gone one step further towards the high-risk game. They offerred "variable annuities," wherein the bulk of the money went into common stocks. Of course, in this case, no guarantees of income were made.

It was clearly stated that the amount of the ultimate portfolio value depended on the growth of the common stocks. Nevertheless, many investors continued to believe that simply because it was a life insurance company, it was safer than a mutual fund.

As a whole, the insurance industry had invested more than $100 billion in common stocks, nearly 10% of their total assets, as compared to 3% back in 1929. In other words, on Black Monday, 1987, they were *three times* more vulnerable to a stock market crash than they had been on Black Tuesday, 1929. Later, many policyholders began to switch out of such variable annuities; and because of this exodus, the insurance companies began to sell common stocks, adding to the large amount of supply overhanging the market. Despite all this, most policyholders remained, still completely vulnerable to the Money Panic.

Finally, only *after* the Dow had lost over half of its peak value, did there begin a movement in the industry to get back to basics and return to the traditional business of collecting life insurance premiums. The central axis of this new strategy, however, was to return to their historical 3-4% in common stocks which, in turn, required the outright sale of some $40-50 billion worth.

As it turned out, the insurance companies sold that much and more. But due to defaults and forced sales of other segments in their portfolios, when all was said and done, they still had nearly 7% of their money in stocks. Twenty years of bad decisions and of excessive risk-taking simply could not be undone in two months or even two years.

Savers underestimated how vulnerable the life insurance companies were to a real estate collapse. It was no secret in those days that insurance companies had been among the primary sources of funds for the office building and shopping center explosion of the 1980s.

In normal times, there's nothing wrong with that. But the real estate debacle, which hit Texas towards the end of the

1980s, was just a sampling of what was ahead for the rest of the country.

When office space went empty—in New York City, Dallas, Los Angeles or anywhere in America—life insurance companies lost a bundle. In the Money Panic, as this problem spread, they lost much, much more.

You'd think they might have learned from past mistakes. But alas, maybe it had just been too long for anyone to remember. Fifty-eight years earlier, at the onset of the Great Depression, the industry held 40% of its assets in mortgages. The mortgage defaults were so widespread that their holdings dropped to 23% by the mid-'30s. Meanwhile, as the industry had to take over bankrupt properties, their real estate holdings nearly quadrupled from $548 million in 1930 to $2 billion in 1935.

Only during the years following the Depression were they finally able to extricate themselves—cutting back their exposure in mortgages to just 15% of their portfolios. But by the late 1980s, they were back to their old ways again. The real estate collapse hit them hard. There was no mystery to this: Whenever the insurance company had to repossess a property, income flows dropped to virtually zero. And the more unwanted properties they got stuck with, the more difficult it was for them to meet contractual obligations.

Americans were further shocked by the surging costs of the AIDS epidemic. In 1986, the industry paid out $290 million in life and health claims for AIDS victims—much more than expected. But, unfortunately for both AIDS sufferers and those who had to pay the bills, *that was just the beginning.*

By the late 1980s, nearly 2 million victims carried the virus in the United States; and by the year 2000, AIDS accounted for 20% of all life claims, costing some $100 billion in *additional claims* just during the last decade of the twentieth century. There can be no doubt whatsoever that it was a social disaster unprecedented in modern history—hitting precisely at a time when the insurance industry itself was in poor financial health.

Finally, the public was shocked to discover that the life insurance industry was not free from outright fraud. I cannot say that fraud was a *common* occurrence. Despite some big strategy errors, most large firms were reputable and well-intentioned. But in the hectic '80s, when deregulation dominated the scene, the incidence of fraud did increase substantially.

The most publicized case was that of Baldwin United. The company had been using its annuity premiums illegally to acquire companies such as MGIC. Throughout all this, Baldwin continued to get high ratings by Best Insurance Reports, which rates insurance companies and their products sold by the major brokerage houses.

Was Baldwin the only one that went astray? Most definitely not, as was later revealed. One of the reasons life insurance companies were considered safe is that they were regulated by state insurance commissioners. The Baldwin United case is of special interest because, even as the fraud was being perpetrated, the insurance commissioners *were* being notified. It was no secret. Yet, no one stepped in to block their acquisition of MGIC. The moral of this story is that insurance commissions typically did not act until it was too late. Baldwin United annuity holders finally had to settle for large losses and reduced income.

But it was merely a foreshadowing of what lay ahead for other insurance investors—fraud or no fraud.

The Best Strategy

If you needed to buy insurance in the late twentieth century, how could you escape these disasters? *You did not complicate matters by using insurance as an investment vehicle.* Rather, you bought only term insurance, completely avoiding whole life or annuity policies. In fact, you could achieve much better safety and liquidity by investing your own retirement portfolios in the areas which escaped the Money Panic.

Unfortunately, many savers didn't find out about all this until *after* they had already invested with insurance companies. They discovered that the insurance companies wanted to charge a hefty penalty for cancellations ("surrender") of annuity plans. Some unfortunate investors got hit with a penalty as high as 8% for the first year, sliding downward each year thereafter.

Did it make sense to pull out anyway? This was a decision only the individual investor could make. If his insurance investment represented a large portion of his wealth, he couldn't afford to take any chances. He had to bail out.

In an effort to discourage cancellations, many insurance companies would of course say that they invested only in the very highest-rated, bluechip firms. For the most part, this was true. The trouble was that in the Money Panic, even the bluechips turned out to be quite vulnerable.

31

The Tax Exemption Trap

After generations of government spending, both by liberals and conservatives, taxes had emerged as a major burden to most Americans and were especially onerous for those who had worked hard to accumulate a retirement nest-egg. Confronted with this growing tax bureaucracy, many citizens sought out investments whose only virtue was tax benefits. They flocked to tax-sheltered real estate, limited partnerships, tax-exempt municipals, and numerous special deals to avoid taxes.

One cannot fault investors for maximizing their gains within the law. The real problem is that the methods available almost invariably involved risks which greatly outweighed the tax benefits.

Tax-exempt bonds were a case in point. If you bought a bond issued by New York City, the State of Illinois or some other local government, you paid no taxes on your interest income. This was especially attractive to investors in a high tax bracket, even after the Reagan Administration lowered the maximum tax rate. But, despite a temporary improvement in the mid-1980s, the municipal bond market was a disaster area during the last two decades of the twentieth century. Before the panic, this was primarily due to higher interest rates and bond market collapses. During and after the panic, the massive defaults by municipalities were the cause. In both cases, the net result was the same: A sinking municipal bond market.

Strangely enough, despite the destruction of their principal during the bad years of the 1980s, most investors thought they couldn't go wrong with top-quality municipal bonds. "I

Graph 25 & 26. Big Deficits Of Local Governments

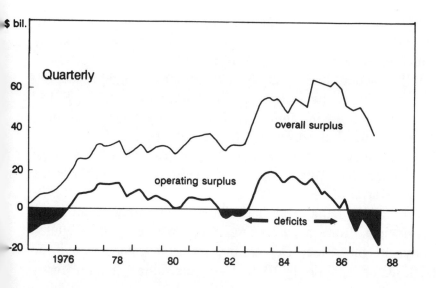

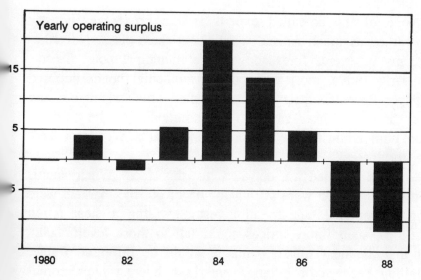

The operating deficits of the municipal governments show up even more ~ly when taken on a yearly basis. Notice the dramatic turnaround from a ~us in 1986 to back-to-back deficits in 1987 and 1988. This coincides with a ~ar plunge in the financial health of corporations, consumers and the nation ~vhole depicted in graphs 4 through 7. Data: Federal Reserve.

can't afford the taxable income if I stick with T-bills," was the common refrain. "Between inflation and taxes, I'm left with practically nothing."

Not true. They still had their principal, even after adjusting for inflation—a privilege not enjoyed by those who stuck by their municipal bonds during the panic.

What about municipal bond insurance? Sadly, the insurance companies that supposedly guaranteed the principal had *their* money tied up in similar vehicles—utility bonds, industrial bonds and some (but not enough!) Treasury bonds.

"What other choice is there?" complained advocates of tax-exempt bonds. "This is the only investment that protects me from the ravages of high taxes."

The tax benefits were indeed real, but nothing protected their principal from a collapsing bond market and a gutted economy. In the Great Depression, some investors wound up with 50, 40 or as little as 10 cents on the dollar. In the Money Panic, they had similar experiences.

None of the so-called experts in the brokerage industry ever breathed as much as one word about these risks. Nevertheless, plenty of events foreshadowed the municipal bond fiascos. In the early 1980s, most who bought municipal bonds suffered huge paper losses in their principal, which often wiped out any income earned or taxes saved. Their solution: "As long as we hold on until maturity, we get our money back. We don't have to *take* the losses!"

No one seemed to be alert to this fact: When munis bought at 100 or 105 were selling for 65 or 60, the markets were sending a silent message to all investors willing to hear it—in the not-too-distant future, prices could fall to those levels again, except that the next time around, it would be different. Rather than falling because of inflation and high interest rates, something you could live with, it would be falling because of the collapsing economy and financial system—something you could *not* endure.

The next big warning of trouble came when the large players began to abandon ship. Salomon Brothers shut down their municipal bond business in 1987. Others soon followed suit. Why the mass exodus from this supposedly lucrative business?

Searching through the old internal documents of some of these firms, I found a memo from a chief executive which reveals what was really behind it—*fear*. Here are some excerpts: "We must exit this business swiftly and promptly in order to avoid the onslaught of lawsuits arising when tax-exempt bonds begin to default, especially *private-use revenue bonds*, the junk bonds of the municipal market. We must exit this business in order to avoid the fallout which will inevitably hit this industry from the sudden deterioration in the finances of state and local governments."

The top graph on page 271 shows the finances of state and local governments on a quarterly basis. The thin line represents the overall municipal budget surpluses *including* the untouchable social and welfare funds. The thick line represents the true state of affairs, the operating budgets *excluding* those funds. Just look at the utterly shocking plunge in finances of the local governments after 1985! And look also at the record deficit chalked up in the most recent period, an annual rate of $15.8 billion!

In those days, some people argued that the quarterly figures were misleading, that yearly totals provided a more accurate picture. True—but the outlook on a yearly basis was even worse: The total deficit for 1988—over $11 billion—was more than just a disastrous reversal from previous years. (See bottom graph, page 271.) It was the worst deficit since the Great Depression, and the economy wasn't even in a recession. What would happen when the economy declined? *Tax-exempt bond investors, no matter how cautious, would be severely hurt.*

Another warning of trouble came from the rating agencies. In 1987, Standard & Poor's and Moody's downgraded two municipal bonds for every one which they upgraded. This would not be so terribly important except for the fact that unsuspecting investors had just purchased municipals in such huge quantities. The issuers raced to beat the restrictions imposed by the Tax Reform Act of 1986, while the buyers were lured in by heavy-handed promotion tactics. By the time the market closed on the last trading day of 1985, state and local governments had issued a whopping $204 billion in bonds— nearly *ten times* the normal volume for an average year in the early 1970s.

As usual, everything looked great at the peak. The yields were excellent, sometimes higher than 30-year Treasury bonds; the states appeared to be in good financial health; and the municipal bond brokers were going great guns. So everyone, issuers and investors alike, "went to town." Furthermore, long-term interest rates fell, boosting the market value of all bonds, including municipals. But in the Money Panic, long *after* the crowd of investors had been locked in, the truth emerged.

If you invested in municipal bonds, you had two types to choose from. You could buy a general revenue bond which would be backed by all the income, property and other taxes collected by the local government. Or you could buy project-type bonds to finance a hospital, a bridge, a housing development or some other government-sponsored enterprise. These were backed exclusively by the revenues of that particular project. If they couldn't make money, you might not get your interest checks.

The brokers, many of whom were aggressively marketing the munis during the mid-1980s, period, failed to mention that the vast majority of the issues were the riskier project-type bonds.

During the Money Panic, investors learned an even harder lesson when the project bonds started to default and both the bonds and the funds tumbled. Most project bonds were municipal bonds in *form* only. In substance, they were nothing more than high-risk private-sector bonds, often no better than junk bonds.

The Tax Reform Act of 1986 greatly reduced their volume and, in that sense, it was beneficial. It put a virtual halt to the practice of issuing low-quality housing, hospital and other private-use issues under the guise of municipal bonds. Unfortunately, a large number of investors were already trapped. During the Money Panic, the market for those bonds turned extremely thin. The brokers who sold the bonds were no longer around to buy them back. Therefore, it was virtually impossible to sell without suffering a large markdown.

This was devastating to retired people whose municipal bonds were their only source of income. Their bonds came with pages of coupons which they clipped off every quarter to get their interest checks. Over the years, this not only became an ingrained habit for many people, it was a definite source of satisfaction and pleasure. Now, thousands of senior citizens refused to accept the reality that their coupons on defaulted municipals were no longer of value. Out of desperation, they continued their quarterly coupon-clipping, and were distraught when no checks came in the mail. They grew especially outraged when they were told that the long-awaited maturity dates might never arrive.

Some formed committees and pressure groups in a desperate attempt to be heard. "Why didn't you warn us?" they shouted. "Why didn't you at least disclose this as a remote possibility?" But in the great din of protest and despair which enveloped the banks, the savings and loans, the credit unions, the insurance companies and the government mortgage agencies, this particular outcry was barely heard.

The Lucky Few

Strangely enough, escaping the dangers of municipal bonds was actually quite simple. The exit doors were clearly marked. And there were few if any obstacles on the way out. On several occasions, bond prices rallied sharply—often to a point where you could get out with a profit or at least with a substantially reduced loss, depending on when you got in.

During these interludes of temporary strength the smart investors liquidated most municipal holdings. Once they got out, they did not look back. They didn't care if prices continued to go up for a while after they sold. They knew that, in the initial stages of a recession, all bond prices could enjoy substantial rallies, but that this would not alter the dire state of local finances. In *Money & Markets*, I put it this way:

To hold on in an attempt to catch these peaks is tantamount to playing a game of chicken with the Debt Monster. Here's why: In the near term, the economic decline is temporarily positive in that the markets believe it will reduce inflation. But soon thereafter, an economic decline will be a major negative, reducing the tax revenues and boosting the social welfare expenses of the local governments. When will this critical switchover occur? It is almost impossible to pinpoint ahead of time, which is why I call it a "game of chicken." My philosophy is simple: better early than sorry.

The advantage of acting early—rather than trying to catch the absolute peak—was this: You had the time to act methodically. Especially in markets where the liquidity was poor, it was important to give your broker limits to buy your municipals at a certain price or better. In this way, you could give him time— perhaps a period of a few weeks—to execute the orders. Otherwise, the actual price you got could be significantly lower than what you expected.

Meanwhile, investors who held municipal bond unit investment trusts, expecting those trusts to serve as an umbrella of protection, were greatly disappointed. They suffered the same drawbacks as direct purchases of tax exempts. When the market value of tax exempts declined, so did the municipal bond investment trusts. Moreover, the market for these trusts was usually not nearly as liquid as advertised! When everyone wanted to get out in a hurry, many brokers abandoned their promised market-making responsibilities, literally closing up shop.

When the economic outlook turned from bad to worse, subscribers who followed our advice were prepared. They quickly shifted their assets from receivables and inventories, from plant and equipment, plus any other cash they could lay their hands on, straight into their Treasury securities. They followed a similar procedure with their personal accounts. Unfortunately, however, no matter how we tried to spread the word, only a minority followed our advice and moved nearly all of their assets into short-term Treasury securities.

However, we didn't want to stay in T-bills forever. There would come a time for shifting out into other areas—first into longer term Treasury securities such as T-notes and T-bonds, and later into stocks and other investments. Ironically, I recommended the first such shift during one of the most frightening periods of the Money Panic.

32

The Gap

Normally, in the real world of markets and economics, things don't go straight down. There are usually rallies which produce a zigzag pattern. But if you examine price charts closely, you occasionally find what technicians call a "gap"—a hole in the chart between the point where one line ends and another begins. The gap implies that no trading took place during that time, that the price suddenly jumped from one point to another on the chart. That is essentially what happened to the world's economies when the Fed cancelled its plan to rescue Metrobank. One moment we hung in midair at the edge of a cliff. the next moment we were well on our way to the rocky bottom.

In earlier stages of the crisis, every critical event seemed to be distinctly separate from the next one. The economies of Brazil and Argentina fell in the mid-1980s. The dollar's slide began in 1985. Oil prices went in 1986; the stock market, in 1987. Each went down the vortex—but in single-file fashion. During the Money Panic, however, the crises seemed to happen simultaneously:

The stock market was crashing again.

Check clearings, reported to us weekly by the nation's clearing houses, took another nosedive.

Business and bank failures continued to spread.

Meanwhile, utilities were losing large portions of their equity. Adding insult to injury, Congress was still busy passing legislation requiring a costly cleanup of acid rain and nuclear waste disposal.

Fannie Mae, the largest corporation in the world, shocked everyone by filing for protection under Chapter 11 of the Federal Bankruptcy Act.

Federal budget cuts, which had been postponed for so long, were finally put into place. The money vanished. Obviously, if the government couldn't *get* enough money, and if the Fed couldn't *print* enough money for fear of a dollar collapse, then it follows that the government couldn't *spend* the money.

Municipal bonds were defaulting. Casualty insurance companies, commercial banks and other big buyers of municipal bonds, suffering sudden and violent cash hemorrhaging, became heavy net sellers.

Insurance companies, credit unions, brokerage firms and entire governments were going under.

The Gap was a sudden "implosion" of the financial system. To this day, it is a phenomenon which no one can fully understand. The changes came so swiftly, and the participants were so busy salvaging their own assets, that few took the time to record the events.

Some say that the acceleration of change was so great that there actually occurred a reversal in the normal sequence of cause and effect—*reactions* preceded *actions*. Banks in trouble were hit with massive withdrawals before any word of that trouble was known. Specific stocks were dumped even before many so-called "insiders" got wind of a bankruptcy. Was this merely due to a hyperactive rumor mill in which information was passed along at a feverish pace? Whatever the cause, one thing was certain: During the Gap, the economy was undergoing a rapid *structural* transformation.

Economists never asked what would happen if consumers became sellers, if major institutions went failed, or if certain pivotal markets suffered Chernobyl-type meltdowns. Yet precisely these kinds of changes took place during the Gap!

Since we really don't know *what* happened during the Gap, the best we can do is speculate. By drawing on diaries and publications, we can see some of the rapid shifts in people's psyches that were precipitated by economic events. One young broker, formerly a hot shot takeover specialist, described his feelings:

I was trapped by an unrelenting feeling of helplessness. It seemed that, no matter what I did and no matter what I said, I had lost control over the events in my life. At one point, I even believed my innermost thoughts had been written in some master blueprint of my destiny.

My feeling of fatalism was reinforced by constant coincidences. Names of people and places. Words. Sights. Sounds. The name of the stock which brought the downfall of my portfolio. The name of the street where I lived.

Of course, there was no master plan. But there *were* strong undercurrents, invisible to the naked eye, tieing together events which, in other periods, might be unrelated.

Media advertising shifted rapidly to get into synch. Network news anchors, intuitively sensing the new environment, changed their pitch. Everyone lowered their voices and toned down their words in a subconscious effort to compensate for the turmoil.

Another undercurrent was the real cost of money—an economic force that transcended all sectors and socioeconomic classes. At the time, this was a big mystery to most people. But looking back at the Money Panic from our vantage point of the early twenty-first century, we can see that it was not an uncommon event in history.

Had Americans looked back to the United States during the 1930s or, better yet, to Britain in the late 1800s, they could have found a faithful guide to the transformations of those hectic years.

Of course, a *direct* comparison with previous depressions had many pitfalls. History did repeat itself, but always with a new twist, a new wrinkle or a new footnote to trip up the amateur analyst.

The astute historian can see the underlying pattern with a tool called "structural-functional analysis." Although it was developed originally for cross-cultural comparisons, I have applied it successfully to the comparison of equivalent points in the long-wave cycle.

Essentially, one matches institutions, behavior patterns and economic functions which, although vastly different in outward appearance, fit into similar slots in the puzzle. Here are a few examples:

1. The "stock pools" of the 1920s were blamed for sudden selling frenzies that drove down prices. There were no stock pools in the 1980s. But program trading, which moved large blocks of stocks in unison, filled the same functional role in the overall scheme of things.

2. The gold standard in the 1930s imposed a strict discipline on monetary policy. In fact it was due to the fear of a flight to gold that the Fed temporarily tightened money in 1933. By the late 1980s and early 1990s, the gold standard was long gone. Therefore, many analysts concluded that things would be vastly different. Not so—this time it was the dollar, and the fear of a flight to other currencies, that imposed a similar discipline.

Nowhere, however, was there more confusion than in the realm of interest rates.

Three Interest Rate Moves

Had economists only looked back one half century to the big interest rate swings of the 1930s, they would have found some of the answers.

As in the 1930s, there were three interest rate phases that devastated the financial markets and whipsawed even the most astute traders of the Western World.

Phase #1 was a sharp decline as the Fed pushed rates down to avert depression and financial collapse.

Phase #2 was an upward surge, an eruption in rates which no one expected. This was called "the spike." And it is a similar move in the late twentieth century which historians associate with the Gap. The Gap began when the spike occurred, and the Gap was over when the spike ended.

The interest rate spike was uncontrollable and unstoppable regardless of the Fed's actions. Its cause is now clear: When the banks and S&Ls closed in growing numbers, this choked off the flow of cash to corporations and other borrowers, producing a "cash drought" that forced the cost of money—interest rates—skyward.

Interest rate *Phase #3*—another decline back to "normal levels"—occurred when a substantial proportion of the debts were liquidated. It was not until this stage that the panic subsided and the nation embarked on the long road to recovery.

The Best Time To Buy Bonds

Both in the 1930s and during the Money Panic, the ideal time to buy long-term bonds was at the tail end of Phase #2, when the Gap or the spike was over and when the great plunge in yields (upsurge in prices) was about to begin.

Unfortunately, however, very few people were able to catch the peak. Most were too preoccupied with other pressing matters or simply too frightened by the rapid cascade of events. Others were dissuaded from buying bonds by their advisors who told them that the country was "going to hell in a hand basket." And even those who were aware of the opportunities ran into trouble when it came to *timing*. Market swings were violent. When yields hit their peak, they didn't stay there for very long. So it was extremely difficult to catch the right moment.

Therefore, the wisest investors moved into long-term bonds in stages. Starting off with 100% of their cash in 3-month T-bills or a money fund that owned only Treasuries, here are the steps that they took:

First, during Phase 1, well before the Gap, they took 20% of their money and put it into Treasury notes with a maximum maturity of five years. "So what if yields go up some more!" they reasoned. "As long as I do not go beyond five years, any decline in prices will be modest; and as long as I still have most of my money in T-bills, I will be able to take full advantage of the higher rates when they become available."

Second, during Phase 2, they took another 20% and put it into Treasury notes which matured within 10 years. Again, even if rates were going higher and prices still lower, it didn't matter. They still had 60% of their money in T-bills.

Third, when they thought Phase 3 was beginning, they took another 20% and put it into 30-year T-bonds. If it turned out they were wrong, they were still earning a hefty yield. And they still had 40% left in T-bills.

Finally, once interest rates really began to fall, they took still another 20% of their cash and bought strip bonds, with maturities ranging from 10 to 30 years. (Strip bonds pay no in-

Graphs 27 & 28. T-Bill And T-Bond Yields (1920-40)

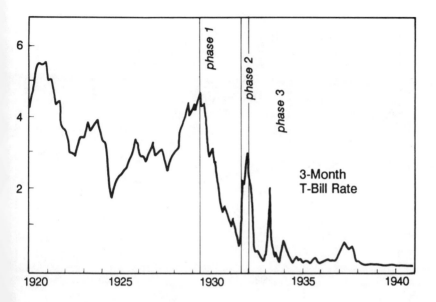

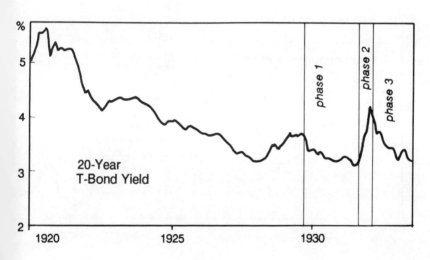

Although important differences were bound to emerge, the pattern of interest-rate movements during the 1920s and '30s provided the only historic guide to what interest rates might do during the Money Panic. Three distinct phases can be discerned. During Phase #1, when the stock market crashed in 1929, interest rates fell sharply. During Phase #2, the height of the banking crisis in the 1930s, they surged back upward. And in Phase #3, they fell back down again. Source: Federal Reserve.

Graphs 29 & 30. Corporate Bond Yields (1920-40)

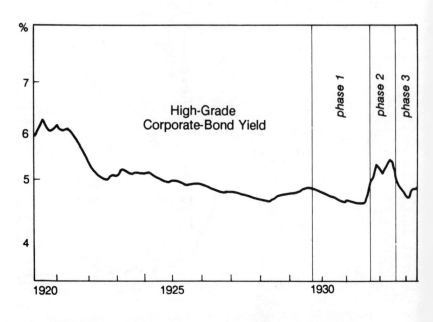

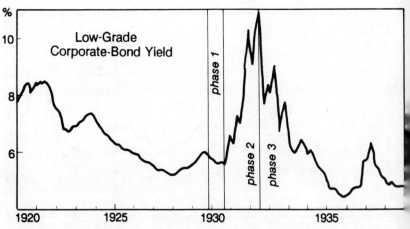

In the 1930s, high-grade corporate bond yields behaved much l
government bond yields . However, in the Money Panic, with so many bluech
in financial difficulties, the pattern was more similar to that of the low-gr
corporate bonds — much lower prices and much higher yields than at any t
in the previous years. (Notice in the bottom graph how low-grade corpo
bond yields surged way above the 1929 precrash highs.) Source: Fed
Reserve.

terest but go up in value more rapidly when interest rates decline.)

When it was all over, their portfolio of keep-safe funds was split into five equal segments—(1) T-bills, (2) T-notes of five years or less, (3) T-notes of ten years or less, (4) 30-year T-bonds and (5) strip bonds. The specific level of the yield they earned wasn't the primary concern. Rather what counted most was that they had protected their principal. In addition, they were earning a good yield above the inflation rate and could shift funds into other opportunities without taking a loss on their bonds.

Some Tough Questions

What indicator could be used for getting a better grasp of the timing? What about corporate bonds? Were high-yielding corporates a good investment during the Money Panic? If not, when would they become attractive and safe? None of these questions could be answered in advance. Rather, as before, the best guide could be found in the patterns of the past. If you were among the few that took the time to study them, here's what you would have found:

Treasury-bill rate. Roughly six decades earlier, in 1929 and 1930, the rates on T-bills fell sharply. That was Phase #1. However, in 1931, the panic caused T-bill rates to soar temporarily (Phase #2). Finally, in the third and final phase of the 1930s, they fell again to new lows.

The experience of the late twentieth century was similar with a few notable differences. Due to the ballooning budget deficit and the acute cash shortages, the fall was not as steep as in 1929-30; and the intermediate spike was greater. If you were a saver in the 1980s and '90s, T-bills were the best medium for safety and liquidity, but they were not always the best vehicle for high yields. By watching the T-bill yield, however, you could glean some valuable clues regarding the best time to move into T-bonds: It was when the T-bill rate temporarily rose well above the T-bond yield and when most people shunned the T-bonds for that very reason.

Long-term Treasury-bond yields. Back in 1929-30 (Phase #1), they declined throughout the stock market crash. But in Phase #2, they easily eclipsed their 1929 highs.

For anyone living in the late twentieth century, the lessons to be learned from this experience were clear: First, it proved that the stock market could go through a long decline despite a slide in T-bond yields. Second, it showed that the interest rate spike could easily reverse much of the decline once a banking panic started. Third, although high yields would return temporarily, it would be very difficult for the average person to catch the peak and lock them in.

High-grade corporate bonds. Back in the '30s, their yields declined during Phase #1 and then surged to new highs during Phase #2. And in the Money Panic, they did the same. The trouble is there were fewer corporate bonds which were able to retain their high rating. In fact, *most triple-As of 1987 had similar balance sheets to the B-rated bonds of 1929!*

Many investors couldn't understand why the price of an "average triple-A bond" was holding up relatively well on their charts while their own "triple-A" was sinking so rapidly. The reason was that as soon as their bond was downgraded, it was no longer included in the average depicted in the charts! Instead, it was relegated to the averages shown in Graph 30—the yield on low-grade bonds.

This is why it was not a very good idea to buy corporate bonds with money you wanted to keep safe. Rather, during the Money Panic, you had to treat most corporate bonds in virtually the same manner as you treated common stocks—as a speculative investment. Those that recognized that reality and took the necessary precautions when buying them, were able to buy them for 40 or 50 cents on the dollar, earn high yields and make substantial profits. Unlike Treasury bonds, however, which were best bought before the end of the Gap, the ideal time to buy corporate bonds was *after* the Gap, when you could sort out the wheat from the chaff. You had to know, with a reasonable degree of certainty, that the bad news on the company was already out, and that there were no more big surprises on the horizon.

Low-grade bonds. The contrast between Graph 30 and the three previous ones is obvious. The yield decline (Phase #1) was much more shallow, and the spike (Phase #2) was much steeper. The same held true in the late twentieth century: After the initial decline, these rates later turned around and easily eclipsed their all-time highs, decimating the equity of investors as their market value collapsed.

Thus, the interest-rate spike became the epicenter of the Gap, disrupting the money supply to all sectors of the economy. Hopes for material well-being were replaced by a struggle for economic survival. Rapid reversals occurred in values, attitudes, feelings, beliefs and actions.

Cries For Relief

Most economic institutions now faced their day of reckoning. Which were solvent, which were insolvent? These questions were asked about individuals, retailers, manufacturers, utilities, banks, universities, foundations, cities, states and even entire nations. The answers had little to do with size or power. Instead, survival usually depended primarily upon the degree of liquidity during the final stage of the boom and the swiftness of protective action taken in the early stage of the panic. The world economy needed a rest, a time for reflection and relief, a cease-fire from the bombardment of events.

The first to feel this need were officials of the savings and loan industry. A few months earlier, while the stock market was plunging through its previous lows, many homeowners could no longer pay their mortgages. As a result, the delinquency rate soared past what was later called the "absurdity threshold," the level at which it became impossible to live up to written contracts, orders and promises of all kinds.

Who could answer all the complaints? How could they handle the legal proceedings against all those who resisted? What criteria would the S&Ls use for choosing the cases to prosecute and the cases to write off as losses? The mortgages, the repossession notices and all the other "paperwork" became just that—a lot of paper and a lot of work. It was an "absurd situation."

A grassroots movement took hold. Out of closed-door meetings held in the S&L offices throughout the country came the word "moratorium." At first, it was only whispered; but it soon was shouted as one of the most virulent public demands in recent memory. Moratorium implied some form of global relief—a major dissolution of the debts. Precisely *how* this would be accomplished no one knew.

In Hartford, Connecticut, and other insurance centers of the world, Sears, ITT, Allstate and others wanted a "policy loan freeze" to prevent the "total disintegration" of their assets. In Los Angeles, savings and loans cried out for relief from withdrawals as the only way to keep their doors open for regular passbook accounts.

Within a few weeks, the strongest demands for a moratorium came from some of the giant corporations. They used the term "debt freeze" with the argument that, if only something could be done to stop the cash drain, business would improve. They also hoped this would be linked to a postponement of payments on interest and trade credit so they wouldn't have to file for bankruptcy and further clutter the courts.

The Federal Reserve again responded with vehement opposition. "Rather than face the reality of their own insolvency, what these firms are asking for is a kind of 'collective bankruptcy' with another name. They want us to somehow abolish or postpone—as if by magic—all the debts they owe to their suppliers and dealers. They forget, as usual, about the other side of the ledger: The creditors. For every firm that's granted relief, another—the one owed the money—is driven further into the hole. Since each has borrowed from Peter to pay Paul, any collective defaults will spread from one sector to the next in a chain reaction of bankruptcies."

According to one senior executive, "The bottom didn't fall out of our market. It was the market that fell out of our bottom! And we're still trying to find it. We have a fleet of ships floundering at sea. We ran out of cash-fuel weeks ago, and now we're throwing the deck furniture into big furnaces called interest costs. But there's still no sign of land." The fleet he was referring to was the electric power industry.

Many of the power companies' big corporate customers were cancelling or reducing their accounts. Some were going bankrupt. Almost all were cutting corners and delaying payments. Meanwhile, smaller accounts—the same families who were delinquent on home mortgage payments—also defaulted on their electric bills. The electric company, along with other utilities, found themselves in much the same position as the savings and loans and the insurance companies—with a "run" on their cash resources.

Bank failures, which surged from 200 in 1987 to an annual rate of 1,000 in the first phase of the Money Panic, reached an annual pace of 2,000. Interest rates, which had been declining for months, again spiked upward. All eyes turned once more to Washington for some solution to the crisis.

33

The Debt Hearings

A great unresolved mystery still facing historians is how the majority of Americans could have believed in the "absolute truths" of those days: That a banking disaster was *absolutely* impossible. That another Depression was *absolutely* out of the question. That the Dow Jones Industrials' rise to 4000 was *absolutely* inevitable.

By this time, however, these "absolute truths" were *absolutely* shattered. There arose a great demand for new truths, new words of wisdom which might somehow replace the old. Americans still asked the same questions which were common throughout the panic: Could the government turn back the stock market crash, the interest rate spike, the consumer panic, the near-collapse of the banking system? What new tricks could be devised?

Most Americans, however, finally recognized that even if there was some cure-all still available, the side effects would be more damaging than the disease. They also took another important step. For the first time, it was finally accepted that the big debts were the root cause of the Money Panic and the ultimate question was finally asked: "How will we ever get rid of the excess debt?"

The Federal Reserve Board, the President's Council of Economic Advisors, the Department of Commerce—all had special research teams seeking an answer. The primary focus of the debate, however, was the U.S. Senate, where a nationally televised Congressional investigation hammered at the problem day after day. Dubbed the "Debt Hearings," these Watergatestyle committee meetings became a constant focus of the media throughout the worst months of the panic.

Spectators crowded the visitors' galleries of Congress to witness the Debt Hearings. TV cameras were everywhere. On the first day, the Chairman of the Senate Finance Committee made an issue over savings. He complained that, while the Japanese saved 20% of their income, Americans saved no more than 5%. So he embarked on a campaign of his own to find out how to get Americans to save more. "All we have to do is boost the savings rates somehow," he said, "and we'll be over the hump." He called expert witnesses and asked them one by one: "What would happen if America had a savings rate like West Germany or Japan?"

The first witness, former Metrobank Chairman Robert Sheppard, replied: "Unfortunately, Senator, the question implies a great deal of wishful thinking. Rather than improve, the U.S. savings rate has plunged. Furthermore, even if we suddenly shifted to a 20% savings rate—without the technological and cultural changes—the near-term results would be disastrous. When someone saves a lot more, he spends less; and when you have less spending, the entire economy suffers. The kind of change you want will help in the long run, but it won't stop the immediate crisis."

"What would happen if the Treasury issued gold-backed bonds?" asked a maverick Republican Senator from the Midwest.

"Excuse my bluntness," responded the next witness, John Hartman, "but you are again avoiding the real, hard solutions. Gold-linked bonds would only help as long as gold itself were attractive. But as soon as gold weakens, it will be like two drunks trying to support each other—a struggling bond market and an erratic gold market."

"Is there no way of satisfying the bond market without an economic calamity?" the Senator from Illinois interjected.

"For argument's sake," Hartman continued, "let's say you find a good gimmick that sells new government bonds—variable rates, zero coupons, partial tax exemptions or whatever. What happens? To the degree that the *new* gimmick does attract buyers for new issues, it automatically damages the market for the *old* government issues. And it just so happens that there are over $2 trillion of those out there."

A new witness came forward. The Senator from Illinois leaned back and said, "Throughout these hearings, we have heard why this or that solution won't work. Are you here to suggest how we can get out of this mess? Or are you here, just like the others, to knock down our ideas?"

"Sir, there is no short-term solution. We are *already* in a money panic, and there is nothing you can do to turn it back— you must let it take its course, intervening only to avoid disorderly markets and to keep the heart of the economy—the financial centers—alive."

"What is the long-term solution?" the Illinois Senator insisted, raising his voice.

"Here it is, Senator. First, we need a period of reduced living standards and increased savings rates. Hard work and sacrifice! Second, we must reorient our production priorities by retooling and recapitalizing. Third, we have to remove the social obstacles blocking technological evolution. We have poor math and science education. We have virtually no preschool teaching by parents. The list of areas for improvement is endless."

The Budget Deficit

Initially, it was felt that the solution was to balance the budget. Somehow, they thought this would finally convince the public and the financial markets of the "soundness of the economic system." As they continued the hearings, however, they discovered two problems with this rationale:

Problem number one was that it would take years to accomplish this goal. In fact, it *required* a money panic—precisely the crisis they wanted to avoid—to create a crisis environment powerful enough to motivate the public and their leaders.

Problem number two was that they had to worry about more than just the *government's* deficits. Government debts were only the tip of the iceberg. In addition, there were trillions in corporate debt, mortgage debt, consumer debt and foreign debts.

How could they balance all those budgets simultaneously? If the government tried to balance its own budget, it created havoc in the budgets of corporations and households. When it tried to help the corporations and consumers, it threw its own budget into disarray. The Committee finally realized that, no matter what was done, the debt problem was out of control.

Large gasoline taxes were proposed, but defeated. If gas revenues flowed like they had earlier in the 1970s, it might have helped. However, with the gas and energy industry in a tailspin and with oil prices still sinking, a high tax rate would produce *less* demand and *lower* revenues for both the energy companies and the government!

Another suggestion was that taxes should be reduced on interest to stimulate savings. But that wouldn't balance the budget either: The immediate impact would be a *bigger* deficit, overwhelming any potential long-term benefits.

Reality proved overwhelming. All solutions ran up against the same wall—a "zero-sum game." This meant that any dollar added to one area had to be taken away from another.

Nevertheless, one group of die-hard Administration optimists clung to the hope that the debt could be naturally paid down over time. Their theory was that, if only confidence could be restored, if only some symbolic action could be taken in the right direction, that would be enough to get back on the right track.

The last witness was the Secretary of the Sound Dollar Committee. "A natural paydown of debts," he began, "only occurs with *noninflationary* growth over a *long* period of time— *real* wealth creation rather than just artificial money and credit. We would have to have both good times and tough sacrifices. Americans would have to change their habits—work harder, spend less and save more. Instead, every time we get some kind of real growth in the economy, we do the opposite. We live it up still more. We pile new debts onto our old debts. And we set ourselves up for an even bigger fall soon thereafter!"

"If that's the case," asked the Senator from Illinois, "then how *will* the debts be liquidated?"

The witness paused, hesitating to say what he believed.

"Well? Don't you know the answer to the question?"

"Yes, sir, I certainly do. A more drastic method of liquidation will predominate."

"Such as?"

"A chain reaction of corporate bankruptcies and reorganizations. A massive shrinking in the banking system. A probable shutdown of our thrift industry."

With rumors flying around Washington and Wall Street of more major corporations and banks going under, this last statement had a ring of truth which shocked the Senate Committee into a momentary silence.

The Senator asked, "You're saying that the best solution is to let the system collapse, and with our blessing? Who's responsible for calling this witness? he exclaimed, glancing back at his fellow committee members.

"Wait, Senator," said the Sound Dollar Committee Secretary calmly. "Bankruptcy is not the end of the world. In fact, there are beneficial housecleaning effects which can later accrue."

As politicians, none of the Senators could see the advantages. All they wanted were suggestions on ways to avoid this crisis. Almost reading their thoughts, the witness continued, echoing the dilemma brought out months earlier at the White House meeting. "Yes, you could bail out the borrowers. But if you do, it will pump up the money supply and the lenders will panic. Yes, you could then bail out the lenders by squeezing the money supply. But then the borrowers would scream in agony! There is simply no more room on the tightrope between these two options."

"How much longer will this last? When do you think this crisis will be over?"

"The longer you try to fight it, the longer it will drag on. The sooner you recognize its inevitability—and work with it— the sooner we can put it behind us."

"Can't you give us a better feel for the timing?"

"No, sir, I cannot. The timing and degree of this crisis— what will happen to unemployment, GNP or inflation—are almost impossible to predict. In federal budget projections, for example, economists now estimate an average unemployment rate of 13%. But it's just a guess they plug into their formulas to

Graph 31. Explaining A Depression With Catastrophe Theory

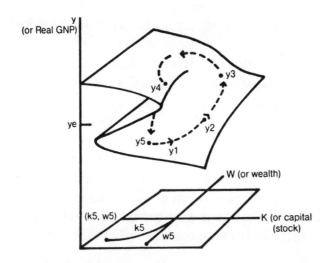

Economists of the twentieth century could account for periodic recessions but could not adequately explain—let alone predict—depressions. In this model, the economy follows a more or less "normal" trajectory from point "y1" to point "y4." But at that juncture, there occurs a definite break with the past as the economy falls through a kind of vacuum or "Gap" to point "y5." Source: Richard G. Zambell, *Hyperinflation or Depression?* pg. 67.

try to arrive at another guess. Anyone who says he can make solid, long-term forecasts in today's environment is just fooling himself."

"Why's that?"

"Because the computer models used are based on a smooth working system which no longer exists. There is no way of plugging in catastrophic events like bank failures. Your models, by definition, must assume there will be *no* major market disruptions, *no* defaults by Third World debtors, *no* large bankruptcies. And yet we know that these events are occurring all around us."

"Is there no economic theory, then, that can handle this crisis, that can give us an inkling of what happens next?"

"Well, sir, there is one, but ..."

The Senator from Illinois sat up in his chair. "Really? Tell me about it."

"It's 'catastrophe theory.' But it's just in its infancy, with few economists or mathematicians trained in its intricacies."

"Please do explain."

"When you blow up a balloon, it expands. If you measure how much air is pumped in, you can predict how big the balloon will grow. This is what economists do with their models. But to predict when the balloon will burst—and explain precisely *why* it happens at that particular moment—is another matter entirely. Most difficult of all is the task of predicting what shape it will take *after* the bust. Computer models simply cannot do it!"

"Why not?"

"Our knowledge and application of mathematics hasn't advanced that far. The behavior of the continuous processes—like the expanding of the balloon or of our economy—can be understood by using calculus, invented 300 years ago. But no one has invented an equally effective form of mathematics for explaining and predicting discontinuous phenomena such as a stock market crash or a bank collapse. One exception might be Rene Thom and 'catastrophe theory.'"

"Tell me more."

"I can't. Very few have ever pursued that line of research. The prevailing view of economists has been that the Great Depression was an accident of history caused by the Fed's policy errors. If it couldn't happen again, why worry about economic theories for predicting it?"

"I see."

"Only now have some people begun to recognize that such depressions are recurring phenomena after all. Unfortunately, it's too late to start constructing new computer models for this crisis—let alone invent the new mathematical theories we'd need to run those models. If we start now, maybe we'll have something ready for the next panic, perhaps fifty or sixty years from now."

The Senator was flabbergasted. "So that's it? We're doomed to enduring darkness?"

"Sir, for whatever it's worth, I've been toying around with this theory a bit and I have constructed a diagram which begins to explain what happens. It shows that the entire theory of business cycles has to be revamped. Instead of a smooth cycle, every fifty or sixty years, there occurs a structural break, leaving a wide gap between the past and the future." (See Graph 31.)

The Senator was fascinated. But again, this model did little more than explain the events and indicate some direction for research. It did nothing to help resolve the immediate crisis.

34
___

Rock Bottom

Not all the news was bad. In spite of the turmoil, the market system and most of the major brokers survived.

Around the time of the 1987 Crash, SIPC, the public corporation which protected investors from brokers that went broke, had $387 million in government and government-backed securities. It had a confirmed line of credit with a consortium of 16 banks for an additional $500 million. And finally, if push came to shove, it had the ability to borrow up to $1 billion from the U.S. Treasury. Would that be enough? Would they need more? And if so, would Congress—already besieged with demands for money from failing banks and S&Ls—provide sufficient quantities soon enough?

If you merely read the headlines during those hectic and panicky days, you'd probably think the answer to this question was "no," that the brokerage industry was in ruins. The financial press, which in previous years had tended to understate the bad news, now did precisely the opposite. Investors were continually bombarded with stories of other investors who had to wait weeks and months for their accounts to be settled. The brokerage industry was portrayed as reckless and irresponsible. Editorials talked about the urgent need for reform and the hopelessness of engineering any reforms during a panic.

Behind the scenes, however, the reality was actually not as bad as it seemed. True, SIPC's bank credit lines didn't help very much. But the other sources of funds—especially their governments securities—were relatively solid. Moreover, since securities held at brokerage firms were themselves liquid (unlike bank deposits), much less money was needed to back them up. In short, SIPC *did* provide adequate backing during the very worst stages of the panic!

For the investor who was willing to take some risk, this was the ideal time to buy stocks in well-capitalized brokerage firms! No one wanted them. Nearly everyone thought the brokers were going broke and "would never recoup." Some even went so far as to say that the entire capitalist system was "doomed" and that the next election would bring a socialist into power. Nothing could be further from the truth! If you bought Merrill Lynch stock at this juncture, you could double or triple your money before long. The same was true for several other firms.

For the investor who wanted to take his money *out* of his brokerage account, however, it was another story, especially if it was with a less reliable firm. He ran into delays and snags. Second, if he had an unusually large account he could be beyond the limit of SIPC protection—$500,000, of which only $100,000 could be in cash. If the firm went under, he could lose the overage.

I wish to stress once again, however, that this was the exception and not the rule. Most major brokerage firms had purchased additional private insurance. Furthermore, because of the back-office paper deluge in the late sixties, the brokerage industry was fully computerized by the time the Money Panic hit. No matter what the Dow Jones Averages did, and no matter how much money the brokers and investors lost, the global network of computers continued to churn out accurate debits and credits, allocating the supply and demand for securities with efficiency and dispatch.

Unfortunately, neither the SEC nor SIPC could prevent the *appearance* of chaos. Nor could they avoid sporadic market gridlock—when trading in key stocks had to be temporarily halted, or when the futures exchanges were closed down due to excessive "volatility" (the official code word for panic). Finally, when it was least expected and pessimism was greater than ever, it happened: The stock market hit rock bottom.

The trading volume in stocks was unprecedented, but the Averages gyrated wildly, getting nowhere. Selling pressure was absorbed whenever the Dow Jones Industrials approached the bottom. It was the beginning of the end for the greatest bear market in American history. It was not, however, the end of the crisis.

Governments all over the world made announcements to rally their economies. France: "It's time for all citizens of the Republic to reinvest their confidence in their country." Britain: "The real recovery will soon begin." Markets ignored them. Rallies collapsed. And the Dow bounced up and down off the bottom for months.

The problem was that few people had any money to reinvest. There were, however, some individuals and small, unknown, institutions that had managed to stay out of stocks, bonds and other commitments throughout the decline. They were ready to get in on the ground floor.

As it turned out, this was the ideal time to buy stocks, *provided you waited for the big dips!* You could pick up solid bluechip companies at prices far below their book value. You could buy into firms with still-excellent prospects for growth at a time when they were shunned by the consensus of Wall Street analysts. And you could secure for yourself a big stake in America's future with a relatively small nest-egg of cash.

Perhaps the biggest bargains of all were the few good prospects in the most battered industries—especially the banks and S&Ls.

Earlier, near the market's peak, investors failed to check whether an S&L or bank was financially strong or not. All they cared about was earnings. So when one went bankrupt, they got caught by surprise.

Now, near the bottom of the market, they made the same mistake in reverse. Even though institutions like Strong Bank, Inc. had one of the very best safety ratings in the country, investors sold its shares anyhow—just because it was a bank. So the price plummeted. However, if you had some cash readily available—in a Treasury-only money fund or a T-bill—you could buy the shares for a pittance now and double your money just as soon as the worst of the banking panic was over. Later, after a recovery in the economy, your investment would be worth even more!

Similar opportunities abounded in small and medium-sized, high-tech companies. Often you'd find a company which held valuable patents and had an inside track on the most promising new technology in the nation ... but which had floundered because of a few financial mistakes—a high-interest loan from a bank, a bond issue that they couldn't keep up with, or uncollectible bills from customers. Or, better yet, you could occasionally find a firm that actually had a healthy financial picture but whose stocks were battered simply because the nature of its business was similar to another, larger firm which had failed. In fact, it was this phenomenon—called "panic by association"—which helped to generate some of the greatest bargains of all!

Which ones were the best? No one had the answer, primarily because most analysts, still shell shocked by the panic, weren't even looking for the bargains. Nor did it matter very much. With the market at rock bottom, you could buy almost anything—even some companies in Chapter 11 bankruptcy—and still make a good profit.

During the prepanic period, if you had erred on the side of caution, placing your money into the safest possible investments, you could now afford to err in the opposite direction. With a modest portion of your assets, you could take some of those extra risks which most investors would consider "wild." Within a relatively short period of time, you'd be richly rewarded with gains several times your initial investment.

However, it was absolutely essential that you continued to keep a portion of your money safe. In those final days of the panic, we were in unchartered waters. No one really knew what would happen next. Until you had solid confirmation that we were on the recovery track, it was unwise to commit all of your assets.

35

The Darkest Day

A furor of protest arose from every town and city in America. Again, the new word, the word that most people did not fully understand—"moratorium"—appeared in the newspapers, on heated TV talk shows and in the Congressional Debt Hearings. It was on posters and the placards of protesters. On Wall Street, on Main Street and from within the White House itself, the plea could be heard.

The Fed Chairman resigned. But his successor did little to stop the turmoil. Federal and municipal employees walked out any time a paycheck was late. Their slogan was simple: "No pay, no work." They weren't bargaining; all they wanted was their regular paychecks. Depositors lined up at bank doorsteps, overflowing into the streets, protesting loudly if their money wasn't produced immediately. The nation was on the brink of chaos.

All eyes focused on one man, the President of the United States. In the weeks following his decision to abandon the Metrobank rescue plan, he had grown increasingly frustrated with the advice of his closest aides. On several occasions he was said to have banged his fist in an unusual demonstration of anger, saying: "I want an alternative plan! I want a constructive, rational plan!" None was forthcoming.

It wasn't until the banking crisis literally spilled onto the streets that the President appointed a new group of experts to various high government posts. Robert Sheppard, the outspoken banker who warned of the coming collapse, was appointed as the new Fed Chairman. John Hartman, the Wall Street bond-market expert, became the new Chairman of the Council of Economic Advisors. They met with the President for a weekend of intensive talks at Camp David.

The peaceful tranquility of the Maryland mountain retreat belied the economic confusion in the world at large. But the President made no effort to mask his desperation.

"The people say they want a 'moratorium,'" the President said, "but no one seems to know what a moratorium really is or what its true consequences would be."

The newly appointed Fed Chairman was the first to respond. "A moratorium is a forgiveness of debts. But that is impossible. People don't realize that they are not just debtors. They are also creditors. If you have money in a bank, you're a creditor. If you own money fund shares, you're a creditor. And creditors don't get paid in a moratorium. No. A moratorium is absolutely out of the question. It cannot and will not take place!

"What we need," continued the Fed Chairman, "is a *general holiday*. In a general holiday, nothing is forgiven. Quite the contrary. We all will have to meet our obligations to the best of our ability. But we stop the panic. We stop this madness before it causes social and political chaos."

"I don't understand."

"The concept is simple. In the commodity markets, when some disastrous event forces corn or wheat to fall by a certain predetermined limit, the exchanges automatically stop trading, imposing a temporary cooling off period. The next morning, the markets are reopened and, hopefully, the panic has subsided. I propose a similar shutdown. We halt withdrawals on all banks and S&Ls. Simultaneously we impose a coordinated freeze on all financial markets and transactions—a temporary stoppage that will last for no more than a few days, perhaps a week at the most."

The President paused for a moment and then sat back in his chair. "It's a final act of desperation!"

"Yes, it is. But there are no other solutions."

"I'm afraid it would be a dark tunnel, and that the only light at the end of that tunnel will be the headlight of a speeding locomotive. How could we ever survive it?"

Sheppard spoke more emphatically. "Sir, you have no choice. You are already in the tunnel. You already have a *de facto* banking holiday, a *de facto* production holiday, a *de facto* market holiday. In addition, you have agricultural surpluses in rural areas and acute shortages in urban areas. Why? Because you have transportation bottlenecks, communication failures and excessive cutbacks of essential services in financially troubled municipalities. You have to do something drastic to slow down the maddening pace of the panic, to gain control, to smooth it out, to restore confidence."

The President nodded slowly and deliberately. "But what do you suggest we do to get the country going again?" he queried.

"First, let me cite what we cannot do. Many people in debt hope that the moratorium will get them off the hook. This cannot be. We cannot wipe out real contractual relationships between real institutions. To clean out debts, all of us— businesspeople, bankers, bureaucrats—have to meet face to face and work it out. We must reorganize and rebuild, even if it means big slashes, cutbacks and greater sacrifices—a long, arduous process we won't accomplish overnight.

"Now here's what we *will* do," Sheppard announced. "We will keep all Treasury markets alive. We will honor—at all costs—our government's obligation to the public. That is the absolute minimum requirement—our financial system's last flame of life which must not be extinguished. President Carter's 1980 experience demonstrated that. Our experience with the failed Metrobank rescue attempt proved it again. We must retain—at all costs—the government's ability to borrow money in the open market. That's one market that can never close down, one debt that must always be repaid no matter what. No matter where you live and no matter who you are, if you are an investor or saver who has bought Treasury securities, you will get your money back, promptly, and on time. And no matter how you bought your Treasuries—through a money fund, a broker a bank or directly through a Federal Reserve branch, you are guaranteed equal treatment."

"And if we don't have the money?" asked the President.

"We borrow more."

"And if we can't borrow more?"

"We raise the rate."

"What about the rest of the economy?" the President asked.

"Except for essential goods and services, our efforts must be focused not on production, but on communication and transportation. While established businesses, schools and corporate groups are temporarily restricted, the news media plus the web of relationships between friends, relatives and neighbors will be needed as society's second line of defense. Telephone switchboards, TV newsrooms and printing presses plus land, sea and air transportation facilities must be kept functioning, regardless of financial difficulties. Congressional debates must be open to the public, regardless of possible inconveniences. The lines of communication between nations must be used to their utmost to coordinate an international holiday, regardless of current trade disputes. You have to—"

Hartman interrupted: "Aren't you forgetting something? Even a disorderly market is a thousand times better than no market at all! Before you close down the markets, you must make sure there is a mechanism in place for opening them back up again. You must find liquid buyers who have been standing on the sidelines and attract them back in to long-term Treasuries, equities, and so on."

"Easier said than done" was the skeptical response from all those present. "Where are the buyers? Where is the liquidity? Who has the cash?"

On this particular day, no one had the answers. But they had no choice but to proceed. They decided to begin with a bank holiday. Then, if that wasn't enough, they would proceed to a temporary stoppage of the financial markets as well. It was the greatest peacetime risk ever taken by any President in the history of our nation.

36

The Bank Holiday

On a hot summer day, Federal Reserve Chairman Sheppard appeared before a select group of the press corps. With dark circles under his eyes, only a hint of emotion and a solemn expression, he announced:

"In order to foster a more equitable distribution of the damages wrought by the financial turmoil of recent months, I will impose an indefinite suspension of FDIC payments to depositors. At the same time, to cool down the pressures on the banks, we are declaring a temporary holiday for the withdrawal of bank deposits."

Normally, reporters would have jumped to their feet, hands raised anxiously, jockeying for position and shouting questions. Instead, the sole response was stunned silence. A holiday for withdrawals was expected by some. But an "indefinite suspension" of FDIC payments?

The AP correspondent stood slowly and asked meekly: "Mr. Chairman, I sense in your statement a contrast between the temporary nature of the holiday and the indefinite, perhaps permanent, nature of the FDIC suspension. Was that contrast intentional? If so, what does it really mean for savers in this country?"

The reporter from the *Wall Street Journal* stood up almost simultaneously with a similar question: "What are the consequences, in dollars and cents, of your comment regarding the 'more equitable distribution of damages'?"

The Chairman's expression became even more solemn than before. "In the past, the damages wrought upon this nation by the financial crisis have fallen almost entirely upon the shoulders of those savers and investors who have entrusted their hard-earned funds directly to the Treasury Department of the United States of America via long-term bonds. They were wise enough to invest in the very safest security of our land. And yet they are being penalized by declines in the market value of their investments. Since they can't afford to sell these bonds at a price which would substantially reduce their capital, they are, in effect, locked out of their savings—savings they desperately need to pay their mortgages, their overhead, their business debts.

"Meanwhile," the Chairman continued, "those Americans who deposited their money in the nation's banks—institutions that are known by all to be involved in foreign loans and merger deals—have been protected. And those savers who sought to get the most yield for their money, ignoring the implied risk, have been sheltered. In order to maintain this fiction—this unnatural imbalance—our Treasury has had to drain its cash resources, our central bank has had to flush the banking system with paper money, and our entire future as a nation has been jeopardized.

"This inequity can continue no longer. The time has come to let the true values flow to the true investors in those values; and to let the true losses be shouldered by those who took the true risks. Truth and equity—rather than deception and fantasy—must be the underlying principle through which this crisis is finally resolved!"

This answer once again left the reporters stunned. Slowly at first, but then in a flash of images, the audience finally realized what had just happened. One columnist later described his thoughts as follows:

> I sat there, frustrated by the Chairman's use of philosophical concepts, struggling desperately to decipher the real meaning of what had just transpired. Suddenly, a scene flashed across my mind of my grandmother sitting before a bank officer. She has come to the bank to withdraw her life savings of $25,000. But instead, he hands over less than $8,000, which supposedly represents all the money due her.
>
> "Oh my God," I thought to myself. "The Chairman just said that the depositors in this country will take the rap for the

banks' losses. They're only going to get so many cents on each dollar, depending on the actual market value of the banks' portfolios. The Fed is going to actually liquidate the assets of the banks wherever necessary. This is worse than the 1930s! Much worse!"

Most economists could not understand why it happened. Yet, if you looked at the numbers on the largest banks and S&Ls you could see the reasons clearly. Most of America's financial institutions had made too many poor investments. When those investments went bad during an economic decline, they lost money. And when the word got around to depositors, they tried to take their money out, which, for the most part, was unavailable either from the bank or the federal insurance companies. You didn't have to have a Ph.D. in finance to figure that one out!

Now, with the truth obvious to everyone, the mood turned from the extreme complacency of the prepanic period to excessive negativism. Americans felt that it was "the worst disaster of all time" and that they could "never" recover.

But with a broader vision of history, they might have realized that it could have been a lot worse. In fact, looking back at those final, climactic days of the Money Panic, we can see many positive elements, the importance of which was not fully appreciated at the time.

First and foremost was the fact that, although hard to come by, paper money still had solid value. This was infinitely better than the crisis which had befallen Germany after World War I when it took 3 *trillion* marks to buy one U.S. dollar.

Second, although most people said that "the doors of the banks and S&Ls were closed," they weren't actually closed. What it really meant was that there was a *freeze on most deposits*. Meanwhile, most other bank business continued. The banks' trust departments and custodial services were largely uninterrupted. Your safety deposit box was immediately accessible. And although some check cashing on NOW accounts was blocked, all commercial check clearing was maintained. Most important, payouts to your checking account from the Treasury Department were kept inviolate.

Third, checks drawn on Treasury-only money funds also emerged as shining stars. Unlike some other drafts, they were accepted—and even actively sought after—by individuals and businesses anxious to sell their products. In the days following the Fed Chairman's announcement, if you wanted to buy an item at your local appliance outlet and offered to pay with a personal check, you'd initially encounter extreme reluctance. But if you mentioned that it was a money-fund check, the clerk would pull out a list of "good money funds." As long as it was on the list, he'd honor it. And as long as your money fund invested solely in Treasury securities, it would be on the list.

The liquidation of bad bank assets and the distribution of each bank's losses according to their actual market values, as painful as it was, did not doom the nation as a whole. Rather, it forced each citizen and each corporation to make the sacrifices necessary to restore the economy. In response, Americans of all income strata had to lower their living standards, work harder and cut costs.

One Senator who was absolutely opposed to the idea changed his views and explained in a speech at the Debt Hearings: "If you're on the roof of a two-story building that's consumed by flames, you have two choices. Either you face certain death by fire, or you jump and endure the broken bones. Any further attempt to prolong the banking disaster would burn the whole economy to the ground. We chose to jump. It was the only way out."

In response, one spectator shouted out from the Senate gallery: "Is it only a two-story building that's burning? Or is it a towering inferno?" The answer wouldn't be known for many months.

Despite the freeze on withdrawals, new mobs of depositors lined up at their banks' doorsteps. Again, the nation was thought to be on the brink of chaos.

Less than twenty-four hours later, the spreading paralysis forced the President of the United States to take the final step. He declared a temporary halt to most nonessential production, distribution and financial transactions—a banking, production and market holiday.

For astute investors, the days preceding this declaration turned out to be the last chance to buy common stocks at the bottom of the greatest bear market in history.

To most Americans, however, it seemed as though the U.S. economy had come to a screeching halt from which it could never recover.

37

The Recovery

The panic selling stopped; eerie tranquility ensued. But in the hearts and minds of the people, fear lingered. Some imagined that some faceless bureaucrat, in a final act of desperation, might set off not only the money presses but the nuclear warheads as well. Authorities were concerned that the general holiday would be haphazard and unregulated. Billion-dollar manufacturers feared that the shutdown might be permanent, while foreign competitors continued to dump goods. Political analysts predicted that the intense economic crisis might bring to power quasi-dictators backed by military juntas; and that any recovery which might ensue would be sabotaged by civil and racial wars.

The President and his new advisors convened again at Camp David. In response to the question "Where is the cash?" Sheppard brought with him a computer print-out which he placed on the table. Hartman glanced anxiously at the names and numbers on the list. His assistant stood up and helped him unfold the long sheets across the table and onto the floor. One column showed cash resources; one showed short-term debts; a third showed quick liquidity ratios.

There was a separate sections for the banks, the strongest S&Ls and the most liquid corporations in America, as shown in Table 15.

However, after scanning it for a few minutes, Hartman was not enthusiastic. "If this list is typical, the task ahead of us will be more difficult than I imagined. Look," he said, stabbing

Table 15. The Most Liquid Corporations In America

Company Name	Liquid. Ratio (%)	Working Capital ($mil.)	Long-Term Debt ($mil.)
Autodesk	1,077.8	105	-
Chicago Milwaukee	1,003.4	304	-
National Presto Industries	889.5	180	6
Amgen	815.4	106	17
Metro Mobile	800.0	83	85
Minnetonk Corp	720.0	79	-
Millicom Inc.	686.7	126	14
Genetech Institute	685.7	132	6
Lac Minerals	635.7	242	63
Cetus Corp.	631.8	125	107
Skyline Corp.	521.1	110	-
Ranger Oil	410.6	162	82
Lyphomed Inc.	404.8	164	103
Golden Nugget	386.8	125	564
Premiere Industries	363.9	248	7
SHL System House	346.7	161	37
LSI Logic	343.2	309	188
Cypress Semiconductor	332.3	112	18
Gulf Resources	323.2	165	96
CBS Inc.	319.7	3,007	962
Farmers Group	300.0	216	202
Comcast	265.7	224	923
Placer Dome	259.3	439	49
Mentor Graphics	251.3	156	-
Coortis Wright	244.2	159	46
Barris Industries	243.1	90	59
Penn Central	240.4	1,154	192
National Patent Development	210.2	162	173
McCaw Cellular Communications	197.2	204	1,722
Microsoft	193.6	229	4
Flight Safety International	191.3	65	40
MEI Diversified	179.1	157	119
Kansas Gas & Electric	178.9	227	1,016
Consolidated Papers	178.5	189	-
Dart Group	173.8	402	152
Hilton Hotels	159.6	207	284
Charter Medical	158.7	94	72
Texaco	158.0	1,055	82
Nacco Industries	157.0	205	353
ICN Pharmecueticals	153.6	211	328
AutoData Proc	150.7	501	256
Commerce Clearing House	145.1	251	16
Toledo Edison	133.6	295	1,321
Int'L Flavors-Fragr	133.5	489	-
Xidex Corp	131.1	249	120

his finger at the computer sheets as he held them up in the air, "when the ratios are good, the quantities are small; and when the quantities are big, the ratios are not so good. This is a far cry from the days of J.P. Morgan, when all the reserves needed to piece things together after a panic could be scribbled on a few pieces of paper."

No matter how big the names and no matter how impressive the numbers, they recognized that it was still just a drop in the ocean of debt which surrounded them. On the other hand, no matter how unimaginably large the task ahead, they also recognized that *something* was infinitely better than nothing.

For a while they discussed some individual investors and entrepreneurs they thought might be able to help.

They talked about Lawrence A. Tisch, head of CBS and Loews. Once described by *U.S. News & World Report* as the "Quiet Billionaire," he had been fundamentally opposed to the fake prosperity Washington helped to build in the late '70s and early '80s. Ignoring criticism from below, he had moved aggressively and consistently to build cash resources, slash unnecessary expenses and, above all, stay out of debt.

They mentioned Howard Stein, head of Dreyfus Corporation, which managed 24 mutual funds. Early on, as an assistant to the founder of the company, Jack Dreyfus, he learned that the stock market is not a one-way street; it goes up *and* down. Unlike many of its competitors, the firm's managers had come through the Crash of '87 largely unscathed. They had kept some 40% of their funds in cash and equivalent. And after the crash, they had increased their cash position still further to 50%.

Also on Sheppard's list was H. Ross Perot. Those who had followed the career of this 57-year-old entrepreneur knew that he built his business and his nearly $3 billion fortune the hard way. He had placed the bulk of his fortune in U.S. Government securities, and never participated in the takeover craze which had swept Wall Street both before and after the crash.

But these and others among the "liquid minority" had not yet volunteered to help.

When they heard that their names were on a list discussed in high places, they were even more hesitant.

"Before any liquid resources are committed," said one in a letter to the President, "certain conditions have to be met."

What were these conditions? The letter referred repeatedly to the "housecleaning process" but complained about the slow progress that was being made. Here are some excerpts:

> Wall Street analysts are saying that the latest round of casualties will be the last casualties, that there is no more need for liquidation. But this is not true. By the end of the boom, there were approximately $11 trillion in debts outstanding in the United States—over $16 trillion if you included Western Europe and Japan. But, at the most, less than one fifth of the private debts have been liquidated thus far. How much has to be cleared out before it is enough? Maybe a third. Maybe even more. We can't say for certain. But we *are* sure about one thing: It is time to halt the chain reaction of panic liquidations and begin a rational, orderly period of reorganization.

Back at Camp David, one Administration official was visibly upset by the slant of the debate. Echoing a widespread concern throughout Washington for the free-enterprise system, he raised his voice in protest. "Are you gentlemen implying that the President should assume dictatorial powers under the cloak of a national emergency? Are you saying he should take over private industry, preside over market transactions?"

What he failed to realize was that the Money Panic had—for better or for worse—made those arguments academic. Due to the sharp declines in tax revenues, many government programs had been reduced to almost empty shells and the government's power—to tax less, spend more, tighten money or ease money—was reduced to a mere shadow of its former self. To think that the government could now assume dictatorial powers was completely unrealistic.

The President was particularly conscious of this change. "The government cannot call a national emergency," he replied, "because we *already* have a national emergency. All the government can do is guarantee law and order, coordinate meetings and provide the information needed to put the pieces back together."

The Administration official also complained about the extremely high cost of money.

The President, turning philosophical, responded with this comment: "This is the first time in history that the cost of money and the cost of things have taken such widely divergent paths. Could it be that the market is trying to tell us something? I'm not an economist. But one thing I have learned is that interest rates represent the market value of money—of credit, faith and trust. The market is telling us that it needs more trust and more faith. At the same time, low prices are telling us that we live in an era of abundance, that we have an almost unlimited ability to produce but have been producing the wrong things.

"Could it be that this crisis is a flash of lightning—giving us a glimpse into a future of stronger human relationships and more abundant material goods? I only hope we can make a more conscious distinction between the two—between people and things. Clearly, to force interest rates down artificially will be tantamount to—"

The President groped for the appropriate metaphor.

Reopening

At last markets reopened. There was no big volume, no fanfare. However, when you looked at the prices, you saw a huge gap from the point at which they closed before the forced holiday and the point at which they were now opening. Although it wasn't too late to buy, it *was* too late for the truly great bargains.

Separately, the Federal Reserve made it clear that any attempts to lower interest rates artificially would be equivalent to "barking at the thunder."

As confidence returned, the big action began. Despite the lack of government intervention, the dollar continued to recover. Thus, the foreign exchange markets—the first to feel the sting of the panic back in the late 1980s—became the first to snap back. The very fact that the banks and markets were functioning was in itself hailed by overseas investors, and a sudden flush of funds, hoarded in cash and Treasury bills, returned to the equity markets.

Would it be enough to sustain a real recovery? Or would the market fall back down again, eventually plunging the nation into another panic and another general holiday?

To this ultimate question, no one has the answer except you, the reader. If you—and other investors like you—endeavor to build cash and reduce debts before the panic, you will join the new "liquid minority" which could lead the nation out of the panic. But to achieve this end, you must take strong, protective steps in the early stages to accumulate liquidity. This liquidity, coupled to the still-solid productive capacity of the industrial nations, can be enough to spark a recovery.

We have seen the great financial blunders of the 1960s and 1970s, the great dilemmas of the 1980s, and the ultimate consequences to those who ignored the warning signs. What happens next will depend upon what you do now. You have the opportunity to not only survive the panic but to greatly increase your wealth even during its most confusing stages.

How To Receive A Free Update Of This Book

I made my last editorial changes to this book on March 19th, 1989. Therefore, by the time you read it, the economic environment will inevitably have changed.

Rest assured that my tables and graphs on the banks and other corporations will remain valid much longer than most company analyses which are commonly published on Wall Street. This is because mine are based entirely on balance-sheet data which are subject to fewer fluctuations than earnings data.

However, in the Money Panic, everything is subject to rapid change. Nothing is sacred. One day in the financial markets, such as October 19, 1987, can transform the entire world. And despite temporary periods of quiet, one week or one month could bring market moves which normally might take years to occur.

This phenomenon will create a wider-than-normal information gap between the day I finished writing this book and the day you finish reading it.

But I have found a way to bridge this gap. Every month I put together a new Money Panic Update package.

The package contains the latest data on the safety of America's largest banks, the strongest banks in each state, the nation's largest S&Ls, the brokers, insurance companies and business corporations. It covers all the important events which have occurred since the day this book was written. And it includes my current views regarding what to expect in the financial markets along with my recommendations on what to do about it.

I strongly believe that The Money Panic Update, especially designed as a companion to this book, is an absolutely essential tool in order to survive—and profit from—this crisis. Best of all, it's free!

Simply send your name and address to Weiss Research, Inc., P.O. Box 2923, West Palm Beach, FL. along with $2 for postage and handling ($20 for overnight service). Or, you may call my office at (407) 684-8100. I will send you this month's Money Panic Update right away.

Acknowledgements

In real life, this book comes to you neither from the future nor from a historian. Rather, it is the product of a team effort and thousands of man-hours by a very extensive research group and computer facility.

Needless to say, I am forever indebted to my father, Irving Weiss, who has imparted to me as much of his experience and knowledge as I could absorb; to my uncle, Al Weiss, who helped to edit each of the 18 drafts; and to Tom Holt, whose many years of successful investing in gold and bonds has helped to enlighten me in those areas.

Frank Ventura, a contributing editor to our newsletters, provided critical materials for several of the chapters on the insurance industry and the banks. Mark Pendergrast contributed the chapter "Use A Strong Broker." Lee Finberg, Alan Radcliff, Jim Powell and Dan Rahfeldt also contributed important sections. Dan Abelow and Linda Heilman made improvements in the book's readability and invaluable suggestions regarding its organization.

At Weiss Research, of course, everyone has played an important role. Dan Derby, Dana Nicholas and Leslie McDonnell provided the computer power. Leslie Underwood, the editor of our *WOW Indexes* newsletter, did the hard part—the word processing of the many drafts and the thousands upon thousands of revisions. Everyone had a hand in the proofreading, especially Jeanette Weiss. And everyone did their share, especially Helen Barrow, who dedicated many weekends to finishing the book on time. The cover design is by Lavonne Hyde.

Finally, this book would have been impossible had it not been for the wonderful hospitality of Alan and Barbara Radcliff who gave me a home away from home and an office away from the hubbub of newsletter writing.